Political and Economic Transition in Russia

Ararat L. Osipian

Political and Economic Transition in Russia

Predatory Raiding, Privatization Reforms, and Property Rights

palgrave
macmillan

Ararat L. Osipian
University of Wisconsin–Madison
Madison, WI, USA

ISBN 978-3-030-03830-4 ISBN 978-3-030-03831-1 (eBook)
https://doi.org/10.1007/978-3-030-03831-1

Library of Congress Control Number: 2018964186

Cover image © Fabrizio Moglia / Getty Images
Cover design: Oscar Spigolon

This Palgrave Macmillan imprint is published by the registered company Springer Nature Switzerland AG
The registered company address is: Gewerbestrasse 11, 6330 Cham, Switzerland

Foreword

Barbarians at the gate! Today, they are gathering at the gates of factories and plants, housing condominiums, collective farms, banks and insurance companies and numerous other enterprises, firms, and organizations. The image of the predatory raider, the Russian predator, becomes emblematic of modern Russia. This image dominates the landscape of business transactions, financial flows, and oil riches in the country that not so long ago was a gray-colored militarized Stalinist Empire.

Who are these aggressively looking men in black or khaki uniforms wielding clubs and batons, spreading tear gas, jumping over fences, and ramming gates? These are Russian raiders. Why do they climb the walls, jump into windows, break through office doors into director's quarters, and roll top managers out of their offices along with their leather armchairs? Because they take over the key positions: the director's office, accounting books, and gates and checkpoints. They secure the perimeter to let their people in and to move the now previous owners out. This is called a corporate hostile takeover, the way it is done in Russia. Iron gates and fireproof safes are unlocked with electric saws and sledge hummers in order to gain access to seals, documents, charters, and cash. It is relatively easy to explain such a dramatic raiding spectacle to an unaware bystander, but it is much harder to understand and explain what is in the background of such swift violent storming actions and battles for property. This book will attempt exactly this, the explanation of fundamentals that lie beneath the bold manifestations of corporate hostile takeovers and other types of raiding.

Private security firms (ChOPs) promise a better protection of property rights to you personally, while Putin promises it to everyone, to the nation as a whole. However, the war against raiding, declared by the state, is about as successful as the war against corruption, if the word *success* is at all appropriate in this context. The future of raiding is not as bleak as some state officials like to picture. Waves of raiding activities follow the waves of privatization and financial crises. Privatization in Russia continues, and so does raiding. Similar to the "Russians are Coming" expression, set in minds of people in the West during the Cold War era, "Raiders are Coming" came into the annals of the Russian modern history for a long time. Opportunistic behavior of raiders and foreign investors is alike. The Russian business climate is harsh, but those who see the opportunity in it may eventually succeed.

Madison, WI

Ararat L. Osipian

Preface

Three decades into the market reforms, Russia is still in the process of creating and developing its market institutions. The Russian economy is the sixth largest economy in the world, sharing the ranks with Germany and Brazil, but it faces serious challenges when it comes to such issues as the legitimacy of property and the protection of property rights. Raiding, along with corruption, is the number one problem in Russia, which worries not only domestic entrepreneurs, but also foreign investors. According to some accounts, this problem, after the financial crisis of 2008, has worsened. A dramatic depreciation of the ruble in 2014 further distracted transnational corporations from investing in Russia. In addition to production facilities, real estate and land are major targets of raiders. Raiding goes far beyond bankrupt private enterprises. Raids are organized against the state enterprises and state property as well. Essentially, anything of value is potentially an object for a raider attack. As Moscow stays in the top ten world capitals to do business in and to invest, Russian raiders may certainly pretend on a top place in the ranking of world raiding, if such ranking would exist.

Three decades ago, at the development of Gorbachev's Perestroika in 1989, cooperatives and individual entrepreneurs manifested the legalization of private property in the USSR,[1] very little and tightly restricted and controlled, and yet private. This was not a genuinely private property, but rather a quasi-private property, tightly controlled by the state and oftentimes assaulted by criminals, including first of all racketeers. It was explained in part by the lack of a proper regulatory frame and market environment. There was a clear lack of market institutions, indeed.

However, in 2019, there are still plenty of problems with property rights which owners of private property face frequently, and the major blame continues to be placed on that same lack of market institutions.

Privatization reforms, property rights, and predatory raiders in post-Soviet Russia, placed in the title of this book, correlate with such notions as virtual reality, volatile rights, and violent raiding. Indeed, this set of notions may be positioned as parallel to the title line. Privatization was done through the creation of virtual reality, when every Soviet state-owned enterprise was reproduced in a parallel dimension called title of property. Shares, privatization vouchers, auctions, and other tools were used to manipulate the status of these enterprises through their virtual being or virtual dimension. Private property rights in Russia are still not well protected. They are vulnerable to both the state and criminal groups and dishonest entrepreneurial raiders. Thus, private property rights are strongly associated with the notion of volatility. Volatile rights to private property do not let owners sleep well. They lost their sleep in part thanks to the growing threat of predatory and aggressive raiding. Raiders in Russia are not those met in the West: they do not limit themselves to the Wall Street strategies and tactics of acquiring shares. Instead, they often resort to violence. Violent crimes, related to private property, including order killings of heads of targeted companies, are no longer exceptionally rare. The use of violence during the storming of offices and enterprises gives justification to associating the notion of violent raiding with raiding actions that take place in Russia.

Property relations are indeed the key to understanding the phenomenon of raiding. Property rights were formed and transformed through the processes of distribution and redistribution of property. The move from predatory lending to predatory raiding signifies the transition from more civilized to more violent forms of property redistribution. In addition, state agencies act similar to raiders: they take property from citizens and turn it to new owners. Sometimes "Raiders are coming" means collector agencies are at work. Terms such as democratization and disintegration are now being replaced with capitalization, arbitration, and commercial dispute resolution.

Corporate raiding as we know it is the way it is presented in western research. Here, golden parachutes and poison pills are included in the defensive strategies of western firms designed to oppose hostile takeovers. The problem of raiding in works of Russian scholars is not well described, and in addition, some large cases of corporate hostile takeovers, such as those of Yukos, TogliattiAzot, and Vympelkom, receive a fair amount of media attention. Organizational forms of raiding in Russia include a familiar structure of client, organizer, and executor. It is hard to say who the real raider is: the client who orders the raiding, the organizer who designs the raiding project and sets the whole thing in motion, or the executor, who actually put it into action.

Not all corporate raids in Russia are done in business offices and law firms; some, in fact many, remind chronicles of ancient sieges or the war of high fences with foot soldiers and firepower. While foot soldiers or storm-troopers and trial lawyers are the front men, there are deeply entrenched institutional actors as well. Prices on raiding and related services, which are sometimes mentioned in the media and surfaced in the reports on raiding in the form of pricelists, point to a strong institutional component of Russian raiding. Private security firms (ChOPs) and the Ministry of the Interior (MVD) exercise their right to defend property from raiders and equally so when it comes to defeating the rightful owners.

Madison, WI — Ararat L. Osipian

Note

1. USSR, The Union of the Soviet Socialist Republics, also known as the Soviet Union.

Note on Translation and Transliteration

I transliterated Russian words using the Library of Congress system, omitting diacritics but using two-letter tie characters. The same system was used for names of well-known people, for whom a certain spelling has become conventional, such as Khodorkovsky or Magnitsky. All translations from Russian original documents and records are my own.

Contents

About the Author

Ararat L. Osipian is Fellow of the Institute of International Education, United Nations Plaza, New York, and honorary associate in the Department of Political Science, University of Wisconsin-Madison, and holds a PhD in Leadership and Policy Studies from Vanderbilt University, where he came as a fellow of the US Department of State. He is the author of *The Political Economy of Corporate Raiding in Russia* and *The Impact of Human Capital on Economic Growth: A Case Study in Post-Soviet Ukraine, 1989–2009* (Palgrave Macmillan, 2009) and studies corruption globally.

Abbreviations

BTI	Byuro tekhnicheskoj inventarizatsii [Bureau of Technical Inventory Registration]
ChOP	chastnoe ohrannoe predpriyatie [private security firm]
Duma	Lower Chamber of the Russian Parliament
FBK	Fond bor'by s korruptsiej [Anti-Corruption Foundation]
FGUP	Federal'noe gosudarstvennoe unitarnoe predpriyatie [Federal State Unitary Enterprise]
FIG	financial-industrial group
FNS	Federal'naya nalogovaya sluzhba [Federal Tax Services]
FSB	Federal'naya sluzhba bezopasnosti [Federal Security Services], former KGB
FSSP	Federal'naya sluzhba sudebnykh pristavov [Federal Services of Court Bailiffs]
Gosduma	Gosudarstvennaya duma [State Duma, Lower Chamber of the Russian Parliament]
Komsomol	Kommunisticheskij soyuz molodezhi [Young Communists League]
LLC	Limited Liability Company
M&A	Mergers and acquisitions
MP	Member of Parliament
MVD	Ministerstvo vnutrennikh del [Ministry of the Interior]
NAK	Natsional'ny antikorruptsionny komitet [National Anti-Corruption Committee]
Narkomfin	Narodny komissariat finansov [People's Commissariat of Finance]
NEP	Novaya ekonomicheskaya politika [New Economic Policy]
NGO	Nongovernmental Organizations
NII	Nauchno-issledovatel'sky institut [Research Institute]
RF	Rossijskaya Federatsiya [the Russian Federation]

ROL	rule of law
RSPP	Rossijskij soyuz promyshlennikov i predprinimatelej [Russian Union of Industrialists and Entrepreneurs]
Sberbank	Sberegatel'nyj bank [State Savings Bank]
SK	Sledstvennyj komitet [Investigations Committee]
ToAZ	TogliattiAzot
USSR	the Union of the Soviet Socialist Republics
VCIOM	Vserossijsky tsentr issledovanij obshchestvennogo mneniya [Russian Public Opinion Research Center]
VEB	Vneshekonombank
YUKOS	YUganskneftegaz and KuibyshevOrgSintez
ZhEK	zhilishchno-ekspluatatsionnaya kontora [Housing Management Unit]

List of Figures

List of Tables

CHAPTER 1

Introduction: Raiding Russia

Corporate Hostile Takeovers

Corporate hostile takeovers, also referred to as corporate raiding, are perceived to be actions with the help of which enterprises are transferred from the hands of less capable managers into the hands of more capable management teams. Corporate raiders have an arsenal of financial and legal tools at their disposal in order to take over enterprises against the will of their ineffective managers and to convert them into more successful firms. The transformation of unsuccessful or poorly managed firms into successful and financially stable ones may occur in cases of hostile takeovers, but not always. Sometimes raiders fail in their task to improve the financial situation of a targeted firm, despite such efforts as restructuring, new management, and investment in technologies and human capital. Sometimes raiders simply blackmail current management in order to profiteer on their rights as minority shareholders; this trick is known as greenmail. Nevertheless, corporate raiders in the western world play a positive role, performing the function of market cleaners. With the help of hostile takeovers, enterprises are released from under the rule of ineffective management teams and transferred to more effective ones. Ineffective, incapable, or financially weak firms are being weeded out from the market. At the end, not only raiders win, but consumers do too.

Corporate raiding denotes a situation on the stock market when an investor, be it a company, investment bank, or a group of investors, is buy-

A. L. Osipian, *Political and Economic Transition in Russia*,
https://doi.org/10.1007/978-3-030-03831-1_1

ing a majority stake or a significant minority stake in a publicly traded company such that it can dismiss the current management team and appoint its own managers. Raiding often occurs when the company's share price has recently fallen significantly, especially if this value depreciation is only expected in the short run.[1] Corporate raiding is frequently called a hostile takeover. Accordingly, a hostile takeover is defined as takeover of a company against the will of the current management and the board of directors by an acquiring company or raider. Hostile takeover is the acquisition of one company by another without the consent of the target company's leadership. Raiders buy stock directly from shareholders, sometimes by offering a particularly high price. The acquiring company may buy up to 5 percent of the targeted company without registering the move with the Securities & Exchange Commission (SEC).[2] The SEC is a US governmental agency that serves at the primary regulator of the securities trade. SEC's functions include ensuring that all trades are fair and that no price manipulation or insider trading occurs, promoting full disclosure, and monitoring mergers and acquisitions (M&A) to ensure competitiveness. The SEC was created in 1934, as part of the New Deal, to prevent excessive speculation.[3]

Another well-known form of corporate raiding is called greenmail. Greenmail literally means receiving a pack of US dollars by mail.[4] In reality, of course, this does not happen. In the corporate world, greenmail describes the situation with the holding of a large block of stock of a targeted company by raiders, with the goal of forcing the targeted company to repurchase the stock at a substantial premium. Why would a joint-stock company buy a block of its shares at a highly inflated price? The targeted company may want to do so in order to prevent a potential hostile takeover in the future. A professional corporate raider buys a certain amount of stock from another publicly traded company and starts blackmailing this company, creating all kinds of procedural inconveniences, and clearly abusing his/her shareholder rights. With no intention of actually buying or managing the targeted company, a greenmail raider merely seeks to profit from the buyback. Greenmail is also referred to as a defensive maneuver, in which the targeted company purchases shares of its own stock from a raider, at a price above that available to other stockholders, who are ordinarily excluded from the transaction. If the raider holds a significant stock of shares, the targeted company may have to borrow funds to finance greenmail stock repurchase.[5] If the targeted company is already in a difficult financial situation, it may end up with substantial additional debt. This is how corporate raiding works in the West.

Introducing some characteristics of Wall Street type raiding may be of help in order to highlight the differences, later in the study, and show how Russian predatory raiding differs from western raiding. Adding some discussion of raiding in other transition countries, especially Ukraine, may also be of help. Ukraine's problems with the rule of law, property protection, predatory raiding, and corruption have persisted for many years. More on divergent paths of different countries in the post-socialist transitioning space, oligarchy, and economic and social consequences of restructuring in Russia and Ukraine can be found in Havrylyshyn (2006, 2017) and Bruk and Lehmann (2012).

Russia continues its nonlinear, extremely slow, and highly controversial move to the market-based economy. It builds market infrastructure and reforms its legislature in order to achieve the level of economic effectiveness on par with developed market economies. Russian enterprises are in much stronger need of more effective management than are their western counterparts. There are corporate predatory raiders that may be found on the changing Russian business landscape, and so western businessmen and politicians may hold a view that they play the same overall positive role for the development of the economy and perform the same functions, as do their western counterparts. Or do they? Unlike in the West, hostile takeovers in Russia are done by quite distinct market operators. Although called raiders, they are very different from their western counterparts. Russian predatory raiders use different tools, utilize different means, pursue different goals, and achieve different ends. There are plenty of semi-legal, quasi-legal, would-be-legal, and clearly illegal tools in their master toolkit.

In order to achieve a more or less high level of the rule of law in the national economy, Russian society first has to transform into a developed market economy and democracy. Such a process takes place in the post-Soviet space and continues for three decades, but its pace varies by region and differs in each former Soviet republic. For instance, the situation with predatory raiding in Central Asia is not clear at all. The landscape of hostile takeovers in this region remains unknown, while the situation with corruption and the rule of law is clearly below any imaginable standard. The mix of different forms of economic activities, varying from semi-feudal, monarchic, and militaristic, to pseudo-market, liberal, and libertarian, leaves enough space for predatory raiding, because raiding as a method of property redistribution can coexist with other noneconomic methods, widely used in such systems.

Ukraine, the second largest of all former Soviet republics, is quite similar to Russia in terms of corporate predatory raiding and equally so it is quite different from western corporate practices. At the same time, there are a few specifics that make Ukraine distinct from Russia. Although these differences are not fundamental, they are nevertheless significant and merit a brief mention. First, due to its on-going political turmoil and war, Ukraine is overwhelmed with the new powerful wave of predatory raiding, with violent clashes being recorded by the media almost daily. Russia is relatively stable in this sense, indicating no major distinct waves of raiding. Second, in distinction of Russia, where Putin propagates his strategy of equidistance in regards to oligarchs, in less centralized Ukraine, the political power is taken directly by oligarchs with no alternative in sight. Finally, the quest for the EU accession, proclaimed as the main political and economic strategy for Ukraine, makes it different from Russia. This latter point is also advanced by Rojansky (2014). However, it is hard to establish the direct link of the joining the EU aspirations with the problem of predatory raiding, since the situation with the rule of law in Ukraine may well be even worse than in Russia. Moreover, in many ways, and especially economically, Russia may find itself on much better terms with EU members than does Ukraine. This includes both major EU players, such as Germany and France, and smaller players, such as Hungary.

What is in the essence of corporate hostile takeovers in Russia? How do Russian scholars highlight the problem of corporate predatory raiding in their works? Why do predatory raiders use illegal tools in corporate hostile takeovers? What is the role of mass privatization of the 1990s in the predatory raiding phenomenon? What are organizational and institutional forms of predatory raiding? What is the legitimacy of the raided property and the private property rights in general? What is the role of state institutions, including law enforcement agencies, in predatory raiding? Is the state a major instrument of legitimization of property rights or legitimization of predatory raiding? What is the purpose of the renationalization rhetoric, and how does it impact the legitimacy of property? If there is a market for predatory raiding and related services, then what are the prices on these services and what do they indicate? Certainly, one book is not enough to cover all of these questions in a comprehensive and convincing manner. Nevertheless, this book takes on the task of touching on all of these questions and finding answers on the key questions.

The major lines of investigation into the phenomenon of predatory raiding may be presented as follows. The book introduces the natural component to the political-economic study. This component serves as a structure for investigation into the specifics of Russian predatory raiding in the broader context. The natural component includes the concept of social Darwinism, which places emphasis on competition of races in the process of natural selection. Survival of the fittest in the Russian context means competition based, to a significant extent, on noneconomic factors. Within the framework of a predatory state the use of noneconomic tools and factors may become dominant. Given the high level of corruption in Russian courts, police and other law enforcement agencies and controlling bodies, predatory raiders welcome the aggressive involvement of the state in economic matters. Russian predatory raiders take corruption for granted, enjoying the opportunities that corruption in state organs opens to them. Of course, corruption is always costly, as the average size of bribes in Russia increases year after year, but the investment may be worth the proceeds. As a result, instead of protective and regulatory state, Russian business ecosystem faces predatory state.

In this research, predatory raiding is defined as the hostile takeover of an enterprise or property that indicates the process of redistribution of property through the use of corruption and fraud. Raiding does not necessarily imply a forceful entry, an assault, a storm of an enterprise, or another object with the goal of taking over this enterprise, object, or property as a result of economic dispute between two economic agents. In certain cases, raiding can be done without violence. In many cases, the storming is a culmination of the raiding campaign that follows court hearings and other legal procedures. In other cases, the storm may be just the beginning of a long and exhausting raiding campaign, including court hearings and appeals, which last for many months. While legal disputes over the ownership of an enterprise continue, the enterprise itself can be stormed and taken back a few times, going from hand to hand.

The invisible hand of the market and indivisible hand of the state point to the duality of the state and its role in the process of legitimization of property and facilitation of predatory raiding. In this sense, the discussion of the possible revision of privatization results may be considered as a gift to the predatory raiding movement. With all the terms of legitimization of property, nationalization, renationalization, de-nationalization, and re-privatization, the public becomes confused. Privatization combines virtual reality, volatile private property rights, and violent raiding and signifies all of these processes. The mass privatization of the 1990s and the waves of privatization that followed signify the unequal distribution of property, and thus worry the masses. At the same time, businessmen are more concerned with the safety and security of their assets, both present and those they may acquire in the course of the future and planned privatization campaigns. The chronology of predatory raiding, which is difficult to extract at this point, may correlate with the waves of privatization.

Raiding in Russia has a distinct predatory character. However, institutions and property rights of businesspeople did not suffer significantly after the financial crisis of 2008. While external management, auctioning, and liquidation are used by predatory raiders, crisis-related bankruptcy and the role of commercial arbitration courts should not be overestimated when it comes to hostile corporate takeovers. Waves of privatization may play a much larger role in the chronology of raiding and peaks of raiding activity than do financial crises. As the process of privatization continues, the invisible hand of the market is complimented with the iron fist of predatory raiders.

The role of the state in a market economy is to oppose the processes, phenomena, and actors that have a negative impact on the national economic system. Predatory raiding in Russia clearly has a destructive character, including its negative impact on the newly emerging system of property rights. It may be assumed by default, then, that the state would aim its bureaucratic machine at restricting, mitigating, and eliminating predatory raiding. However, it would be misleading to suggest that the Russian government is by definition the antipode of raiding, actively opposes raiding, and prosecutes predatory raiders. On the contrary, there are quite a few examples in Russian history when the state legitimated raiding and encouraged and indeed rewarded predatory raiders. Such legitimation is especially typical for raiding outside the state domain, that is, not to the detriment of the country where raiders are based.

The Russian state rarely misses the opportunity of filling the state treasury with the help of raiding and racketeering against property owners who happen to fall out of the regime's favor. Historically, Russian tsars were eager to fill their coffers with the help of outright looting that has been later framed in a more civilized term of confiscation of property. Violence and threat of violence was a norm, especially as it was done in the name, and to the favor, of the state. At that time, personal riches of the leader and state treasures were one and the same thing. Recent forced deindustrialization and evolution of grey markets left its print on Russians' perceptions about the changing role of the state.

Raiding is, first of all, an economic problem, and only then a legal one. Even though the legal approach to the problem of corporate raiding is logically explained and justified, it is incomplete. Hence, the monopoly of such an approach to the problem of corporate raiding is misleading. This is especially true for Russia, where fundamental factors of economic development and growth play a much more significant role, even on the surface, than do legal frameworks. It is true that raiding should be studied within the legal frame, because it is accompanied by at least three major factors that come from the legal dimension. These factors are as follows: predatory raiding involves crime, legal gaps allow predatory raiding, and corruption in courts and law enforcement facilitate predatory raiding. But at the same time raiding is predominantly an economic problem. Accordingly, the priority in research on predatory raiding should shift more toward the economic aspects of raiding. Predatory raiding in Russia should be a subject matter for research done by economists, rather than almost exclusively by legal scholars.

The basis of predatory raiding in Russia is not exclusively in imperfect laws, the presence of legal loopholes, rudiments of Socialism, or court corruption. Predatory raiding is being built on an economic fundament. Accordingly, the solution to the problem of raiding should be sought not in improving legislation and struggle against corruption in courts, but in the national economy. The institutional structure is important, but it is nothing more than a regulatory super-structure of the national economy. Institutions are called to reduce transaction costs that emerge in the process of the functioning of the national economy.

Institutions are operational in protecting property rights. Indeed, institutions influence economic processes, but their influence on fundamental economic advances is not as significant as neo-institutionalists would like to present. Institutions themselves are formed under the pressure of fundamental economic processes and reflect changes in economic realities. This is characteristic of both legal and illegal institutions. In the problem of predatory raiding, this reflectivity manifests itself in the reactive character of measures undertaken by the government in order to oppose and prevent predatory raiding.

As foreign investors continue to consider Russian markets as a potentially very promising field for their investments, they should keep in mind the threat of predatory raiding. Foreign investors are not immune from the risk of being raided. It is also important that they understand what type of raiding they may face in Russia. Unlike the corporate raiding in the

US and other established market economies, in Russia they may face an explosive blend of violent hostile takeovers, storming and assaults, police inaction, and dubious court decisions.

Scholarly Reflections on Hostile Takeovers

The wave of corporate hostile takeovers that has swept across the US and covered most of other market democracies in the 1980s and early 1990s found its reflection in numerous scholarly publications, including Auerbach (1988), Auerbach and Reishus (1988), Bradley and Wakeman (1983), Coffee, Lowenstein, and Rose-Ackerman (1988), to name but a few. Due to its significance, the phenomenon of corporate hostile takeovers gained so much attention that, by the early 1990s, scholars have produced a plethora of publications focused on specific aspects of hostile takeovers (see, for instance, Chaplinsky & Niehaus, 1994). Such specific aspects included defensive strategies of corporations deployed in order to repel hostile takeover attempts (Banerjee & Owers, 1992; Barclay, 1986; Barnatan, 1991; Berkovitch & Khanna, 1990), protection of confidential business information (Calamari, 2002), hostile bank takeovers (Baradwaj, Fraser, & Furtado, 1990), changes in executive careers and compensation due to hostile takeover bids (Agrawal & Walkling, 1994), restructuring (Cundiff, 2002), and defense strategies that maximize shareholder wealth (Pearce & Robinson, 2004).

Internal conflicts are also part of scholarship on corporate hostile takeovers (Chang, 1990; Coffee, 1988; Committee on Government Operations, 1988). The scholarship on corporate hostile takeovers also targets specific industries. For instance, Byrd and Stammerjohan (1997) investigate success and failure in the market for corporate control with the evidence from the petroleum industry. As Bhagat, Shleifer, and Vishny (1990) point out, corporate hostile takeovers of the 1980s may symbolize the return to corporate specialization.

Since corporate hostile takeovers extended far beyond the US, international comparisons became inevitable. Such comparisons involve, first of all, matching the US with other developed economies, including the UK (Armour & Skeel, 2007) and Germany (Donath, 1994). Studies of corporate hostile takeovers also include single country case studies other than the US, including Japan (Alger, 2006; Huckaby, 1991) and the UK (Cooke, Luther, & Pearson, 2003). All of these are largest developed market economies.

The sprawling topic of corporate hostile takeovers moves into politics and other segments of social life. For instance, Anderson (2006) considers anti-unionism and the neoliberal politics of urban school reform in New York through the lens of hostile takeover. McCarthy (1997) goes even further, considering the dilemma of judging the school privatization as a friendly or hostile takeover. In such instances, the term "hostile takeover" is frequently used for opportunistic reasons that have little to do with the corporate world.

Willingly or not, scholarship produced locally in Russia in many ways repeats that produced in the US three decades ago. However, it repeats the western scholarship only superficially: Russian scholars do not use sophisticated mathematical modeling or econometric analysis. Hostile takeover of enterprises and property in Russia remains a black box. Smetankina (2007) asks the question, "What is raiding?" while Skidanova (2009b) considers raiding in Russia as a social phenomenon. Indeed, limiting corporate hostile takeovers in Russia to corporate issues would be a mistake. The phenomenon has its extended legal, political, and social dimensions.

Russian scholarship on corporate hostile takeovers starts with comparisons of local realities and Wall Street practices. Andreeva (2001) addresses the organizational aspects of M&A by comparing western experiences and Russian realities. This is unavoidable in such a bureaucratized society as Russia. Bandurin and Zinatulin (1999) describe economic and legal regulation of corporations in Russia, while Konstantinov (2008) suggests that corporate raiding is not fraud. To the contrary, Shnaider (2007) considers raiding as a criminal phenomenon. Nikonova (2009) addresses both the civil and criminal aspects of corporate hostile takeovers. Borisov (2008) calls hostile takeovers a legalized robbery. Similarly, Dmitrieva (2007) considers raiding as a phenomenon of the criminalized economy. Luchin and Kashkin (2009) go even further, considering corporate and property raiding in Russia a threat to the constitutional order.

According to Zhelnorovich (2007), presence of the criminal raiding in Russia is the indicator of institutional deficit of the Russian economy. Whether deficit or deficiency, this phenomenon is here to stay. In fact, not only criminal raiding manifests insufficiency of institutions and laws, but the phenomenon itself becomes institutionalized within a frame of informal institutions, rules, and regulations. In the case of extreme, widespread aggressive and criminally charged corporate hostile takeovers can potentially make the state apparatus partially defunct.

Any significant action brings to life a counter action. As it is in western scholarship, defensive strategies of corporations deployed in order to repel hostile takeover attempts are popular among Russian scholars (Demidova, 2007a, 2007b; Krichevsky & Kiryushkin, 2007; Rudyk, 2006). Rybakova (2008) even suggests proactive measures against hostile takeovers in the higher education sector, advising on how to protect universities from raiders. Similar to western scholarship, internal corporate conflicts are also part of scholarship on corporate hostile takeovers in Russia (Gololobov, 2004; Hrabrova, 2000; Skidanova, 2009a). Studies of corporate raiding also become a matter of church development and that of historical analysis (Thyrêt, 2010). At the same time, such specific issues as protection of confidential business information, hostile bank takeovers, and changes in executive careers and compensation due to hostile takeover bids have yet to find their place in works of Russian scholars.

The topic of corporate hostile takeovers is time sensitive; it depends on certain periods and economic developments, of which crises are perhaps the most significant ones. Demekhin (2010) and Skidanova (2009c) describe mechanisms of hostile takeovers during the economic crisis of 2008. Yalanzhi (2009) figuratively calls crisis raiding in Russia attack of the clones. The issue of aggressive hostile takeovers and defenses against them made its way into popular magazines, such as *Ogonek* (Mlechin, 2009), which is also explained by the post-crisis period. Even before the economic crisis of 2008, hostile takeovers were considered as an immanent feature of the Russian economy (Skidanova, 2006) and a normal practice of the modern Russia (Faenson & Pimanova, 2007). The main arguments of these authors reflect the tenor of the literature on corporate raiding from the late 2000s.

The issue of corporate hostile takeovers attracts the attention of scholars far beyond the US, reflecting on global ties of modern national economies and the process of globalization in general. Russia also influences its neighbors, and this influence finds its reflection in works on corporate hostile takeovers in post-socialist countries other than Russia, including first of all Ukraine (Belikov, 2007; Riabchuk, 2003; Varnalij, 2006; Varnalij & Mazur, 2007). Not only specific industries, but even specific cases of corporate hostile takeovers catch the eye of Russian scholars. Such is the case of Togliattiazot, a large industrial enterprise attacked by the raiders in the 2000s (Andriyanov, 2007). The case of Togliattiazot has become a textbook example of corporate raiding in Russia, a white book of corporate resistance. The issue of corporate hostile takeovers extends to textbooks

(Tikhomirov, 2006) and terminological dictionaries (Borisov, 2007) and transforms into literary works (Astakhov, 2007). Informational space on corporate hostile takeovers is supplemented with independent nongovernmental websites about raiding, such as Zahvat.ru (literally, takeover). Such websites disappear and reappear in different forms and formats.

Finally, there is a small but growing block of the scholarly works of western scholars focused on the raiding of property and corporate hostile takeovers in Russia. These include, first of all, the seminal work of Firestone (2008) and Carbonell, Foux, Krimnus, Ma, and Safyan (2009), and, lately, Frye (2014, 2017), Gans-Morse (2012, 2017), Markus (2012, 2015), and Osipian (2012, 2018). It is surprising that property raiding in Russia had to wait for so long to finally gain some attention from western scholars. And it may be even more surprising, given the attention that the issues directly related to raiding have been in focus since the early 2000s. These issues include property rights, protection of investments, court system and contract enforcement, shadow economy, tax evasion, the gangster state, and corruption in Russia, and scholarly reflections on these issues reached their peak well over a decade ago, in the mid-2000s. A good example of this high level of attention would be a special publication of *Fifth Nobel Symposium in Economics* focused on the economics of transition (see Berglof & Roland, 2007).[6]

The book also connects to the recent quantitative scholarship on corporate predatory raiding in Russia; for example, a recent literature arguing that predatory pressure by state officials has become less important in recent years, with regulatory pressure becoming more important, or a literature on how businesses try to organize and defend themselves against corporate raiders. Starting with works of Osipian (2012), Yakovlev, Sobolev, and Kazun (2014), and Kazun (2015a, 2015b), scholars attempt to quantify the phenomenon of predatory raiding in Russia and explain its impact on the economy. In order to investigate predatory raiding in Russia, Rochlitz (2014) builds a database of 312 cases of corporate raiding that took place during 1999 to 2010, with the help of a systematic analysis of national and regional newspaper archives. A set of indicators that come from official Russian statistics and the media is used to estimate the extent of property rights insecurity, state predation, and business-related violence that take place in the country.

Russia is known not only for its high levels of corruption, but also for its large shadow sector in the national economy. Violent pressure on businesses, exerted by the predatory state, can influence firms' willingness to stay in the shadow or informal sector of the economy. Using evidence from Russia's numerous regions, Rochlitz (2017, p. 173) finds that,

> [p]hysical violence in a given region is positively correlated with the number of people working outside the corporate sector, but negatively with the degree of competition from the informal sector. On the other hand, insecure property rights for entrepreneurs and investors increase the amount of competition from the informal economy.

The author points out that the findings are consistent with a theory where "firms seek the protection of the formal economy against different types of physical violence in regions with decentralized predation, but hide in the informal economy against predatory state officials and corporate raiders in regions where predation is centralized" (Rochlitz, 2017, p. 173).

The question of whether raiders are hurting the overall economy or making it more efficient by weeding out weaker firms is an important one, but the data required to address this issue in Russia directly simply does not exist. At the same time, there are studies that demonstrate how administrative corruption undermines entrepreneurship and economic opportunities (see, for instance, Krylova, 2018). The author investigates the vulnerability of individual entrepreneurs and confirms the involvement of public officials in the illegal raiding of small businesses.

While the market for corporate M&A in the US and other developed democracies has been researched by scholars to the highest level of sophistication, there is a lot to do in terms of discovering the phenomenon of corporate hostile takeovers in the post-Soviet space. Furthermore, the level of scholarship has to be upgraded both quantitatively and qualitatively. Russian scholars have to produce a larger quality of research on hostile takeovers while using more sophisticated methods of analysis. There is a hope that the phenomenon of corporate hostile takeovers in the post-Soviet space will attract more attention from both western and local scholars.

In setting this particular volume in existing literature on predatory raiding in Russia, one may want to acknowledge the distinction between research books and scholarly books. While Markus (2015), Frye (2017), and Gans-Morse (2017) produced clear-cut research volumes, this is a scholarly volume, being more generalist and more appealing to broader audiences of scholars. At the same time, this volume is distinct from Sakwa's (2009) book on Khodorkovsky, Putin, and the Yukos affair. While the former is reasonably broad in scope, the latter is focused on one particular major case of state-orchestrated predatory raiding, placed in the context of freedom, broadly interpreted.

The scholars are too slow and in the case of Russian predatory raiding, even too late. These books have been written in large parts around 2000s, and use the data from that period. Fortunately for scholars, not much has changed in Russian raiding since the 2000s, and thus their work remains not only up to date, but in demand.[7] All these books differ in approaches, structure and content. Osipian (2018) focuses on corruption, coercion and control model, economically active bureaucracy, and inverted character of raiding. This makes the volume more theoretically loaded. This book is about privatization, legitimacy, and specifics of the raiding business, which makes it more applied and thus more appealing to broader audiences. While the former concentrates on relations of predatory raiding and the state, the latter focuses on the core of raiding itself. This study starts from the late 1980s and traces raiding through the 1990s, 2000s, and 2010s.

Some scholars aim at a standard research structure that would include formulating a clear research question, theoretical framing, hypotheses to be tested, methodology, and interpretation of the results. This would characterize a research volume, while this is a scholarly volume. This book brings together materials that exist in various reports and journal articles into a unified account and places more emphasis on scholarly synthesis, involving more scholarly sources. The book relies on a number of sources, including interviews and surveys that come from the media and other scholars. At the same time, this study went through a lot of media reports, some of which feature results of surveys, interviews, and research reports. There are other online sources as well. The book has a lot of endnotes, but these are just the tip of the iceberg. In this sense, the book is based at least to a certain extent on original research.

The book uses plenty of data, collected primarily from media reports, but other sources as well. Thousands of media reports related to predatory raiding, including video footage, were analyzed starting 2007. Some scholars hire Russian companies to conduct surveys, trust these companies, and rely on answers of respondents, all of which can be subjected to scrutiny on the grounds of honesty and reliability. This study works with media, laws, and data posted by official Russian agencies. Scholars would probably agree that the data required to address the issue of harm caused by predatory raiding simply does not exist. This is because the raiding phenomenon is even more elusive than that of corruption. Corruption can be at least partially traced through court decisions, while raiding only vaguely expresses itself through corrupt actions.

The nature of the subject matter of this study, that is, predatory raiding in Russia, is very elusive. It is not exactly property rights; it is not exactly crime; it is not exactly the state; and it is not exactly corruption; it is something in between these and some other determinants. That is why one may have an impression that there is not enough focus in different studies on raiding. Choosing just a few research questions and making one or two central arguments and aligning the chapters along these arguments remains a challenge.

The Structure

The structure of this book reflects the logic of inquiry into the matter of corporate hostile takeovers in Russia. This study considers predatory raiders in the context of zoomorphism, the shaping of something in animal form or terms. The Russian predator, ascribed with animal characteristics, hunts for most lucrative businesses, properties, and land. This volume is structured in the following way. Chapter 2 departs from the literature surveyed on the context of predatory raiding in Russia, presented in the introductory chapter. This study introduces the notion and concept of predatory raiding and suggests that it may serve as an explanatory model for corporate, property, and land raiding in Russia. Building on previous scholarship, this study conceptualizes the predatory character of corporate hostile takeovers in Russia and links it with the coercive nature of the ruling authoritarian regime. The introductory chapter outlines the problem, scholarly literature that exists on the topic, and presents the structure of the inquiry. Earlier chapters are more conceptual, while the later ones are more practical. This study juxtaposes Soviet parasites against post-Soviet predators and starts with Chap. 2, focused on the emergence of Wild-West capitalism in Russia.

Chapter 2 considers how the new social archetype—Communist cowboy capitalists—captured Russia in the course of economic reforms during the late 1980s and early 1990s. It further links the concept of social Darwinism with predatory hostile takeovers. The chapter emphasizes that the struggle for survival or competition that takes place in modern Russian business ecosystem is based on the use of noneconomic factors, including direct violence. Predatory raiders actively use corruption and violence as two dominant forms of state-society and state-business relations.

During Joseph Stalin era, the Soviet people were the object of predation, the prey of the totalitarian regime. But in addition to this major predator, there were parasites, most of which were petty and multiplied in millions. Chapter 3 studies parasites who lived off the people's body by practicing embezzlement of socialist property, nepotism, cronyism, and gift-giving as a camouflaged bribery. It argues that despite the partial disintegration of the Soviet Union, modern Russian state retains the role of the major predator. This one overwhelming predator helps predatory raiders to overpower—both legally and financially—a strong and successful business. Chapter 3 argues that a profitable business can fall prey to a predatory raider only through the involvement or direct interference of an external force, exogenous factor, an overwhelming aggressive power such as that of the predatory state. Corrupt bureaucrats collude with predatory raiders, forming an unlawful symbiosis in order to expropriate profitable businesses and other valuable assets to their personal benefit.

The way this study came to zoomorphism and related terminology is as follows. A few scholars have used the term "predatory" in relation to raiding in Russia. However, not one of those few scholars who work on the issue moved beyond the term itself. This study decided to look into what "predatory" actually means in nature, and how it may be applied to Russian raiders. Of course, at this stage, it is more allegoric than scientific, that is, this study is not going deep into biology in search for explanations. Comparing various types of Soviet and post-Soviet economic actors to animals in a proper research manner would be quite a task of interdisciplinary nature. Nevertheless, some basic comparisons are interesting and may attract the reader.

The phenomenon of predatory raiding cannot be considered without first looking into the earlier forms of property distribution, including first of all Russia's mass privatization. This study analyzes privatization reforms and crisis raiding. Chapter 4 starts with the mass privatization of the 1990s and argues that despite several attempts done by scholars, establishing the chronology of predatory raiding remains a challenge. If such a chronology is to be formed, it will inadvertently connect to stages of privatization as the unequal distribution of property. Chapter 4 argues that the predatory raiding of the 2000s and 2010s as a form of redistribution of property is certainly not the first wave of property redistribution that rolled over Russia. The mass privatization of the 1990s combined with corruption created perfect breeding grounds for predatory raiders.

Chapter 5 analyzes future prospects of raiding evolution and suggests that prognosis for predatory raiding movement in Russia is optimistic, at least for raiders. The rationale for discussing any topic largely depends on its magnitude and meaning for the future. In this sense, defining perspectives of predatory raiding movement is much more than just fortunetelling. Russian business ecosystem is not ready to weed out predatory raiders, and the state has no interest in doing this either. Chapter 5 discussed future of predatory raiding within a theoretical framework, labelled as a revolutionary theory of permanent lawlessness. When the rule of law is not the state's priority, the decline in predatory raiding is unlikely.

Contrary to the assurances of the ruling political regime about a significant decline in predatory raiding, numerous media reports on hostile takeovers point to the opposite. In both Moscow and Russia's numerous regions, raiding activities related to large corporations and small businesses are reported regularly. In addition, there are plenty of reports on raiding public property and personal property. Both federal and municipal properties become the target of predatory raiders. Furthermore, corruption as a fundamental base for predatory raiding continues to flourish throughout Russia, including its largest and most developed cities and most distant regions and provinces. Even official reports indicate a steady rise in the size of the average bribe in Russia year after year. It becomes obvious that only a dramatic reduction in corruption can put an end to predatory raiding, but such a change is highly unlikely in the foreseen future.

This study moves the investigation of predatory raiding phenomenon from future prospects of predatory raiding to a more fundamental question, that of legitimacy of property and illegality of predatory raiding. This question is addressed through the perspective of the possible revision of privatization results. Chapter 6 considers the state as an instrument of legitimization and raiding being taken over or privatized through political raiding. In the case of Russia, the state is privatized by extended families and clans of former Communist elites in Moscow and its regions. The state, captured by clans, transforms from the institution into a tool that may be rented out as needed, including to predatory raiders. This situation brings to the fore a question of whether claims about the process of state building in Russia may be valid. When the state as the major regulatory institute does not perform its major functions, helping the predatory raiders instead, transaction costs increase. When the ruling political regime loses its credibility, the legitimization of property rights becomes problematic.

Chapter 6 also presents the duality in the position of both Russian businesses and the state. While the results of the initial mass privatization of state assets in the 1990s are dubious, businesspeople are very interested in using the state apparatus to secure their property. At the same time, other businessmen, including those who were late for the initial giveaway of state property, use the state as the legitimized violence machine for the redistribution of property. For them, predatory raiding with its violence and corruption turns quite handy. These two diverging positions correspond to the duality of the state. The state guarantees security of property rights, and at the same time the state sees the possibility to deny it. Redistribution of economic assets that may be initiated or orchestrated by the ruling political regime threatens the existing property arrangements.

The threat of predatory raiding has the potential to become a single most important source of additional transaction costs in Russia. In western discourse on corporate raiding, along with an increase in transaction costs, raiders are also considered "forest wolves" that help to get reed of ineffective owners. Chapter 7 clarifies whether predatory raiders in Russia can be considered as positive and useful market agents, with the phenomenon of raiding considered as a useful institution to the market-type transition economy. Is it true that raiders act not only in their own best interests, but also to the benefit of the economic system overall, as follows from the "invisible hand of the market" concept of Adam Smith? Do raiders strengthen the national economy? Simply put, is it true that predatory raiders serve as "market cleaners"? This chapter also clarifies institutional aspects of raiding, by considering such issues as legitimacy of property rights and illegality of raiding.

A periodically mentioned potential threat of renationalization that comes primarily from the state and is voiced by different political groups keeps the legitimacy of property rights on both the political and business agendas. Chapter 7 argues that a high level of concentration of property rights on the means of production remains the main obstacle for economic and democratic development in modern Russia. Russia needs both the further privatization of state property and a much more significant dispersion of property rights among the large and diverse population strata. At the same time, any claims about property redistribution, dispersion, renationalization, or other possible actions in regards to property rights worry the business community. Russian ruling political regime does not guarantee the stability of property rights and may serve the interests of predatory raiders.

This study considers organizational and institutional forms of predatory raiding in Russia. It starts with Chap. 8, which analyzes the business of hostile takeovers. Predatory raiding in Russia is a specific business, connected to other related businesses and state structures. In addition to banks and financial-industrial groups, there are firms that specialize in raiding. Organizational forms of raiding demonstrate the division of functions and include the structural chain that consists of the client, organizer, and executor. In this chain, predatory raiders can occupy any position in this chain or simply play a role of sub-contractors in a hostile takeover. Predatory raiders take over enterprises to own them or sell them. Due to the violent nature and storming of enterprises by predatory raiders, modern history of the Russian raiding movement may be labeled as the chronicles of ancient sieges or the war of high fences.

Finally, Chap. 9 continues on the issue of organizational forms and participants of predatory raiding. Predatory raiders that take part in violent storming and the defense of stormed enterprises are regarded as foot soldiers of the raiding movement. They have their qualitative characteristics, including, first of all, firepower and prices charged for raiding services. Both law enforcement agencies and private security agencies exercise their right and duty to protect private and state property. The mass privatization of the 1990s brought to life the need to protect private property on a massive scale. At the same time, state law enforcement agencies were no longer capable of or willing to protect private property. The state lost its monopoly on the physical protection of property. Private security firms partially replace the state in its function of protecting private property.

In addition to protecting private property, private security agencies also take part in hostile takeovers, performing the function of violent stormtroopers. And so do some law enforcement officers, working on the side of predatory raiders. Corruption in the law enforcement agencies, judiciary, and other related state bureaucracies helps predatory raiders to target successful and financially sound businesses as well as federal and municipal properties of high-market value. Services of corrupt state agencies are reflected in some reported price lists. Based on the prices posted, one may conclude that predatory raiding is a costly activity that requires a significant initial investment.

Notes

1. Raiding. Farlex Financial Dictionary. Retrieved January 12, 2017, from https://financial-dictionary.thefreedictionary.com/Corporate+Raiding
2. Hostile takeover. Farlex Financial Dictionary. Retrieved January 12, 2017, from https://financial-dictionary.thefreedictionary.com/hostile+takeover
3. Securities & Exchange Commission. Farlex Financial Dictionary. Retrieved January 12, 2017, from https://financial-dictionary.thefreedictionary.com/SEC

4. A greenback is a slang term for US paper dollars.
5. Greenmail. Farlex Financial Dictionary. Retrieved January 12, 2017, from https://financial-dictionary.thefreedictionary.com/greenmail
6. Berglof, Erik, & Roland, Gerard (Eds.). (2007). *The Economics of Transition: The Fifth Nobel Symposium in Economics.* New York: Palgrave Macmillan. Publications, including this edited volume, are authored by well-known political economists and appeared before in leading scholarly journals. For instance, Johnson, Simon, McMillan, John, & Woodruff, Christopher. (2007). Property Rights and Finance. In Erik Berglof and Gerard Roland (Eds.). *The Economics of Transition: The Fifth Nobel Symposium in Economics* (pp. 213–242). New York: Palgrave Macmillan, was initially published in *American Economic Review*, 92(5), pp. 1335–1356. Other works in the collection include: Johnson, Simon, McMillan, John, & Woodruff, Christopher. (2007). Courts and Relational Contracts. In Erik Berglof and Gerard Roland (Eds.). *The Economics of Transition: The Fifth Nobel Symposium in Economics* (pp. 243–297). New York: Palgrave Macmillan; Friedman, Eric, Johnson, Simon, Kaufmann, Daniel, & Zoido-Lobaton, Pablo. (2007). Dodging the Grabbing Hand: The Determinants of Unofficial Activity. In Erik Berglof and Gerard Roland (Eds.). *The Economics of Transition: The Fifth Nobel Symposium in Economics* (pp. 298–334). New York: Palgrave Macmillan; Johnson, Simon, McMillan, John, Kaufmann, Daniel, & Woodruff, Christopher. (2007). Why Do Firms Hide? Bribes and Unofficial Economy. In Erik Berglof and Gerard Roland (Eds.). *The Economics of Transition: The Fifth Nobel Symposium in Economics* (pp. 335–359). New York: Palgrave Macmillan; Treisman, Daniel. (2007).The Causes of Corruption: A Cross-National Study. In Erik Berglof and Gerard Roland (Eds.). *The Economics of Transition: The Fifth Nobel Symposium in Economics* (pp. 360–423). New York: Palgrave Macmillan.
7. For instance, Stanislav Markus is now working on his second book, titled *The Politics of Wealth Offense: Oligarchs and the State in Developing Democracies*, with contracts already extended by Cambridge University Press and Oxford University Press.

References

Agrawal, A., & Walkling, R. (1994). Executive Careers and Compensation Surrounding Takeover Bids. *Journal of Finance, 49*(3), 985–1014.

Alger, C. (2006). Livedoor Looking Glass: Examining the Limits of Hostile Takeover Bids in Japan. *NYU Journal of Law and Business, 3*, 309–329.

Anderson, N. (2006). Hostile Takeover: Antiunionism and the Neoliberal Politics of Urban School Reform in New York. *Working USA: The Journal of Labor and Society, 9*(2), 225–243.

Andreeva, E. (2001). Organizatsionnye aspekty sliyanij i pogloshchenij: zapadnyj opyt i rossijskie realii [Organizational Aspects of M&A: Western Experiences and Russian Realities]. *Economic Strategies, 1*, 5–6.

Andriyanov, V. (2007). *"Tol'yattiazot" protiv reiderov. Belaya kniga* ["Togliattiazot" Against Raiders. White Book]. Moscow: The Russian Union of Producers.

Armour, J., & Skeel, D. (2007). Who Writes the Rules for Hostile Takeovers, and Why? The Peculiar Divergence of US and UK Takeover Regulation. *Georgetown Law Journal, 95*, 1727–1794.

Astakhov, P. (2007). *Reider* [Raider]. Moskva: EKSMO.

Auerbach, A. (1988). *Corporate Takeovers: Causes and Consequences.* Chicago: University of Chicago Press.

Auerbach, A., & Reishus, D. (1988). Taxes and the Merger Decision. In J. Coffee Jr., L. Lowenstein, & S. Rose-Ackerman (Eds.), *Knights, Raiders, and Targets: The Impact of the Hostile Takeover* (pp. 300–314). New York: Oxford University Press.

Bandurin, A., & Zinatulin, L. (1999). *Economiko-pravovoe regulirovanie deyatel'nosti korporatsii v Rossii* [Economic and Legal Regulation of Corporations in Russia]. Moscow: BUKVITSA.

Banerjee, A., & Owers, J. (1992). Wealth Reduction in White Knight Bids. *Financial Management, 21*(3), 48–57.

Baradwaj, B., Fraser, D., & Furtado, E. (1990). Hostile Bank Takeover Offers: Analysis and Implications. *Journal of Banking & Finance, 14*(6), 1229–1242.

Barclay, C. (1986). Defensive Strategies to Hostile Takeover Attempts: The Impact of Norlin Corp. v. Rooney Pace. Inc. *Northern Kentucky Law Review, 13*, 69–75.

Barnatan, T. (1991). ESOPS as a Defensive Weapon When a Hostile Takeover Rears Its Ugly Head. *Wayne Law Review, 38*, 1877–1897.

Belikov, O. (2007). Reiderstvo v Ukraini: realii s'ogodennia [Raiding in Ukraine: Realities of Modern Days]. *Juridychny zhurnal, 4*, 105–109.

Berglof, E., & Roland, G. (Eds.). (2007). *The Economics of Transition: The Fifth Nobel Symposium in Economics.* New York: Palgrave Macmillan.

Berkovitch, E., & Khanna, N. (1990). How Target Shareholders Benefit from Value-Reducing Defensive Strategies in Takeovers. *Journal of Finance, 45*(1), 137–156.

Bhagat, S., Shleifer, A., & Vishny, R. (1990). Hostile Takeovers in the 1980s: The Return to Corporate Specialization. *Brookings Papers on Economic Activity, 21*, 1–84.

Borisov, Y. (2007). *Kratky tolkovy slovar' korporativnogo reidera* [Brief Terminological Dictionary of a Corporate Raider]. Moscow: Gedeon.

Borisov, Y. (2008). *Reiderskie zahvaty: uzakonenny razboj* [Raiding Takeovers: A Legalized Robbery]. Moscow: Piter.

Bradley, M., & Wakeman, L. M. D. (1983). The Wealth Effects of Targeted Share Repurchases. *Journal of Financial Economics, 11*(1–4), 301–328.

Bruk, T., & Lehmann, H. (Eds.). (2012). *In the Grip of Transition: Economic and Social Consequences of Restructuring in Russia and Ukraine*. London: Palgrave Macmillan.

Byrd, J., & Stammerjohan, W. (1997). Success and Failure in the Market for Corporate Control: Evidence from the Petroleum Industry. *Financial Review, 32*(4), 635–659.

Calamari, P. (2002). Protection of Confidential Business Information. In E. Wallach (Ed.), *Corporate Raiding, Retention & Restructuring*. New York: Practicing Law Institute.

Carbonell, B., Foux, D., Krimnus, V., Ma, E., & Safyan, L. (2009). Hostile Takeovers: Russian Style. *Knowledge Wharton*, April 20. Retrieved August 3, 2009, from http://knowledge.wharton.upenn.edu/article.cfm?articleid=2217

Chang, S. (1990). Employee Stock Ownership Plans and Shareholder Wealth: An Empirical Investigation. *Financial Management, 19*(1), 48–59.

Chaplinsky, S., & Niehaus, G. (1994). The Role of ESOPs in Takeover Contests. *Journal of Finance, 49*(4), 1451–1471.

Coffee, J. (1988). Shareholders Versus Managers: The Strain in the Corporate Web. In J. Coffee Jr., L. Lowenstein, & S. Rose-Ackerman (Eds.), *Knights, Raiders, and Targets: The Impact of the Hostile Takeover* (pp. 77–134). New York: Oxford University Press.

Coffee, J., Lowenstein, L., & Rose-Ackerman, S. (1988). *Knights, Raiders, and Targets: The Impact of the Hostile Takeover*. New York: Oxford University Press.

Committee on Government Operations. (1988). Corporate Raiding of Worker Pension Plans: Hearing Before a Subcommittee of the Committee on Government Operations, House of Representatives, One Hundredth Congress, Second Session, September 28, 1988. Washington, DC: U.S. G.P.O.

Cooke, T. E., Luther, R. G., & Pearson, B. R. (2003). The Information Content of Defense Documents in UK Hostile Takeover Bids. *Journal of Business Finance & Accounting, 25*(1–2), 115–143.

Cundiff, V. (2002). Corporate Restructuring. In E. Wallach (Ed.), *Corporate Raiding, Retention & Restructuring*. New York: Practicing Law Institute.

Demekhin, A. (2010). Tehnologii reiderstva v usloviyah ekonomicheskogo krizisa [Raiding During the Economic Crisis]. *Yurist*, February 2. Retrieved February 2, 2010, from http://www.gazeta-yurist.ru/article.php?i=982

Demidova, E. (2007a). Hostile Takeovers and Defenses Against Them in Russia. *Problems of Economic Transition, 50*(5), 44–60.

Demidova, E. (2007b). Vrazhdebnye pogloshcheniya i zashchita ot nikh v usloviyakh korporativnogo rynka Rossii [Hostile Takeovers and Defenses Against Them in Russia]. *Voprosy ekonomiki, 4*, 70–84.

Dmitrieva, E. (2007). Reider kak yavlenie kriminalizirovannoi ekonomiki [Raider as a Phenomenon of the Criminalized Economy]. *Sledovatel', 6*, 40–44.

Donath, R. (1994). On the Way to US-Style Hostile Tender Offers in Germany – The European Attempt to Harmonize the Takeover Law and Its Impact on German Company Law. *Annual Survey of International & Comparative Law, 1*, 91–110.

Faenson, M., & Pimanova, A. (2007). *Reiderstvo (nedruzhestvenny zahvat predpriyatij): praktika sovremennoj Rossii* [Raiding (Hostile Takeover of Enterprises) the Practice of the Modern Russia]. Moscow: Alfa-Press.

Firestone, T. (2008). Criminal Corporate Raiding in Russia. *The International Lawyer, 42*(4), 1207–1230.

Frye, T. (2014). Legality and Violence in Russia: An Introduction. *Post-Soviet Affairs, 30*(2–3), 87–88.

Frye, T. (2017). *Property Rights and Property Wrongs: How Power, Institutions, and Norms Shape Economic Conflict in Russia*. New York: Cambridge University Press.

Gans-Morse, J. (2012). Threats to Property Rights in Russia: From Private Coercion to State Aggression. *Post-Soviet Affairs, 28*(3), 263–295.

Gans-Morse, J. (2017). *Property Rights in Post-Soviet Russia: Violence, Corruption, and the Demand for Law*. New York: Cambridge University Press.

Gololobov, D. (2004). *Aktsionernoe obshchestvo protiv aktsionera: protivodejstvie korporativnomu shantazhu* [Joint-Stock Company Against a Stock-Holder: Resisting the Corporate Blackmail]. Moscow: Yustinform.

Havrylyshyn, O. (2006). *Divergent Paths in Post-Communist Transformation: Capitalism for All or Capitalism for the Few*. London: Palgrave Macmillan.

Havrylyshyn, O. (2017). *The Political Economy of Independent Ukraine: Slow Starts, False Starts, and a Last Chance*. London: Palgrave Macmillan.

Hrabrova, I. (2000). *Korporativnoe upravlenie: voprosy integratsii* [Corporate Governance: Integration Issues]. Moscow: Alpina. Retrieved February 2, 2010, from http://www.latribune.fr/actualites/economie/international/20110718 trib000636854/les-enfants-de-la-nomenklatura-russe-s-exercent-a-la-lutte-des-places-.html

Huckaby, T. (1991). Defensive Action to Hostile Takeover Efforts in Japan: The Shuwa Decisions. *Columbia Journal of Transnational Law, 29*, 439–459.

Kazun, A. (2015a). Violent Corporate Raiding in Russia: Preconditions and Protective Factors. *Demokratizatsiya: The Journal of Post-Soviet Democratization, 23*(4), 459–484.

Kazun, A. (2015b). Reiderstvo v regionakh Rossii: indikatory i factory [Raiding in Russia's Regions: Indicators and Causes]. *Mir Rossii, 24*(3), 33–60.

Konstantinov, V. (2008). Reiderstvo – ne moshennichestvo [Raiding Is Not Fraud]. *Zakonnost, 11*, 38–43.

Krichevsky, N., & Kiryushkin, R. (2007). *Risk reiderstva: sushchnost', otsenka, upravlenie* [Risk of Raiding: Essence, Estimates, Management]. Moscow: Marketing.

Krylova, Y. (2018). *Corruption and the Russian Economy: How Administrative Corruption Undermines Entrepreneurship and Economic Opportunities*. New York and London: Routledge.

Luchin, V., & Kashkin, D. (2009). Reiderstvo: ugroza konstitutsionnomu stroyu Rossii [Raiding: A Threat to the Constitutional Order of Russia]. *Zakon i pravo, 1*, 8–11.

Markus, S. (2012). Secure Property as a Bottom-Up Process: Firms, Stakeholders, and Predators in Weak States. *World Politics, 64*(2), 242–277.

Markus, S. (2015). *Property, Predation, and Protection: Piranha Capitalism in Russia and Ukraine*. New York: Cambridge University Press.

McCarthy, M. (1997). School Privatization: Friendly or Hostile Takeover? *Journal of Education Policy, 1464–5106, 12*(1), 61–69.

Mlechin, L. (2009). Nado byt' sil'nym [One Has to Be Strong]. *Ogonek, 12*(3–9), 23.

Nikonova, N. (2009). *Reiderstvo: grazhdansko-pravovye i ugolovno-pravovye aspekty* [Raiding: Civil and Criminal Aspects]. Sankt Petersburg: Legal Center Press.

Osipian, A. (2012). Predatory Raiding in Russia: Institutions and Property Rights After the Crisis. *Journal of Economic Issues, 46*(2), 469–479.

Osipian, A. (2018). *The Political Economy of Corporate Raiding in Russia*. London and New York: Routledge.

Pearce, J., & Robinson, R. (2004). Hostile Takeover Defenses That Maximize Shareholder Wealth. *Business Horizons, 47*(5), 15–24.

Riabchuk, M. (2003). *Dvi Ukrainy: real'ni mezhi, virtual'ny viiny* [Two Ukraines: Real Frontiers, Virtual Wars]. Kiev: Krytyka.

Rochlitz, M. (2014). Corporate Raiding and the Role of the State in Russia. *Post-Soviet Affairs, 30*(2–3), 89–114.

Rochlitz, M. (2017). Violent Pressure on Business and the Size of the Informal Economy: Evidence from Russian Regions. In A. Polese, C. Williams, I. Horodnic, & P. Bejakovic (Eds.), *The Informal Economy in Global Perspective: Varieties of Governance* (pp. 173–193). New York: Palgrave Macmillan.

Rojansky, M. (2014). Corporate Raiding in Ukraine: Causes, Methods and Consequences. *Demokratizatsiya: The Journal of Post-Soviet Democratization, 22*(4), 411–443.

Rudyk, N. (2006). *Metody zashchity ot vrazhdebnogo pogloshcheniya* [Defense Methods from Raiding]. Moscow: Delo.

Rybakova, E. (2008). Preduprezhdenie reiderskih zahvatov vuzov [Proactive Measures Against Raiding Takeovers of HEIs]. *Juridicheskoe obrazovanie i nauka, 4*, 39–45.

Sakwa, R. (2009). *The Quality of Freedom: Khodorkovsky, Putin, and the Yukos Affair*. New York: Oxford University Press.

Shnaider, N. (2007). Reiderstvo kak kriminogennoe yavlenie [Raiding as a Criminal Phenomenon]. In *Legal Problems in the Modern Russia* (pp. 182–187). Collection of Conference Talks. Omsk: Omsk State University.

Skidanova, L. (2006). Nedruzhestvennye pogloshcheniya kak cherta rossijskoj ekonomiki [Hostile Takeovers as a Feature of the Russian Economy]. *Aktual'nye problemy sovremennoj nauki, 4*, 1–3.

Skidanova, L. (2009a). Nedruzhestvennye pogloshcheniya kak raznovidnost' korporativnogo konflikta [Hostile Takeovers as a Type of Corporate Conflict]. *Chelovek i trud, 10*, 54–55.

Skidanova, L. (2009b). Reiderstvo kak sotsial'ny fenomen [Raiding as a Social Phenomenon]. *Collections of the Russian State Pedagogic University, 117*, 309–314.

Skidanova, L. (2009c). Raiding During the Crisis: A New Wave. *Conference Proceedings of the Third All-Russia Anti-Crisis Forum "Russian Consumer Market"*, Moscow.

Smetankina, U. (2007). Chto takoe reiderstvo? [What Is Raiding?]. *Vlast, 1*, 37–42.

Thyrêt, I. (2010). Economic Reconstruction or Corporate Raiding? The Borisoglebskii Monastery in Torzhok and the Ascription of Monasteries in the 17th Century. *Kritika: Explorations in Russian and Eurasian History, 11*(3), 490–511.

Tikhomirov, B. (2006). *Reiderstvo: uchebnoe posobie* [Raiding: A Textbook]. Sankt Petersburg: Academic.

Varnalij, Z. (2006). *Tin'ova ekonomika: sutnist', osoblyvosti ta shlyahi legalizatsii*. Kiev: NIDS.

Varnalij, Z., & Mazur, I. (2007). Reiderstvo v Ukraini: peredumovy ta shlyahi podolannya. *Strategichni Pryoritety, 2*(3), 129–136. Retrieved April 2, 2009, from http://www.niss.gov.ua/book/StrPryor/3/17.pdf

Yakovlev, A., Sobolev, A., & Kazun, A. (2014). Means of Production Versus Means of Coercion: Can Russian Business Limit the Violence of a Predatory State? *Post-Soviet Affairs, 30*(2–3), 171–194.

Yalanzhi, E. (2009). Reiderstvo: ataka klonov [Raiding: Attack of the Clones]. *Shchit i Mech*, №29 (1189), August 7. Retrieved August 7, 2009, from http://www.simech.ru/index.php?id=8942

Zahvat.ru. Russian Independent Non-governmental Website About Raiding. Retrieved from http://www.zahvat.ru/

Zhelnorovich, A. (2007). Reiderstvo v Rossii – pokazatel' institutsional'nogo defitsita rossijskoj ekonomiki [Raiding in Russia: The Indicator of Institutional Deficit of the Russian Economy]. *Rossijskaja justitsiya, 8*, 6–10.

CHAPTER 2

Wild-West Capitalism in the East

Communist Cowboy Capitalists

Wild-West capitalism in the East may sound somewhat awkward, but it has been voiced so many times that it has become a textbook maxim and a commonly accepted label. It has also become a characteristic of transitioning Russia and other former Soviet republics. Why would the Wild West apply to the Communist East that had been hidden behind the iron curtain not so long ago? No doubt, Hollywood westerns, including first of all *Stagecoach* and *The Magnificent Seven*, were very popular among Soviet people. But that should not be the reason for the Wild West to apply to the post-Soviet capitalism in the East. Apparently, this is because of its violent nature, injustice, lawlessness, weak role of the state in regulating socioeconomic processes, or, simply put, the dominance of brutal force above everything else. All of these factors may be found in other transitioning societies as well, but in Russia they are dominant. High murder rates, constant criticism of the justice system and dubious court decisions, a multitude of crimes that go unpunished or even unnoticed, and an overwhelmingly corrupted state apparatus are all characteristic of the post-Soviet Russia.

There was never a shortage of books trying to explain post-Soviet realities (see, for instance, Chubais, 2001; Sachs & Pivovarsky, 1994; Treisman, 2011, and most recently, Treisman, 2018, and Aleksashenko, 2018) and to show the way for Russia to survive and carry on its special mission in the new world order (see, for instance, Dugin, 1997, 2010; Medvedev, 2001). From doomsday to prosperity to imaginary chosen destiny, all dramatic

A. L. Osipian, *Political and Economic Transition in Russia*,
https://doi.org/10.1007/978-3-030-03831-1_2

scenarios were written and substantiated by both local and western scholars. The prosperity scenarios all promised market-based democracy and wellbeing. The way out from Stalinist tyranny lay through the set of much advertised market reforms. However, from the economic standpoint, reforms that took place in Russia could hardly lead to any positive changes in the lives of regular citizens.

The steps undertaken by the Russian government over the last three decades were not aimed at building a market economy or democracy in the country. Indeed, in Aleksandr Solzhenitsyn's words,

> It would have been difficult to design a path out of communism worse than the one that has been followed. Our government declared that it is conducting some kind of great reforms. In reality, no real reforms were begun, and no one at any point has declared a coherent program. The name of "reform" simply covers what is blatantly a process of the theft of the national heritage. In other words, many former communists, very flexible, very agile, and others who are basically almost confidence tricksters, petty thieves coming in from the sides, have together in unison began to thieve everything there is from the national resources. It used to belong to the state, … but now under the guise of privatization, all of this has been pocketed. (Pearce, 2011, p. 35)

The thieving nature of Russian privatization in the 1990s and 2000s is beyond any argument. The question remains how these thieves aligned with state bureaucrats managed to realize this economic crime of the century. The Wild-West framework may work as an explanatory tool for the question of how things happened rather than why they happened this way. In Adachi's (2010, p. 1) words, "Russia in the 1990s was referred to frequently as 'the Wild East', a phrase that conjured up images of untamed frontiers—of lawlessness and disputes settled not by the courts, but by violence, and a land of opportunity affording an environment of high risk and high returns."

Although in the East, Wild-West capitalism in Russia had a direct western connection. A word should be said about the visitors from the West who also searched for "high returns" in the "high risk" environment of the Russian market. One such hunting expedition in a risk-saturated environment resulted not only in the fortune earned, but also in the Sergei Magnitsky Act[1] and a personal feud between William Browder and the Russian government.[2] Those willing to take the risk of doing business in Russia should be prepared to incur big losses—both financial and human—

as a cost tied to uncertainty. This was true in the 1990s and remains true today. Russian business environment is not only highly profitable, but also aggressive and threatening. The competition that takes place here extends beyond the usual limits of economic competition, with cost reduction strategies and dumping prices. In Russia, the term *cut throat competition* is not always limited to a figurative meaning. In this sense, Russia's Wild-East capitalism is no different from the Wild West.

The issue of property rights in transition economies, including that of Russia, has become an immanent part of scholarship on post-Communist states (see, for instance, Benham & Benham, 1997). Shlapentokh and Arutunyan's (2013, p. 16) major point that, "the cause of all of the major differences between the Soviet and post-Soviet regimes, as well as the cause of the differences among authoritarian regimes in general, lies in the radical differences in property relations: the dominance of public property in one case and of private property in another," is well taken by those aspiring to understand and describe the nature of raiding. It is of no surprise then that property rights are at the center of scholarship on corporate raiding in the post-Soviet Russia.

The institutionalization of Russian Wild-West-type entrepreneurs came with the formation of financial-industrial groups (FIGs) and privately owned commercial banks. FIGs were large players on the newly emerging market. Moreover, in many ways, FIGs themselves formed these markets, offering new services and products to a society accustomed to near-total deficit. At the same time, FIGs were preoccupied with the privatization of state enterprises, much less so their modernization.[3] The newly reformed Russian banking system, which did not have commercial banks since the Bolshevik revolution, was also preoccupied with activities not so typical for Western banks. Instead of attracting deposits from the population and issuing loans to individuals and private enterprises, private banks were created on the body of state enterprises in order to siphon off the state money and reassign assets to private hands. Legal processing of shady dealings, privatization, transfer of money to the West, nonreturn of export revenues, currency exchange speculations, serving accounts of shell companies, and working with offshores—all these activities were in the arsenal of Russian banks. Scholars have addressed the issue of Russian banking system in the 1990s.[4] Three decades into the reforms, it has become clear that the new Russian banking system was created not to be part of the market economy, but to serve the acquisition and redistribution of state property, including through mass privatization.

The newly created tools of privatization and commercialization were not limited to FIGs and commercial banks. The already existing institutions, including those in the fundament of the statehood, were turning to commercialization. In fact, they have done so actively and with much commercial success. Commercialization of state bureaucracies through illicit ways, including primarily corruption, came to the fore of the transitional agenda. This issue was also addressed by scholars, including local academics, in the 1990s and 2000s. Commercialization of the service by the law enforcement officers was done on a systemic basis and has become a norm. At the same time—and quite expectedly—the problem of legality in law enforcement persists (see, for instance, Kolennikova, Kosals, & Ryvkina, 2004; Romanova, 2000). News on big cases of corruption that involve high-ranking police officers and prosecutors continue to appear in the media for the entire period of economic transition.

Communist bosses arrived at the start of the reforms fully equipped to rob their own citizens. Even first commercial banks were formed before the Soviet Union's collapse and were managed by Communists.[5] These banks were nothing more than parasites feeding off the living body of the state. According to Hoffman (2002, p. 48), "In the year before the Soviet Union collapsed, more than half of all the deposits were from the state. The other half came from cooperatives and other disparate organizations and nascent businesses." All commercial activities conducted during late Perestroika were either done by Communist cadres directly, or had close ties to the Party apparatus and state functioneers. Communist Party cadres throughout the now former socialist bloc started accumulating wealth at an astronomic pace (see, for instance, Hanley, 2000; Hellman, 1998). It is even more surprising that the Communist Party of the Soviet Union was banned in 1991 by then President Boris Yeltsin. Apparently, Communist bosses banned themselves in order to finalize the transformation into business moguls and make the transition complete and irreversible.

The reforms of the late 1980s and early 1990s allowed Soviet Communist Party cadres to keep their property, thus indicating that no real revolution or change of power took place. Communists were not eliminated as a political class, nor were they diminished in their rights, including property rights. As Shlapentokh and Arutunyan (2013, p. 22) point out, "This stood in great contrast to what happened during the violent revolutions in both Russia and China, when the old ruling class lost all their material assets, including their apartments, furniture, or jewels." The change was not a bottom-up grassroots process, as Communist leaders tailored the reform to their personal and clan interests. Figuratively speaking, new cowboys were actually old Communists.[6]

Former Communist bosses were not the only cowboys riding the horse of Wild-West capitalism in Russia. Stripping the state of its assets while distracting the attention of the Soviet people with the talks about market rationality and democratic changes, this turned out to be the Trojan horse, indeed. Criminal groups, including organized crime, were also directly involved in the process of market reforms. Kireev (2007, p. 39) gives the succinct description of major roles and functions of organized crime groups in the post-Soviet Russia:

> At first, criminal groups engaged predominantly in physical protection, convoying of export–import operations, and fraud prevention. But with the development of market relations and the rapid growth in the numbers of transactions, the functions of strong-arm partners became more complex and diverse: these ranged from collecting information about a firm's contractors to resolving corporate disputes, and representing the interests of a business in dealings with state agencies. Strong-arm entrepreneurs were able to perform these business functions through the skillful use of organized criminal structures and information. Strong-arm intermediation involved cooperation between commercial and criminal structures on an irregular basis. In the majority of cases, entrepreneurs turned to criminal structures to recover a debt, convert funds into cash, or resolve a business dispute.

More than three decades after the start of the reforms, Russia can hardly be seen as a market-based democracy. Shlapentokh (2007) goes even further in his critiques, calling contemporary Russia a feudal society, and he is not alone in this critical estimate. A new perspective on the post-Soviet era, presented by the author, suggests that despite some liberal changes, private property led to strong and explicit feudal elements within the society. Similar to Russia, market reforms continue in China too. Unlike Russia, China has not abandoned its Communist ideology. Furthermore, in 2018, the Chinese Communist Party voted for no time limits for the ruler, making it an autocracy similar to Russia.

There are also numerous issues with land appropriations, property rights, corruption, and raiding. The legislation is being adopted along the course of reforms, as the country is ruled by the Communist Party. And yet, predatory raiding based on state corruption is not one of the major characteristics of Chinese economy and society. The answer to this puzzle may be in that post-Soviet Russia is a distributive and redistributive society with a rent-oriented state bureaucracy. Communist China, on the contrary, is a productive system, with redistribution not being a dominant determinant. This is the major distinction between the two countries. In this frame, Wild-West capitalism with its predatory raiding, unsanctioned violence, and corruption is only secondary.

Social Darwinism and Hostile Takeovers

Wild-West capitalism also refers to social Darwinism, especially as related to the economy.[7] Social Darwinism, the theory that human groups and races are subject to the same laws of natural selection as Charles Darwin had perceived in plants and animals, applies to Russian business environment as well. Social Darwinism was popular about a century ago and, with Russian predatory raiding on the rise, it may well enjoy a revival in popularity. According to the theory, the weak were diminished and their cultures delimited while the strong grew in power and in cultural influence over the weak. Social Darwinists held that the life of humans in society was a struggle for existence ruled by the "survival of the fittest."[8]

Social Darwinism emphasizes the competition between races in the process of natural selection. Competition that takes place in the post-Soviet space occurs with the use of noneconomic tools and factors. In fact, within the framework of a predatory state, these noneconomic factors dominate economic ones. The raiding movement in Russia embraces the idea of state interference so long as it means that court decisions and police actions can be bought. Predatory raiding is unnatural because, unlike in social Darwinism, raiders welcome the interference of the state–not the protective and regulatory state, but the predatory state.

Scholarly works on raiding in transition economies—and these are just a few sources, most of which are published recently—focus extensively, and almost exclusively, on property rights. It is property rights that form the conceptual base, a launching pad for investigations into the specifics of post-Soviet raiding. Abrams (2014), Frye (2017), Gans-Morse (2012, 2017), and Markus (2012, 2015, 2016) are all good examples of such a focus, having placed "property" in the titles of their works. Aside from raiding, property rights is a stellar point of research on the post-Soviet transition (See, for instance, Frye, 2004, 2006). It is not hard to explain why property rights occupy so much space in the works of scholars who want to investigate and understand the phenomenon of Russian raiding. Neither Marxists nor supporters of materialist determinism, they nevertheless allocate property rights the key place in their research, and rightly so. Raiding revolves around property, valuable economic assets, and implies operations within a given system of property relations.

The issue of raiding in Russia extends far beyond a conventional understanding of corporate raiding, or asset-grabbing, as Hanson (2014) puts it. But it also extends far beyond a mere discussion of property rights and the mechanisms of their protection. Raiding in Russia is a socioeconomic, legal, and political phenomenon that has yet to be properly framed and researched.

Corruption is the single most important breeding ground for predatory raiding. Corruption as a noneconomic means is used by different agents to advance their interests. Businesses monopolize certain segments of the market in order to maximize profit, state bureaucrats harvest bribes from their clientele, and raiders hijack and resell vulnerable businesses and other economic assets. More than two decades ago, Leitzel (1997) suggested that, despite the barriers the state and mafia extortion create for economic development, there has been a massive increase in private economic activity in Russia. The author also pointed out that the legal norms governing interactions between private businesses and the state in the US may not fit Russian realities: "In such circumstances, high levels of corruption that allow citizens to buy services from government officials for a bribe in the same way they can buy bread at the grocers may not be such a bad outcome" (Leitzel, 1997, p. 128).

This grease-the-wheels approach appears to be somewhat dated, but in the mid-1990s it was popular. Corruption that brought to life raiding can hardly be appreciated in line with "not such a bed outcome, after all." It is clear that Leitzel (1997) points to adaptation, that is, people adapted to the new rules of the game imposed on them externally. But the result of this adaptation is obviously bad. Corruption and predatory raiding on top of it not only increase transaction costs in the national economy and its share in the cost structure of produced products and serviced, but also create a sense of instability and lawlessness. Unstable environments with high transaction costs and low reliance on existing laws are counterproductive and not welcoming of businesses, including those initiated by foreign investors.

Raiding is defined as a relationship that emerges between economic actors regarding the alienation and appropriation of property, when alienation is done against the will or without the consent of the previous owner and without proper compensation, and where appropriation is covered with layers of legality (Osipian, 2018, p. 15). Predatory raiding is defined as the hostile takeover of an enterprise or property that indicates the process of redistribution of property through the use of corruption and fraud. Raiding does not necessarily imply violence, but it always anticipates the application of administrative power, the use of force, be it private force, state force, or a combination of both.

Kireev (2007, p. 32) defines raiding as "systematic activity by stable formal or informal groups, aimed at obtaining the ability to use and distribute (control) assets belonging to other economic actors." According to Abrams (2014, p. 1), criminal corporate raid is "the takeover of a private business through the use of force, whether by means of direct violence or the help of the state." This definition limits the scope of raiding in two significant directions. First, by focusing exclusively on private business, the definition leaves aside the entire mass privatization and all the raiding associated with it. The privatized state or public property simply falls outside the definition, as it is not private business. Furthermore, even aside from the initial and continuing privatization, many public enterprises and properties become the targets of raiders. These are excluded by Abrams' (2014) definition as well. Second, the element of corruption is being missed here, while it is crucially important. The detachment from corruption makes the definition counterproductive. Neither direct violence nor the help of the state in raiding activities is possible without corruption.

Corruption acts as an overarching concept and connecter to ancillary concepts with which it is regularly connected, including state capture, patronage, clientelism, patrimonialism, and particularism (Rothstein & Varraich, 2017, p. 15). Simply put, when it comes to raiding in Russia, corruption may not be taken out of the equation. The literature on political and economic transition in Russia reaffirms the key role that corruption plays in society. Scholars correlate and connect problems of legislative politics and economic power, rule of law, economic crime, blat, kinship, and informal connections, as they affect Russian realties and trends in development (see, for instance, Chaisty, 2006; Ledeneva, 1998; Ledeneva & Kurkchiyan, 2000; Sachs & Pistor, 1997).

In its state structure, Russia combines both legal-rational and patrimonial features. Sakwa's (2010, 2013) notion of the dual state was adopted in most recent works on Russian business and the corporate world (see, for instance, Godzimirski, 2018). The issues of legality and violence in Russia, associated with predatory raiding, are in the focus of Frye (2014), Kazun

(2015a, 2015b), Markus (2015), and Sakwa (2011). Based on evidence from Estonia, Poland, Slovakia, and Ukraine, Abrams (2014) explains variations across post-Communist countries in the frequency of criminal corporate raiding and the effectiveness of property rights institutions by the harm that soft budget constraints do.

Kazun (2015a, 2015b) utilizes a database of 543 cases of violent corporate raiding in Russia's regions from 2011 to 2013[9] in order to test several hypotheses: violent corporate raiding is widespread in regions (1) with well-developed industrial, construction, and trade sectors; (2) rent-oriented law enforcement agencies cooperating with raiders; and (3) low numbers of nongovernmental organizations (NGOs). The findings show that the level of violent raiding is connected to the economic appeal of a given region. Violent raiding is also positively correlated with the level of rent-oriented behavior of regional law enforcement agencies. As the anti-raiding response, Kazun (2015a, 2015b) suggests developing civil mechanisms for the protection of entrepreneurs. Such civil mechanisms may be institutionalized in business associations and other NGOs.

In order to estimate the scale of predatory raiding, which will at the same time shed light on the nature of this troubling phenomenon, Hanson (2014, p. 7) follows statistics on the number of cases on economic crimes investigated by the police and brought to trial in Russian courts:

> The number of cases started in Russia in 2012 (150,000), the number closed (5,000) and the number brought to trial (30,000), quoted by Titov, leave 115,000 unaccounted for. Where, Titov asked, are these cases? The retired Supreme Court judge Vladimir Radchenko replied enigmatically that corruption had a lot to do with this oddity about the numbers. This suggests that a large number of deals are cut whereby the victims of these charges buy themselves out of trouble.

Protection of businesspeople through the protection of their property rights from both predatory raiders and a predatory state has become a hot topic. This topic gains popularity amid continuous allegations of the state's interference with business ownership structures. One conclusion to be derived from the growing discussion on relations between the business community and the state is that Russian businesspeople need protection. And, of all businesspeople, the most prominent are, no doubt, the oligarchs. The topic of oligarchs and corruption in modern Russia can hardly be beaten in terms of popularity. Excellent scholarly works on relationship between oligarchs and the state in Russia have been produced by both local and western scholars (see, for instance, Guriev & Sonin, 2009; Hanson & Teague, 2005; Markus, 2017a, 2017b; Markus & Charnysh, 2017; Sakwa, 2008, 2014).

A clear lack of true market reforms gave rise to oligarchs and, not surprisingly, oligarchs are the ones opposing and preventing the completion of the reforms. This is characteristic of not only Russia, but other countries that emerged in the post-Soviet space. Market reforms in Ukraine remain half-way, and so does democratization. As Havrylyshyn (2017, p. 202) suggests, "Ukraine has suffered from pervasive and persistent corruption, poor ROL and weak institutions because such an opaque environment is best for the oligarchate." Indeed, it is the oligarchs who shape the business and political environment around their interests, and not the other way around. As the author points out, the rule of law (ROL) in Ukraine is at a very low level, and thus both the market reforms and democratization appear to be problematic.

Oligarchs appear to be the fittest, those who reached the finish line of natural selection, the peak of post-Soviet socioeconomic evolution. In natural selection, the fittest are those who demonstrate the most reproductive success. How would this be applied to post-Soviet oligarchs? Do they multiply, and if so, in which way? Do they multiply physically, through multiple marriages and production of multiple offspring? Do they multiply financially, though the amassment of wealth? Do they multiply organizationally and structurally, through the multiplication of their business activities, branches, firms, and by acquiring assets in different sectors of the national economy?

Aside from the fittest—the oligarchs—there are millions of large and small entrepreneurs in the post-Soviet space. They also need to protect themselves and their businesses, and for that reason they frequently form associations. The institutionalization of collective action through legislatively formed organizational arrangements can help businessmen resist autocrats and eventually help attract and retain private investors (Gelbach & Keefer, 2012). "Capitalists of All Russia, Unite!" is the slogan advanced by Markus (2007) in regards to businesses in the state-dominated post-Soviet space. Western scholars address the process of formation and the role and place of business associations in Russia (see, for instance, Duvanova, 2007, 2013), and link business associations with the issue of property rights protection against the predatory state. Pyle (2006, 2011) studies organized business, political competition, and property rights in Russia, and addresses the role of business associations. The author points out that one recent estimate puts the numbers of business associations nationally at close to 5000.[10] It is hard to say how many of these associations are actually active and function according to their stated goals, but the number itself is large.

Yakovlev, Sobolev, and Kazun (2014, p. 179) express an opinion that negotiating property protection between small and medium-sized businesses and the ruling state bureaucracy may lead to a change in the composition of these ruling coalitions that will include representatives of successful medium-sized business under two conditions:

> First, they must not be merely based on the initiative of individuals, but also must reflect the interests of wider social groups. Second, the initiatives must be backed by efficient organizations capable of ensuring the monitoring and enforcement of the agreements concerning the new rules of the state-business relationship. These organizations must be able to exert considerable pressure on their counterparties within the powers that be in the event of violation of those agreements.

Pyle (2011) suggests that there is plenty of evidence that Russia's newly emerged business associations work to strengthen property rights, although this evidence in anecdotal. The author suggests that the role of these business associations is twofold: "Many of their efforts in this regard involve either shining a light on the less flattering features of the business-government interface or improving the flow of policy-relevant information between the business community and state officials" (Pyle, 2011, p. 13). Krylova (2018) calls collective resistance to administrative corruption on the side of individual and small entrepreneurs "Entrepreneurial Spring." Information exchange between the business community and the state may also be facilitated by business ombudsmen, appointed by the government.

Markus (2012) investigates the issue of how businesses can secure their properties by involving other stakeholders under the conditions of predator-saturated environments and weak states. The author uses an original survey of 516 firms in Russia and Ukraine, as well as interview-based case studies, to address the issue of securing property rights and establishing the rule of law in the transitional economy. Most states in the developing world lack the requisite time horizons and institutional capacity to make credible commitments. Markus (2012, 2015) argues that businesses can enforce their property rights without seeking protection and arbitrage from organized criminal groups. Instead, businesspeople can form alliances with other groups of stakeholders, such as foreign investors, community residents, and labor collectives. In the author's view, these groups of stakeholders can impose costs on the potential raiders through a variety of political strategies, allowing firms to defend their property rights not only from private predatory raiders, but also from the predatory state.

International investors, including large institutional investors with international reputations, may be very useful in protecting the property rights of Russian joint-stock companies, of course, if they will be willing to do so. In support of this argument, Markus (2008, p. 91) offers his interview with the head manager of the Emerging Markets Equity Funds at Fidelity Investments:

> a lot of Russian companies like to have EBRD [European Bank for Reconstruction and Development] as shareholder because it provides protection... if you find that EBRD has a stake in a company, it's hard to shake down a company because you'll have all EU governments involved, and it's a pain..., so they [the Russian state officials] don't do it.

More and more scholars are willing to embrace the idea of good businesses[11] and that Russia—in best Shleifer's traditions—is a "normal country."[12] Others are inclined to support this view. Peaceful Russian businesses confront the violence of the predatory state and other—less significant—predators; honest Russian businessmen attempt to establish connections with political personalities in order to secure themselves and their businesses from state attacks. This approach, which has become a very popular narrative, is voiced in Markus (2008), Pyle (2011), Sakwa (2013), and Yakovlev et al. (2014). Calls for business associations as a cornerstone of the resistance movement are usual in this context (Markus, 2007, 2012). Their eager embrace of a victimological narrative as applied to Russian businesspeople nevertheless leaves the door open for some questions and disagreements.

It is true that Russian businesspeople fall prey to predatory raiders, including the predatory state, and do so quite frequently. In fact, it would be fair to say that Russian businesspeople are living on borrowed time thanks to their political connections, but they face the constant risk of being overpowered by predatory raiders who may have stronger political pool. The fall of Yukos and imprisonment of Mikhail Khodorkovsky is a good example in support of this thesis on permanent vulnerability. However, the public and scholarly discourse on predatory raiding often misses the fact that many of these respected businesses of today are nothing more than criminal enterprises of yesterday. Same applies to respected businessmen and property owners—many had started their entrepreneurial careers by committing economic and other serious crimes, including violent crimes. Some killed people, including personally, while others ordered and paid for killings.

Concluding Remarks

Social Darwinism emphasizes competition in the process of natural selection. Competition that takes place in modern Russia is based on the use of noneconomic factors, including direct violence. Moreover, noneconomic factors dominate over economic ones. Russian raiders use state functions of the predatory state in order to achieve their goals. The high level of corruption allows predatory raiders to buy services and decisions of prosecutors, judges, and police officers in order to organize successful hostile takeovers of private businesses and public property. State interference in economic life is considered a norm and, as long as this state of the affairs continues, Russian predatory raiders are not doomed to extinction in the foreseeable future. Predatory raiders in Russia rely on external, noneconomic forces, of which the most welcomed is that of the predatory state.

Those few scholarly works that focus on raiding in transition economies focus extensively, and almost exclusively, on the protection of property rights of private owners. It is property rights that form the conceptual base to investigate the post-Soviet predatory raiding. Predatory raiding, as any form of raiding, is indivisible from property and occurs in a given system of property relations that exist in the country. Given the paramount importance of reforming property relations in transitioning societies, predatory raiding in Russia is nevertheless much more than just a story about property rights violations. Predatory raiding in Russia is an action, a show of force, and at the same time a manifestation of structural deficiencies of the state apparatus.

Notes

1. Gray, Rosie. (2017). Bill Browder's Testimony to the Senate Judiciary Committee. *The Atlantic*, July 25, 2017. Retrieved January 6, 2018, from https://www.theatlantic.com/politics/archive/2017/07/bill-browders-testimony-to-the-senate-judiciary-committee/534864/
2. Flynn, Sean. (2017). Bill Browder, Putin Enemy No. 1. *GQ*, November 17, 2017. Retrieved January 6, 2018, from https://www.gq.com/story/bill-browder-putin-enemy-number-1

3. On the analysis of the role of Russian financial-industrial groups (FIGs) in transition, see, for instance, Johnson, Juliet E. (1997). Russia's Emerging Financial-Industrial Groups. *Post-Soviet Affairs*, 13(4), pp. 333–365.
4. On the analysis of the role of the Russian banking system in transition, see, for instance, Johnson, Juliet. (2000). *A Fistful of Rubles: The Rise and Fall of the Russian Banking System*. Ithaca, NY: Cornell University Press.
5. It is during the Soviet era, in 1990, that the Party legally allowed offshore businesses, enacting a special law. The offshore scandals have been going on since then. The first legal private businesses were not cooperatives, legally allowed only in 1988, but creative centers of the Young Communist League, abbreviated as Komsomol, legally registered in 1986. The first private commercial bank in the USSR was founded as early as in 1988. On August 24, 1988, a private commercial bank was registered in a distant Kazakh city of Chimkent. Mikhail Khodorkovsky's Menatep was registered 25th. By the end of 1988, there were 41 registered private commercial banks—one year later, over 1500. The first legal Soviet millionaire, Artem Tarasov, was a member of the Communist Party (for more, see: Stogov, Il'ya. (2007). *Milliardery* [Billionaires]. Moscow: Labirint. Retrieved May 6, 2017, from https://www.e-reading.club/bookreader.php/68577/Stogov_-_Milliardery.html).
6. William Browder, a vivid critic of Putin's regime and one of Russia's declared enemies, has a strong Communist family background. Browder is the CEO and co-founder of the Hermitage Capital Management, an investment fund that moved to Russia in the 1990s and was the largest foreign portfolio investor in the country. Browder is the grandson of Earl Browder, a Communist from Kansas who moved to the Soviet Union in 1927, staying for several years and marrying a Russian. He returned with his wife to the US to lead the Communist Party, and even ran for US presidency in 1936 and 1940 (see, for instance, Levy, Clifford J. (2008)). An Investment Gets Trapped in Kremlin's Vise. *The New York Times*, July 24, 2008. Retrieved May 6, 2017, from http://www.nytimes.com/2008/07/24/world/europe/24kremlin.html?hp=&pagewanted=all

   Browder said, in an interview, "I had a lot of my family in me, and tried to find a way of connecting my past to my future." (see, for instance, The Weekend Interview: The Man Who Stood Up to Putin. *The Wall Street Journal*. May 9, 2014. Retrieved May 6, 2017, from https://www.wsj.com/articles/the-weekend-interview-the-man-who-stood-up-to-putin-1399674165?mg=reno64-wsj&url=http%3A%2F%2Fonline.wsj.com%2Farticle%2FSB10001424052702304885404579552120262256240.html&tesla=y).
7. The social Darwinists believed that the process of natural selection acting on variations in the population would result in the survival of the best

competitors and in continuing improvements to the population. Societies were viewed as organisms that evolve in this manner. The theory was used to support laissez-faire capitalism and political conservatism. Class stratification was justified on the basis of "natural" inequalities among individuals, for the control of property was said to be a correlate of superior and inherent moral attributes, such as industriousness, temperance, and frugality. Attempts to reform society through state intervention or other means would, therefore, interfere with natural processes; unrestricted competition and defense of the status quo were in accord with biological selection. The poor were the "unfit" and should not be aided; in the struggle for existence, wealth was a sign of success. Social Darwinism. *Encyclopædia Britannica*. Retrieved May 6, 2017, from https://www.britannica.com/topic/social-Darwinism

8. Phrase "survival of the fittest" was proposed by the British philosopher and scientist Herbert Spencer. "This survival of the fittest, which I have here sought to express in mechanical terms, is that which Mr. Darwin has called 'natural selection', or the preservation of favoured races in the struggle for life." Spencer, Herbert. (1864). Principles of Biology, vol. 1, p. 444, as sited in Stucke, Maurice E. (2008). Better Competition Advocacy. *St. John's Law Review*. Retrieved June 5, 2017, from https://works.bepress.com/maurice_stucke/1/
9. The database is assembled by the Center of Public Procedures "Business against Corruption."
10. William Pyle's interview in July 2005 in Moscow with the Director of the Department for Cooperation with Business Associations at the Chamber of Commerce of the Russian Federation.
11. The idea that Russian businessmen present the demand for law becomes more and more popular. The demand itself is said to be growing. See, for instance, Gans-Morse, Jordan. (2017). *Property Rights in Post-Soviet Russia: Violence, Corruption, and the Demand for Law*. New York: Cambridge University Press.
12. Shleifer, Andrei. (2003). *A Normal Country: Russia after Communism*. Cambridge, MA: Harvard University Press.

References

Abrams, N. (2014). *Political Thugs: Criminal Corporate Raiding and Property Rights in Early-Capitalist Eastern Europe*. Ph.D. Dissertation, University of California, Berkeley.

Adachi, Y. (2010). *Building Big Business in Russia: The Impact of Informal Corporate Governance Practices*. New York: Routledge.

Aleksashenko, S. (2018). *Putin's Counterrevolution*. Washington, DC: Brookings Institution Press.
Benham, A., & Benham, L. (1997). Property Rights in Transition Economies: A Commentary on What Economists Know. In J. Nelson, C. Tilly, & L. Walker (Eds.), *Transforming Post-Communist Political Economies* (pp. 35–60). Washington, DC: National Academies Press.
Chaisty, P. (2006). *Legislative Politics and Economic Power in Russia*. Basingstoke: Palgrave Macmillan.
Chubais, A. (2001). *Privatizatsiya po-rossijski* [Privatization a la Russe]. Moscow: Vagrius. Retrieved May 9, 2012, from http://www.chubais.ru/show_prn.cgi?/current/public/publik_1.htm
Dugin, A. (1997). *Osnovy geopolitiki: Geopoliticheskoe budushchee Rossii* [The Foundations of Geopolitics: The Geopolitical Future of Russia]. Moscow: Arktogeja.
Dugin, A. (2010). *Konets ekonomiki* [The End of Economics]. Sankt Petersburg: Amfora.
Duvanova, D. (2007). Bureaucratic Corruption and Collective Action: Business Associations in the Post-Communist Transition. *Journal of Comparative Politics, 39*, 441–461.
Duvanova, D. (2013). *Building Business in Post-communist Russia, Eastern Europe, and Eurasia: Collective Goods, Selective Incentives, and Predatory States*. New York: Cambridge University Press.
Frye, T. (2004). Credible Commitment and Property Rights: Evidence from Russia. *American Political Science Review, 98*, 453–466.
Frye, T. (2006). Original Sin, Good Works, and Property Rights in Russia. *World Politics, 58*, 479–504.
Frye, T. (2014). Legality and Violence in Russia: An Introduction. *Post-Soviet Affairs, 30*(2–3), 87–88.
Frye, T. (2017). *Property Rights and Property Wrongs: How Power, Institutions, and Norms Shape Economic Conflict in Russia*. New York: Cambridge University Press.
Gans-Morse, J. (2012). Threats to Property Rights in Russia: From Private Coercion to State Aggression. *Post-Soviet Affairs, 28*(3), 263–295.
Gans-Morse, J. (2017). *Property Rights in Post-Soviet Russia: Violence, Corruption, and the Demand for Law*. New York: Cambridge University Press.
Gelbach, S., & Keefer, P. (2012). Private Investment and the Institutionalization of Collective Action in Autocracies: Ruling Parties and Legislatures. *Journal of Politics, 74*(2), 621–635.
Godzimirski, J. (2018). *The Political Economy of Russian Aluminium: Between the Dual State and Global Markets*. New York: Palgrave Macmillan.
Guriev, S., & Sonin, K. (2009). Dictators and Oligarchs: A Dynamic Theory of Contested Property Rights. *Journal of Public Economics, 93*(1), 1–13.

Hanley, E. (2000). Cadre Capitalism in Hungary and Poland: Property Accumulation among Communist-Era Elites. *East European Politics and Societies, 14*(1), 143–178.

Hanson, P. (2014, March). *Reiderstvo: Asset-Grabbing in Russia*. Russia and Eurasia PP 2014/03. Chatham House. Retrieved August 12, 2017, from http://www.chathamhouse.org/sites/default/files/home/chatham/public_html/sites/default/files/20140300AssetGrabbingRussiaHanson1.pdf

Hanson, P., & Teague, E. (2005). Big Business and the State in Russia. *Europe-Asia Studies, 57*, 657–680.

Havrylyshyn, O. (2017). *The Political Economy of Independent Ukraine: Slow Starts, False Starts, and a Last Chance*. London: Palgrave Macmillan.

Hellman, J. (1998). Winners Take All: The Politics of Partial Reform in Postcommunist Transitions. *World Politics, 5*(2), 203–234.

Hoffman, D. (2002). *The Oligarchs: Wealth and Power in the New Russia*. New York: Public Affairs.

Kazun, A. (2015a). Violent Corporate Raiding in Russia: Preconditions and Protective Factors. *Demokratizatsiya: The Journal of Post-Soviet Democratization, 23*(4), 459–484.

Kazun, A. (2015b). Reiderstvo v regionakh Rossii: indikatory i factory [Raiding in Russia's Regions: Indicators and Causes]. *Mir Rossii, 24*(3), 33–60.

Kireev, A. (2007). Raiding and the Market for Corporate Control: The Evolution of Strong-Arm Entrepreneurship. *Problems of Economic Transition, 50*(8), 29–45.

Kolennikova, O., Kosals, L., & Ryvkina, R. (2004). Kommertsializatsiya sluzhebnoj deyatel'nosti rabotnikov militsii [Commercialization of the Service by the Law Enforcement Officers]. *Sotsiologicheskie issledovaniya, 3*, 73–83.

Krylova, Y. (2018). *Corruption and the Russian Economy: How Administrative Corruption Undermines Entrepreneurship and Economic Opportunities*. New York and London: Routledge.

Ledeneva, A. (1998). *Russia's Economy of Favours: Blat, Networking and Informal Exchange*. Cambridge, UK: Cambridge University Press.

Ledeneva, A., & Kurkchiyan, M. (2000). *Economic Crime in Russia*. London: Kluwer Law.

Leitzel, J. (1997). Rule Evasion in Transitional Russia. In J. Nelson, C. Tilly, & L. Walker (Eds.), *Transforming Post-Communist Political Economies* (pp. 118–130). Washington, DC: National Academies Press.

Markus, S. (2007). Capitalists of All Russia, Unite! Business Mobilization Under Debilitated Dirigisme. *Polity, 39*(3), 277–304.

Markus, S. (2008). Corporate Governance as Political Insurance: Firm-level Institutional Creation in Emerging Markets and Beyond. *Socio-Economic Review, 6*(1), 69–98.

Markus, S. (2012). Secure Property as a Bottom-Up Process: Firms, Stakeholders, and Predators in Weak States. *World Politics, 64*(2), 242–277.
Markus, S. (2015). *Property, Predation, and Protection: Piranha Capitalism in Russia and Ukraine.* New York: Cambridge University Press.
Markus, S. (2016). Sovereign Commitment and Property Rights: the Case of Ukraine's Orange Revolution. *Studies in Comparative International Development, 51*(4), 411–433.
Markus, S. (2017a). Oligarchs and Corruption in Putin's Russia: Of Sand Castles and Geopolitical Volunteering. *Georgetown Journal of International Affairs, 18*(2), 26–32.
Markus, S. (2017b). The Atlas That Has Not Shrugged: Why Russia's Oligarchs Are an Unlikely Force for Change. *Daedalus, 146*(2), 101–112.
Markus, S., & Charnysh, V. (2017). The Flexible Few: Oligarchs and Wealth Defense in Developing Democracies. *Comparative Political Studies, 50*(12), 1632–1665.
Medvedev, R. (2001). *Vremya Putina? Rossiya na rubezhe vekov* [The Time of Putin? Russia on the Border of Centuries]. Moscow: Prava cheloveka.
Osipian, A. (2018). *The Political Economy of Corporate Raiding in Russia.* London and New York: Routledge.
Pearce, J. (2011). *Solzhenitsyn: A Soul in Exile.* San Francisco: Ignatius Press.
Pyle, W. (2006). Collective Action and Post-Communist Enterprise: The Economic Logic of Russia's Business Associations. *Europe-Asia Studies, 58*, 491–521.
Pyle, W. (2011). Organized Business, Political Competition, and Property Rights: Evidence from the Russian Federation. *Journal of Law, Economics and Organization, 27*(1), 2–31.
Romanova, A. (2000). Sostoyanie zakonnosti pri osushchestvlenii pravoohranitel'noj deyatel'nosti sotrudnikami organov vnutrennikh del [Legality in Law Enforcement]. In A. I. Dolgova (Ed.), *Prestupnost' i vlast'* [Criminality and Power] (pp. 48–49). Moscow: Russian Criminological Association.
Rothstein, B., & Varraich, A. (2017). *Making Sense of Corruption.* New York: Cambridge University Press.
Sachs, J., & Pistor, K. (Eds.). (1997). *The Rule of Law and Economic Reform in Russia.* Boulder, CO: Westview Press.
Sachs, J., & Pivovarsky, A. (1994). *Ekonomika perehidnogo periodu* [The Transition Economy]. Kyiv: Osnova.
Sakwa, R. (2008). Putin and the Oligarchs. *New Political Economy, 13*, 185–191.
Sakwa, R. (2010). The Dual State in Russia. *Post-Soviet Affairs, 26*(3), 185–206.
Sakwa, R. (2011, December 5). Raiding in Russia. *Russian Analytical Digest: State-Business Relations and Modernization* (105), 9–13.

Sakwa, R. (2013). Systemic Stalemate, Reiderstvo, and the Dual State. In N. Robinson (Ed.), *The Political Economy of Russia* (pp. 69–96). Lanham, MD: Rowman & Littlefield.

Sakwa, R. (2014). *Putin and the Oligarch: The Khodorkovsky-Yukos Affair*. New York: I. B. Tauris.

Shlapentokh, V. (2007). *Contemporary Russia as a Feudal Society: A New Perspective on the Post-Soviet Era*. New York: Palgrave Macmillan.

Shlapentokh, V., & Arutunyan, A. (2013). *Freedom, Repression, and Private Property in Russia*. New York: Cambridge University Press.

Treisman, D. (2011). *The Return: Russia's Journey from Gorbachev to Medvedev*. New York: Free Press.

Treisman, D. (Ed.). (2018). *The New Autocracy: Information, Politics, and Policy in Putin's Russia*. Washington, DC: Brookings Institution Press.

Yakovlev, A., Sobolev, A., & Kazun, A. (2014). Means of Production Versus Means of Coercion: Can Russian Business Limit the Violence of a Predatory State? *Post-Soviet Affairs, 30*(2–3), 171–194.

CHAPTER 3

Parasitism and Corporate Predation

Parasites in Soviet and Post-Soviet Russia

In the Stalinist regime, the role of the predator was monopolized by the state. The state exercised total control over the human life, including in both economic and noneconomic spheres. The totalitarian regime was the only predator preying on its own people. At the same time, there were parasites who lived off the people's body. Some of these parasites emerged during the New Economic Policy [Novaya ekonomicheskaya politika, NEP], while others formed and existed under Leonid Brezhnev's "developed socialism" that has later become known as *zastoy* or, literally, the "slowdown." Despite its attempts at redistributional justice and equality, the Soviet system was saturated with predators and parasites of all types (see, for instance, Bernstam & Rabushka, 2003). The major form of grand-scale parasitism during the entire Soviet era was embezzlement. Embezzlement was not only on a grand scale, but on a small scale as well, including in the retail sector and the underdeveloped service sector. Department stores, shops, groceries, farmers' markets, restaurants, and cafeteria were classic examples of the services industry that suffered from petty embezzlement (see, for instance, Duhamel, 2010).[1]

The predominance of embezzlement may be explained by the dominance and indeed near monopoly of the state over productive assets. Thus, the major task of a given crook was embezzling from the state. According to Kondrat'eva and Sokolov (2009, p. 134), there was always control over

A. L. Osipian, *Political and Economic Transition in Russia*,
https://doi.org/10.1007/978-3-030-03831-1_3

materially responsible civil servants and fight against embezzlement and theft in the Soviet system, and this control was always problematic.

In many instances, embezzlement was not in cash, but in kind. A classical form of petty embezzlement was *nesuny*, a widespread phenomenon of the socialist economy. *Nesuny*, literally, carryout people, were petty thieves who stole things from their workplaces. Shlapentokh (2007, p. 140) contends that the Russians "regularly stole from their workplaces, despite the efforts of the Soviet state to protect public property. While pilfering from factories, collective farms, construction sites, and offices was perceived as morally acceptable, stealing the belongings of individuals was strongly condemned." The majority of socialist workers could be qualified as *nesuny*; just about everyone was taking home something from the workplace, including goods, prefabricated products, working tools, and uniforms that belonged to the state. At the same time, taking home something from the workplace was considered as a near-entitlement. In public opinion, if that would be done by someone other than the worker himself/herself, that would be a theft of state property. But if it is done by the worker at his/her workplace, then it was considered ok and well tolerated by the public, at least in modest amounts. And that is precisely what made *nesuny* phenomenon parasitic. Petty embezzlement was mostly confined to personal consumption, and the losses suffered by the economy due to the *nesuny* problem were moderate. The restrictions on personal consumption played the controlling function over people's lifestyles. Sources of income had to be justified by the household (Alexeev, 1988).

Parasitism was not limited to embezzlement and bribery. Nepotism and cronyism could be found in job placements, entering public universities with limited access, and obtaining scarce goods and services. Such practices were known as *kumovstvo* and *blat*. *Blat* meant the access to a limited resource or asset based on informal connections. Blat as a form of rent-seeking behavior is described in Spiridonov (2000), Pleines (2000), and Ledeneva (2008a, 2008b). The Soviet economy, often characterized as the shortage economy or economy of deficit (Kornai, 1980), where the access to goods and services was limited by production capacities, chronically suffered from *blat*. Birdsall (2000, p. 170) suggests that *blat* was coupled with the Soviet system of property rights and distribution, and point to the parasitic nature of this phenomenon: "Due to the nature of the Soviet order blat can be seen as parasitic on the Soviet economy, but at the same time as a natural reaction of ordinary people to the rigidities of the regime." Thus, the author confirms the presence of not only a significant socioeconomic stratum of parasites in the Soviet totalitarian regime, but also the entire sprawling culture of parasitism.

The multiplying parasitic structures that grew in the 1990s were not something new to Russia. The Russian economy had already had rich experiences with the corruption and abuse of public property during the period from 1921 to 1928, when the NEP was designed and implemented by the Bolsheviks. NEP was intended to introduce some market reforms and revitalize the economy, devastated by World War I and the Civil War that followed the October Revolution of 1917. Along with the positive results for the growing national economy, NEP brought a growing culture of corruption and mismanagement, as confirmed in works of Fitzpatrick, Rabinowitch, and Stites (1991), Kudriavtsev (1991), and Goland (1998). Small private enterprises and producers used the difference between prices set by the state and market prices to accumulate wealth, while feeding from large state enterprises. There were absurd cases when truckloads of goods were leaving a state enterprise through one gate and entering it back through the other gate, "supplying" the product at a much-inflated rate.

Many corrupt schemes used in the transition economy of the 1990s were but exact blueprints of corrupt schemes used during NEP: "The newly emerged parallel structures that played a role of intermediaries were often nothing other than parasites. They grew on the body of Soviet enterprises as mushrooms grow on trees" (Osipian, 2010, p. 828). Studies of theory and history of the shadow economy in the Soviet Union were done by Soviet era exiles (Simis, 1982), and later by contemporary Russian scholars (see, for instance, Latov, 2001). Some scholars even acknowledged the existence of a Soviet mafia similar to its Italian counterpart (Vaksberg, 1991). And this is given that the Soviet authorities always prided themselves in the declared absence of professional criminal groups in the USSR.

National entrepreneurs of the Soviet era, Perestroika, and the post-Soviet period normally did not have the skills for creating and managing economically effective and efficient businesses. This deficiency has become even more apparent under the introduction of market reforms. Still, this shortcoming in managerial skills would have been even more obvious under the conditions of the free market, if such would ever emerge in the post-Soviet Russia. So-called *tsekhoviki*, who held semi-legal workshops and produced consumer goods in the Soviet era, could not possibly be profitable, thanks to the lack of their economic knowledge and business skills. Indeed, such knowledge was simply absent, and their business skills were quite simple at best. They were able to generate profits thanks only to six factors which will be discussed below. All of these factors have little or nothing to do with the art of entrepreneurship.

First, economic operations of *tsekhoviki* were focused on the production of consumer goods. The Soviet system was distinctive for its lack of many kinds of consumer goods and services. *Tsekhoviki* filled the niche in the consumer market left unfilled by the socialist-planned administrative national economy, regulated and owned by the state. Second, goods, produced by semi-legal workshops, were easy to sell even though they were of relatively low quality. This gave high velocity of money, also called velocity of circulation, quick and substantial commodity turnover, and a speedy return on invested capital.

Competition and corruption were two defining factors in *tsekhoviki* operations. Absence of the former and presence of the latter gave *tsekhoviki* a very welcoming environment, best trading conditions, so to speak. Thus, third, *tsekhoviki* did not have to work under the pressure of tough competition, simply because there were no competitors. Fourth, the semi-legal character of the workshops and their commercial activities anticipated not only the high transaction costs of operation, but also a difficult entry into the market for potential private competitors. *Tsekhoviki* were negotiating their operations and indeed their very existence with the organs of state oversight, based on personal connections and bribery. Thus, corruptibility of state bureaucrats also played a role in this business. This feature can hardly be related to ideal free market conditions.

Fifth, *tsekhoviki* carried only minimal economic costs. They did not pay necessary contributions to their workers' pension funds or health insurance, because all of these functions were taken over by the state. Moreover, *tsekhoviki* often tried to use the equipment of state factories illegally, for free, or for a bribe, hiring their workers to work nights or on weekends. And finally, sixth, *tsekhoviki* were parasites on the body of the state. They bought raw materials and supplies from the state enterprises at state prices, which were normally reduced. Moreover, they tried to buy stolen supplies for an even lower price or steal the raw materials and supplies from state enterprises. At the same time, they sold their products at black market prices, that is, much higher than those in state department stores. It is obvious that under the conditions of perfect competition, open market, absence of corruption, or black and gray markets, such entrepreneurs would have to either change their strategies or become ineffective and go out of business.

There is a commonly shared view that *kooperatory* [cooperators] of the Perestroika period were talented entrepreneurs, but this is not exactly true. Cooperators of Perestroika were somewhat similar to *tsekhoviki* of the Soviet era. They organized profitable small enterprises under conditions very distant from what is known as an open and free market. In fact, they benefited from nonmarket conditions. Similar to *tsekhoviki*, cooperators continued the mission of filling the niche of consumer goods that were in short supply in the Soviet economy. The novelty that cooperators used had less emphasis on production of goods and more reliance on provision of services. As poor as the Soviet economy was in terms of consumer goods, it was even poorer in terms of consumer services. Producing and selling services turned out to be a gold mine for cooperators, at least in the short run. But that was enough, because Perestroika did not last long.

The economic success of cooperators may be explained by the chronic deficit of consumer goods and services coupled with a significant amount of savings at the public's disposal. Simply put, people had money, and they were ready to spend it, but there was not much on which to spend it. The demand for consumer services significantly exceeded the available supply. All the prices were regulated by the state, and in fact set by the state. Thus, a typical balancing mechanism of the market economy, reaching price equilibrium between supply and demand on consumer goods and services, did not work here. Therefore, increasing prices in order to diminish the demand was not an option.

As a result of such supply and demand "scissors," commission stores, cafes, pubs, railway station fast food stands, cafeterias, laundries, flower stands, tobacco kiosks, and paid public restrooms turned out to be highly profitable enterprises. It was hard to imagine paid public restrooms in a socialist society, where even heart surgery was free, but according to the Roman Emperor Diocletian, who set similar services in ancient Rome, "money does not smell." Soviet money did not depreciate or suffer inflation and, thus, any losses due to inflation did not threaten the cooperators. Instead, they enjoyed access to cash, so unusual for typical Soviet enterprises, where all transactions were managed through state bank accounts.

However, with the fall of Communism, the situation has changed. The disintegration of the Soviet Union, hyperinflation, mass privatization, including privatization of large enterprises and entire branches of the economy, left behind *tsekhoviki* and cooperators. Formation of market conditions for entrepreneurs, and market economy in general, demanded entrepreneurs of a new type. Unfortunately, this new type of entrepreneurs did not exist in the country. Individuals, quite skillful in profiteering and cashing out on shortages and deficits, parasites on the body of the Soviet economy, turned out to be unable to work effectively under market conditions. They continued to function on a predominantly nonmarket basis.

Inability to manage firms effectively in market conditions does not leave those holding onto productive assets and economic power with much choice but to take over property and rely on the rent-oriented structure of economic relations. As a result, the luxurious lifestyle is guaranteed to just a few. These few owners enjoy a luxurious lifestyle not because of economic efficiency and profitability of enterprises, but based on a high level of concentration of already accumulated significant economic assets in the hands of just a few members of the society. An entrepreneur in the classical definition is a work-loving, savvy, rational individual who is not afraid to take initiative and face reasonable economic risks.

In distinction of this classical type of entrepreneur, Russian entrepreneurs do not show similar qualities. They are not particularly characterized by entrepreneurial spirit, managerial skills, love of work, or even less so being savvy. To the contrary, they emphasize their luxury lifestyle and prolific spending on assets that have nothing to do with economic production. The French political theorist, Montesquieu (1892, Book V, Chapter 7, section 6) said, "When a democracy is founded on commerce, private people may acquire vast riches without corruption of morals... because the spirit of commerce is naturally attended with that of frugality, economy, moderation, order and rule."[2] Montesquieu's saying would hardly apply to any of Russia's nouveaux riches, nor would modern Russia qualify to be named a "democracy founded on commerce."

Glaz'ev (1997, p. 116) points out that as a result of strong criminalization of the mass privatization of state property and orientation of the participants of the privatization process on speculative and high profits, another important mechanism of economic growth was blocked. This mechanism includes economic motivation of the owner of the means of production. Organizers of the privatization campaign and their business partners oriented themselves to speculative and high revenues obtained from resale of shares of significantly undervalued enterprises. The author also points out that the majority of privatized enterprises still do not have owners interested in their development. At the same time, the state budget lost hundreds of trillions of rubles in potential revenues from privatization.

Speculative and unreasonably high revenues and profits were part of the general orientation of the early businessmen, when they preferred to steal rather than buy cheap. A rate of profit of around 20 percent, considered a good deal in the western world, would not even be taken seriously by the early Russian entrepreneurs. They were looking at rates of return of hundreds of percent, with little initial investment, and a fast money turnout. The good way of reducing the cost of production was not to buy supplies at reduced prices, but to steal them or to bribe those who can let the entrepreneur to steal them.

An understanding of this problem is present not only among the masses, but among the leadership of the law enforcement agencies as well. The Deputy Chief of the Investigations Committee [Sledstvennyj komitet, SK] Oleg Logunov, says that,

> The economy which received a new development impulse in the 1990s of the last century was not a market economy. The winner was not the one who produced goods or services of better quality at a lower price, but the one who bought protection from bureaucrats or even criminal groups in exchange for bribes. Competitors were eliminated either by killing them or through administrative pressure… The group of entrepreneurs who achieved the entrepreneurial Olympus in this way is unable to exist in different conditions. These people are unable to produce high quality goods and services. They are as dangerous as those who accept bribes, because they impede economic development.

Logunov thinks that contemporary corruption was born thanks in part to businessmen who perverted and corrupted bureaucrats.[3]

Logunov is right, in that not all corruption that exists in the realm of state-business relations is driven by state bureaucrats demanding bribes and kickbacks from businessmen. In many instances, businessmen initiate corrupt transactions, offering bribes and making bureaucrats overstep or abuse their authority. Even more so Logunov is right about Russia's prosperous businessmen when it comes to their ability to compete successfully in an open market environment. Oftentimes those who own big businesses have little to do with real entrepreneurial talents.

Parasitism in the Soviet era was not limited to ***nesuny***, ***tsekhoviki***, ***blat*-users**, street-level bureaucrats with their gift-receiving ambitions, petty embezzling crooks, and other characters of the shadow economy. The Soviet ruling class, known as ***nomenklatura*** (see, for instance, Karatuev, 1998; Voslensky, 1984), although not nearly as numerous, was not less harmful to the economy. *Nomenklatura* related to *nesuny* about the same way as grand corruption relates to petty corruption. The elitist Soviet *nomenklatura* was parasitic to the society as it produced little but consumed a lot. Gorbachev's Perestroika was certainly not a revolution, nor was the attempt of market reforms in the early 1990s. Despite the significant transition to private property, the old leadership structures did not lose their power. To the contrary, in many respects, the process of individual power accumulation gained momentum. Furthermore, the ruling political class did not lose its material privileges or personal assets, including flats, summer houses or *dachas*, cars, furniture, and gold. Simply put, there was no witch hunting for now ex-Communist leaders. Yesterday's Communist leaders were today's entrepreneurs, being first in line for acquiring state property at nominal prices.

> [t]he new rules did not restrain the access of anybody in the party apparatus from the acquisition of big property. They allowed the nomenclature to use their positions (for instance, as a minister or the director of a big factory), as well as their rich social capital, to be among the first who could privatize state property for their own benefit. The large sums of money that started to flow to former apparatchiks made the old party privileges unimportant, and provided "new Russians" with benefits the likes of which were unthinkable in Soviet times, when the ruling elite could not even permit itself extravagances. (Shlapentokh & Arutunyan, 2013, p. 22)

This rich social capital in Soviet and post-Soviet Russia included, primarily, kinship, personal connections, knowledge of the current situation and projects for development, and involvement in illicit activities as well.

Soft budget constraints, which are the centerpiece of Abrams' (2014, p. 1) analysis of predatory raiding in the post-Soviet space, "ended up enriching and empowering a class of political thugs whose comparative advantage lay solely in their political connections, not their capacity for productive economic activity. Having accumulated their initial fortunes by stealing state assets, it was a natural and logical step to begin stealing them from others in the form of raiding." In the course of state-organized "market" reforms, high-ranking state bureaucrats known as Communist Party cadres converted into Russian oligarchs, and this conversion signified the transition from socialist parasites to post-socialist predatory raiders. The parasitic and nonproductive lifestyle of Russian oligarchs, distinct with conspicuous consumption, leaves no chances for a positive image in the public space.

The mass media—both Russian and international—is quite prolific in developing stories and distributing news about the extravagant spending of Russian oligarchs. For instance, the media eagerly reports about yet another Russian oligarch completing a luxury yacht that will become the largest and most expensive yacht in the world, beating in value and size the previous record, also belonging to a Russian oligarch. A real entrepreneur, even if he/she operates with hundreds of millions or even billions of dollars, would not spend $450 million on a personal yacht.[4] To the contrary, he/she would invest this money into production in order to generate profit and then likely reinvest it.

Russian oligarchs prefer to invest in property, because they are simply unable and unwilling to work effectively. They rely on preserving their wealth in such assets as real estate, yachts, planes, land, and art, but these assets are not productive. They do not create added value. Moreover, Russian oligarchs acquire and keep all their assets abroad, in countries where private property is sometimes even more sacred than the state itself. For instance, London has become a sanctuary city for Russian oligarchs. Furthermore, some of these oligarchs are no longer friendly to the Kremlin, posing as political exiles and entering into a publicized feud with the Russian authorities.[5]

No Predator Without a Prey

The acceptance of social Darwinism calls for natural analogies to predatory raiding. Definitions of predation are not in short supply. This study will offer just a few to set the agenda. *The Merriam-Webster Dictionary* defines predation as the act of preying or plundering, also known as depredation; a mode of life in which food is primarily obtained by the killing and consuming of animals.[6] Predation and depredation derive primarily from the Latin verb *praedari*, meaning "to plunder," an ancestor to words "predator" and "prey."[7] The Biology Online Dictionary suggests that predation is a form of symbiotic relationship between two organisms of unlike species, in which one of them acts as predator that captures and feeds on the other organism that serves as the prey.[8] Accordingly, a predator is an organism that preys upon other organisms.[9] And there is no predator without a prey. Prey is the animal being hunted or the organism being eaten.[10]

The term *predation* first appeared in English in the seventeenth century, and is most commonly used in contexts relating to nature and ecology in order to describe the methodical, almost automatic destruction of life.[11] Since then, terms "predation" and "predator" have seen a much broader application. There is no longer a need for one species to eat another to qualify as a predator. Terms "corporate predator," "social predator," and "sexual predator" are good examples of such a use. Predatory raiders, the term that originates from zoomorphism, certainly add to this list. Zoomorphism is the shaping of something in animal form or terms. Zoomorphism, reverse of anthropomorphism, denotes the tendency of viewing human behavior in terms of the behavior of animals.[12] The term zoomorphism is derived from the Greek *zoon*, meaning animal, and *morphe*, meaning shape or form. The Russian predator, ascribed with animal characteristics and supported by the state, hunts for most lucrative businesses, property, and land. This image may be purified or extracted from the mosaics of post-Soviet transformation with the help of court cases, legal documents, interviews, results of surveys, media reports, and videos posted on social media.

Predators exist within a certain food chain. In nature, food chains normally include primary producers, herbivores, primary consumers, secondary consumers, and tertiary consumers. In business, one can also observe primary producers, those who transfer the product from producers to consumers, and consumers. The problem for businesses begins when the state, acting as a predator, becomes a tertiary consumer. All organisms in a food chain, except the first organism, are consumers, that is, organisms that eat other organisms. On the one hand, there are myriad shell firms that register and disappear in one day with no use to the society, and nevertheless permitted by the state. On the other hand, there are solid and well-established reputable businesses being raided, hijacked, and resold or destroyed.

In corporate M&A, including the hostile ones, assets are being transferred and consumed in production. In the case of Russia, the focus is on the transfer of assets, much less so on production. Similarly, in a food chain, there is also reliable energy transfer through each step of the consumption pyramid. However, all the energy at one stage of the chain is not absorbed by the organism at the next stage. The amount of energy transferred from one stage to another decreases. The same rule applies to predatory raiding—given the high transaction costs and frequently the inability to manage or even sell assets at market prices, predatory raiders or new owners lose a lot in value of the assets.

Complexity is yet another characteristic of food chains. Interconnected food chains that exist in certain natural areas with loosely defined borders form a food web. As complex as food webs, that is, networks of food chains may be in nature, corporate ownership structures that include partners, suppliers, subsidiaries, shell firms, and offshores are even more complex. State regulatory agencies represented by economically active bureaucracies further complicate the corporate food web.[13] The Russian predator has yet to find its place in the food chain of post-Soviet business environment.

Western raiders are not homogeneous, depending on what specific types of raiding methods they use. For instance, raiders who use green mail remind one-time parasites looking to benefit from a large body of a corporation. Others are more akin to vultures or scavengers, detritivores or decomposers. Russian raiders are clear predators. Western raiders attack the sick body, or help to decompose a dying body, and do so by a set of financial and organizational operations known as restructuring. They separate dead flesh from that with a perspective of growth and development and form new businesses accordingly. Russian predatory raiders attack healthy, most lucrative businesses and assets. Quite frequently, they do not even know what to do with them afterwards: how to reshape them, how to restructure them, or how to make them effective.

By working in teams, groups of potential prey often manage to chase away predators. The core of different defense strategies employed or recommended to businesses lies in collective action. However, due to the competitive nature of every individual business and the business environment in general, the possible scope of collective action is naturally restricted by self-interest. If businesses compete, each of them individually will not be interested in co-operating with others in order to strengthen the common defensiveness against possible predatory raiding attacks. Modern Russian business environment has quite a few illustrations of this self-interest prevailing over the incentives of taking part in collective action.

Browder welcomed the arrest of Khodorkovsky and did not even make a secret out of him being pleased with the misfortune of the head of Yukos. Moreover, he did not deny this—his stance at the time when Yukos was made an icon of big business victimization by the Russian predatory state.[14] Many years later, Browder apologized,[15] but that apology came when neither Browder nor Khodorkovsky had any business left in Russia. The former moved his money to the US and Britain, while the latter was effectively expelled from Russia as a result of some secret negotiations between Russia and the West. Simply put, they were not competitors anymore. In fact, both were working toward the same goal, to discredit Putin's regime. It is thus interesting to observe how corporate predators convert into political victims.

The feeding positions in a food chain or web are called trophic levels. The trophic levels in an ecosystem form ecological pyramids. Ecological pyramids are schematic diagrams that depict how energy, biomass, or numbers of consumers decrease from lower to higher trophic levels. If one is to assume that predatory raiders are tertiary consumers, then their numbers will be much smaller than those of secondary and primary consumers, not to mention producers. Predatory raiders as final consumers can only grow in numbers if businesses as their potential prey grow in numbers even more significantly. Thus, the expansion of the business ecosystems is necessary to create a base for Russian predatory raiders to multiply. This expansion was initially achieved through privatization and creation of numerous private businesses and property owners. However, if this process is to stop, then the growth in raiding movement can only continue thanks to redistribution of assets. In any case, the number of assets potentially available for hostile takeovers has to increase.

Predator and prey evolve and coexist or co-habituate together, at least as long as the latter can keep a safe distance from the former. The prey is a necessary part of the predator's environment. If the predator does not find enough prey to feed itself, the predator moves, changes the area of habitation. Russian predatory raiders emerged in Moscow, following the mushrooming of commercial banks, cooperatives, small private businesses, and, later, joint-stock companies or corporations. As all advanced business activities took place in Moscow, predatory raiders with their asset redistribution function were best fit in Russia's capital city. The most expensive land and the possibilities for its hostile takeover also kept predatory raiders in Moscow. However, as predatory raiders multiplied and some financial and legal firms re-emerged as professional raiding companies, predatory raiders moved to provinces, discovering new opportunities in Russia's numerous and distant regions, rich with property, natural resources, and land.

Individual organisms in an ecosystem or community interact in many different ways. This interaction may benefit both individuals, or the interaction may benefit one organism to the detriment of the other. An interaction between two organisms that benefits one organism to the detriment of the other is regarded as an antagonistic interaction.[16] The interaction between the predator and prey is a classic example of an antagonistic interaction. In a business community, predatory raiders and businesspeople find themselves in a naturally antagonistic interaction. In the post-Soviet space, cooperator and racketeer and businessman and predatory raider are basic examples of antagonistic interaction of dependent agents.

These forms of loose coupling and antagonistic interaction express the philosophical principle of unity and struggle of opposing forces. In Russian transitioning economy, cooperator bore racketeer, and businessman bore predatory raider. Businessman as an owner and predatory raider as anti-owner manifest an antagonistic interaction in the system of property relations that emerged and developed in post-Soviet Russia.

Predation, herbivory, and parasitism are specific types of antagonistic interactions. In predation, one organism kills and consumes another. In an economic ecosystem, a predatory raider kills the targeted enterprise. Predation provides energy to prolong the life and promote the reproduction of the organism that does the killing, the predator, to the detriment of the organism being consumed, the prey. Predation influences organisms at two ecological levels. At the level of the individual, the prey organism has an abrupt decline in fitness, as measured by its lifetime reproductive success, because it will never reproduce again. At the level of the community, predation reduces the number of individuals in the prey population.[17] This brings to life the controversy between the mode of survival and the opportunity for expansion. Predators kill in order to survive, but need an increase in prey population in order to multiply. Similarly, predatory raiders kill businesses, but at the same time can sustain themselves and multiply only if the number of businesses grows.

Tsekhoviki were parasites, but not predators, and certainly not big ones. The real predator was the state—the Stalinist totalitarian regime, that is. Modern Russian raiders are predators, but they are not independent, nor are they self-sufficient. Their activities rely in many ways on that same state. Thus, although no longer a totalitarian regime, the state apparatus remains the major predator, helping raiders prey on attractive businesses and properties. This is of no surprise, as the state in Russia has preserved many features characteristic of the Stalinist regime. Russia's ruling political regime is the direct descendant of Stalinist apparatus. The country is distinct by its repressions toward peaceful protest and opposition, and the society had not experienced any democratic changes for many years. Instead, there is an ever-tightening control over the population, media, and political opposition.

Feige (1997) describes underground economic activities and institutional changes that took place in transition economies. The author differentiates between productive, protective, and predatory behavior of economic agents. Feige (1997, p. 27) points out that, "The prevalence of amorphous property rights and lax controls over state assets made the theft of state assets a pervasive predatory activity. Low administrative salaries combined with powerful governmental authority created rent-generating opportunities for bribery and corruption to flourish." Thus, there were substantial economic incentives to engage in economic crimes, but there were penalties as well.

In the post-Soviet Russia, mass privatization of state assets was the first hunting, where state assets became prey. It is interesting that unlike in market economies, where assets belong to firms and have individual owners, the post-Soviet privatization was depersonalized, since all assets belonged to the state. This de-personification creates the impression—at least initially—that privatization was not exactly predatory raiding. As predatory raiding is associated with the hostile takeover of economic assets from certain firms or individuals, privatization as predatory raiding could be confusing. Hijacking the all-people's property was appearing as taking something that belonged to everyone in general and no one specifically. The absence of the institute of private property reinforced this confusion. Indeed, there was the absence of any private property, let alone the well-established institution of private property that would protect rights of private property owners.

According to the massive sociological survey conducted by VCIOM in 2017, 39 percent of Russians live in fear for their life and property.[18] They are afraid of predators, be they the corrupt state or criminal predatory raiders. This is of no surprise, since corporate raiding in Russia is not about corporations or, to be precise, not only about corporations. Corporate raiding in Russia is about the strong preying on the weak. And it does not matter whether the weak is a shareholder, a small business owner, or simply a dweller in an apartment or house he/she owns. General population remains a victim, although the Stalinist regime is formally gone. Victimology gains popularity among Russian scholars (Rivman, 2002; Varchuk & Vishnevetsky, 2002; Yakovlev, 2001). As Rojansky (2014, p. 441) points out regarding hostile takeovers in the post-Soviet space, "Raiding is hardly just a crime of the wealthy against the wealthy—relatively poor people have had their apartments or land stolen, and small entrepreneurs have been divested of their businesses and simultaneously lost all of their savings." The constant fear of predatory raiding transforms Russian citizens into victims of predatory state, in which the autocratic ruling political regime decides who to punish and who to reward. In conditions of this kind, no personal or private property may be considered secure.

As the Russian saying goes, "Justice should be with fists." But so does injustice. Firestone (2010) calls it armed injustice. The author investigates complex crimes against property in post-Soviet Russia. These crimes are committed by abusing laws, including by law enforcement agencies. Law enforcement agencies in Russia are known for fabricating criminal cases against businessmen. They do it on orders, and such orders are placed and paid for by competitors. In other instances, blackmail and extortion may be the reason for law enforcers to file baseless criminal charges. Firestone (2010, p. 556) defines fabricated cases as "cases commissioned by third parties as a way of sabotaging business competitors… and criminal cases initiated by law enforcement for extortionate or other improper purposes." Such actions of the law enforcement agencies not only damage the business ecosystem, but undermine the very notion of Russian statehood.

Predation has become a very popular concept, including in the West. Different types of economic behavior found in different sectors of the national economy are frequently referred to as predatory. The modern terminology showcases predatory pricing, predatory lending, predatory practices, and such. This applies in housing market, student loans, financial operations, investment banking, and other sectors of the national economy. As society develops, so does the perspective on predation and the sectors where it applies. Predation reached the shores of the academia as well, with numerous recent references to publishing ethics and predatory practices, including, lately, mushrooming predatory journals.

Along with the popularity of predation as a concept of socioeconomic behavior and as a term, predatory raiding also gains popularity. In Russia, the media is eager to label all sorts of unfriendly actions that happen in political and social life as acts of raiding. For instance, Sakwa (2011) points out that, "Raiding … has become not only an economic phenomenon, but also something permeating social life. The term is used to describe all sorts of attacks by one agency against another." The widespread use of the term raiding and its application to different aggressive actions indicates that the culture of predation saturates not only the economy, but Russian society overall.

Predatory behavior has a negative impact on its targets. Naturally, then, comes the anti-predatory response. This response comes from potential prey, that is, businesses and property owners. This response also comes—at least nominally—from the state. The anti-predatory is called to neutralize the predatory. The key characteristic of predation is the predator's direct impact on the prey population. Selective pressures (coevolution) imposed on one another often leads to an evolutionary arms race between prey and predator, resulting in various antipredator adaptations.[19] These trends and strategies find their reflection as related to predatory raiding as well. Russia has so many shell companies that register and disappear overnight that it is even hard to say what impact—quantitatively—predatory raiders have on the prey population, that is, on large, medium, and small businesses. Both large corporations and street vendors still exist in Russia. As far as antipredator adaptation strategies are concerned, these are mostly on the defense side.

Companies—small and large—design defense strategies against potential predatory raiding attacks. In large companies, these are done with legal tools; in small ones, physical protection is the priority. Protected windows, secure locks, reinforced gates, high fences, and armed security personnel are all tools with which companies and small businesses try to protect their physical assets from predatory raiders. But the predators attack from within too. In the area of corporate governance, several predatory practices had become widespread in Russia. In many such cases, the management of joint-stock companies demonstrates predatory behavior. Among such practices, Adachi (2010, p. 1) delineates the following:

> Selling the company's products at below-market prices to entities controlled by insiders; designing a convoluted ownership structure that included a network of offshore entities; increasing charter capital and offering newly issued shares exclusively to insiders; executing hostile takeovers through bankruptcy proceedings; withholding information about the timing and venue of shareholders' meetings; and barring shareholders from exercising their voting rights at meetings.

These might be the expressions of the evolutionary arms race between prey companies and predatory raiders, but they also transform minority stockholders into victims of the company management's dictate. Damage to shareholders through the restriction of their lawful rights converts the top management into predators. If they harass minority shareholders, deprive them of their shares, and by doing so gain total control over the enterprise, they may be regarded as internally bred predatory raiders. While investigating the development of big business in post-Soviet Russia in the 1990s, Adachi (2010, p. 1) identifies "operational specifics of informal business practices in corporate governance, such as share dilution, asset stripping, transfer pricing, restricting shareholders' voting rights, and bankruptcies to order." Such practices are explained not only by legislative imperfections, but also by a fundamental controversy between the management and minority shareholders.

In addition to anti-predation, predation also brings to the fore victimization and victimology. In Kireev's (2007, p. 38) words, "Prior to 2003–4 relations between raiders and businesses likewise reflected the 'aggressor–victim' model, as a rule in the context of bilateral conflicts between top management and the raiders." In addition to predatory raiders, company managers, including first of all former Soviet directors, have victimized minority shareholders. Such victimization was detrimental to the investment environment and business ecosystem overall.

Problems with minority shareholders' rights persist. Adachi (2010) points to the role of abusive practices in the world of Russian corporate governance, suggesting that the impact of such abusive practices on the companies involved as commercial entities was ambiguous. The author suggests that informal corporate governance practices had an adverse impact on Russia' business and investment climate, as "they were corporate governance abuses and worked against the rights of shareholders, whose protection is a cornerstone of globally accepted standards of good corporate governance" (Adachi, 2010, p. 3).

Russian raiders are unnatural predators. In nature, predators prey on the weakest; they attack the smallest, youngest, oldest, or sick animals. These are the easiest prey. Russian raiders attack the most lucrative businesses that at the same time lack defensive capabilities. Figuratively speaking, they attack the fattest animal with the smallest horns. This is precisely what gives Russian raiders a predatory character. In the West, corporate raiders aim at weak firms that can hardly be named lucrative businesses. They stage hostile takeovers in order to restructure these firms and sell them in parts or convert them into profitable enterprises. In other instances, western raiders penetrate large corporations in order to blackmail them through different inconveniences allowed by the law. In case of Russia, the rule of law is a very relative concept, and thus, predatory raiders have much more room for maneuvering when it comes to aggressive actions. At the same time, their actions aimed at irritating a large corporation will not have much legal protection, unless the predatory raiders are backed by a top state bureaucrat, judge, or law enforcement agency.

In an ecosystem, predation is a biological interaction where a predator feeds on its prey. Predators may or may not kill their prey prior to feeding on it, but the act of predation often results in the death of the prey and the eventual absorption of the prey's tissue through digestion. It could also constitute a chase, stalking, or attack on the prey. Thus, predation is often, though not always, carnivory.[20] Most Russian raiders are carnivores, that is, meat eating. One would expect that being vegan or vegetarian is not very popular among Russian predatory raiders. But this is certainly not the major similarity between them and natural predators in focus. Video recordings offer a good glimpse at the hunting habits of Russian corporate predators. Documented evidence of hostile takeovers in Russia that include video chronic and brief description materials may be found online. Videos show raiding of industrial plants,[21] large businesses,[22] medium businesses,[23] TV companies,[24] banks,[25] markets,[26] public utility companies,[27] factories,[28] public transportation companies,[29] farmers' markets,[30] cafes,[31] and other businesses.

Concluding Remarks

During the Stalinist era, the role of the predator was monopolized by the totalitarian political regime. The Soviet people were the object of predation, the prey. The state exercised total control over the human life, including in both economic and noneconomic spheres. At the same time, there were parasites who lived off the people's body. The major form of parasitism during the entire Soviet era was embezzlement, both grand scale and petty. The dominance and indeed near-monopoly of the state over productive assets explained the predominance of embezzlement under the Soviet socialism. However, parasitism was not limited to embezzlement and gift-giving as a camouflaged bribery. Nepotism and cronyism were present in job placements and promotions, receiving education in public universities, gaining access to consumer goods and services under the conditions of near-total deficit, and even obtaining membership in the Communist Party.

Despite the visible dissolution of the Soviet Union, modern Russian state retains the role of the major predator. In nature, a predator can rarely catch or overpower a strong, healthy, alert, and defensive prey. Similarly, no predatory raider can overpower—both legally and financially—a strong and successful business that operates on legal grounds. The only way a self-sustainable and profitable business can fall prey to a predatory corporate raider is with the help of external force, exogenous factors, or overwhelming aggressive power. Although predatory raiders frequently resort to the use of violence, especially when a hostile takeover peaks in a storming of the targeted enterprise, violence is not the major argument of raiders. In Russia, this key role of overwhelming external force is assumed by the state. The state holds the monopoly on power, coercion, and legal justice. Different state bodies make decisions obligatory for execution and execute them. Corrupt bureaucrats collude with predatory raiders, forming an unlawful symbiosis in order to expropriate profitable businesses and other valuable assets to their personal benefit.

In corporate M&A, including those done by predatory raiders, assets are being transferred and consumed in the process of production. In the case of Russia, the emphasis is made on transfer of assets rather than on economic production. Similarly, in a food chain, there is also a reliable energy transfer through each step of the consumption pyramid, with the amount of energy transferred from one stage to another decreasing. The same rule applies to predatory raiding. Given the high transaction costs and quite frequently the inability to manage or even sell assets at market prices, predatory raiders or new owners lose a lot in value of the assets.

Notes

1. The book by Luc Duhamel refers in its title to the anti-corruption campaign led by the KGB in Moscow, the author's main focus is on the corruption in Soviet trade. In this sense, the scope of the research is quite limited, because neither corruption in Moscow nor the KGB's struggle against corruption was limited to trade. At the same time, the author extends its scope far beyond Moscow, often referring to cases of corruption in Russia's regions and other former Soviet republics. The author emphasizes the role of the KGB in Soviet society and economy: "While the party fell into deeper stagnation with Brezhnev's enfeebled ability to rule, the KGB continued to be one of the few organizations on the rise. Brezhnev relied more and more on Andropov to solve thorny problems" (p. 58). He says that large department stores and grocery stores were under the constant surveillance of KGB officers. Emelyanov, the prosecutor general of Russia, helped the KGB in organizing the anti-corruption brigade and prized the firmness and harsh methods of KGB investigators. Duhamel, Luc. (2010). *The KGB Campaign Against Corruption in Moscow, 1982–1987*. Pittsburgh: University of Pittsburgh Press. See also Osipian, Ararat. (2011). Book review of Luc Duhamel (2010). *The KGB Campaign Against Corruption in Moscow, 1982–1987*. Pittsburgh: University of Pittsburgh Press. *Global Crime*, 12(3), pp. 236–238.
2. Danner, Peter. (1996). Gain-seeking: The economoral nexus. In Edward O'Boyle (Ed.). (1996). *Social Economics: Premises, Findings and Policies* (pp. 47–56). New York: Routledge, p. 49.

3. MVD predlagaet sazhat' vzyatkodatelej, dazhe esli oni sami prishli v militsiyu s zayavleniem [MVD offers to sentence bribe givers, even if they voluntarily came to the police]. *Newsru.com*, July 26, 2009. Retrieved July 26, 2009, from http://www.newsru.com/russia/26jul2009/nmj.html
4. Burford, Rachael, Barnes, Luke & Burke, Dave. (2017). The face of luxury: First sneak peek inside Russian oligarch's £360 million Super Yacht A shows chair in the shape of a giant HEAD. *Daily Mail*, May 6, 2017. Retrieved May 6, 2017, from http://www.dailymail.co.uk/news/article-4480054/Peak-inside-Russian-oligarch-s-360million-Super-Yacht.html#ixzz56ptVQYkW
5. Leppard, David. (2011). London exiles to name 'corrupt' Kremlin aides. *The Sunday Times*, January 29, 2012.
6. Predation. Merriam-Webster Dictionary. Retrieved September 24, 2017, from https://www.merriam-webster.com/dictionary/predation
7. Depredation. Merriam-Webster Dictionary. Retrieved September 24, 2017, from https://www.merriam-webster.com/dictionary/depredation
8. Predation. Biology Online Dictionary. Retrieved September 24, 2017, from http://www.biology-online.org/dictionary/Predation
9. Predator. Biology Online Dictionary. Retrieved September 24, 2017, from http://www.biology-online.org/dictionary/Predator
10. Prey. Biology Online Dictionary. Retrieved September 24, 2017, from http://www.biology-online.org/dictionary/Prey
11. Depredation. Merriam-Webster Dictionary. Retrieved September 24, 2017, from https://www.merriam-webster.com/dictionary/depredation
12. Zoomorphism denotes the tendency of viewing human behavior in terms of the behavior of animals contrary to anthropomorphism, which views animal or nonanimal behavior in human terms.
13. On economically active bureaucracies, see Osipian, Ararat. (2018). *The Political Economy of Corporate Raiding in Russia*. London and New York: Routledge.
14. According to Tom Buerkle (2015), "Browder's biggest mistake was considering Putin to be an ally. The president had tipped the Gazprom case in Hermitage's favor by sacking the company's CEO and installing Alexey Miller with a remit to secure the company's assets. Browder even welcomed the 2003 arrest of Yukos Oil Co. boss Mikhail Khodorkovsky, seeing it as the beginning of the end for a small group of oligarchs that had stolen the country's wealth. 'I was cheering because I thought things were finally going to get back to normal,' he says. 'One down, 21 to go.'" Buerkle, Tom. (2015). Bill Browder Puts Putin on Notice with Exposé of Corruption. February 13, 2015. Retrieved July 22, 2017, from https://www.institutionalinvestor.com/article/b14z9tm3ghykk1/bill-browder-puts-putin-on-notice-with-expos%C3%A9-of-corruption

15. "I should start out by saying to Mikhail that I apologize for in any way supporting the way in which Putin has victimized him [Khodorkovsky]." "It is a shocking travesty of justice the way he has been persecuted and re-persecuted in the most obvious and unpleasant way. What I didn't understand was that it was an attempt for Putin to become the biggest oligarch and to steal from anyone else who had any success, and he did it in the most vociferous way to Mikhail Khodorkovsky." Bill Browder, speaking in an interview as part of the Decade of Injustice video series to mark the 10th anniversary of Khodorkovsky's arrest, August 14, 2013. Retrieved July 22, 2017, from https://www.khodorkovsky.com/resources/browder-bill/
16. Stevens, Alison. (2010). Predation, Herbivory, and Parasitism. *Nature Education Knowledge*, 3(10), p. 36. Retrieved July 22, 2017, from https://www.nature.com/scitable/knowledge/library/predation-herbivory-and-parasitism-13261134
17. Stevens, Alison. (2010). Predation, Herbivory, and Parasitism. *Nature Education Knowledge*, 3(10), p. 36. Retrieved July 22, 2017, from https://www.nature.com/scitable/knowledge/library/predation-herbivory-and-parasitism-13261134
18. VCIOM: 39% rossiyan zhivut v strakhe za svoyu zhizn' i imushchestvo [VCIOM: 39 percent of Russians live in fear for their life and property]. *Newsru.com*, February 22, 2017. Retrieved February 22, 2017, from http://www.newsru.com/crime/22feb2017/39prcdreadofcrime.html
19. Predation. Wikipedia. Retrieved May 6, 2017, from https://en.wikipedia.org/wiki/Predation
20. Predation. Wikipedia. Retrieved May 6, 2017, from https://en.wikipedia.org/wiki/Predation
21. This video shows the storming of Angarskcement cement plant in Siberia, Russia, in February 2006. Retrieved September 24, 2010, from http://rutube.ru/tracks/1431294.html?v=635ffea061d1f457d0068014a1b64a91
22. This is a series of videos of a hostile takeover of a large retail enterprise. The headquarters of Lenta, one of the largest retail chains in Russia, are being stormed by raiders. St Petersburg, Russia, September 29, 2010. Retrieved September 1, 2011, from http://www.youtube.com/watch?v=6XMa1oXk4I0&feature=player_embedded; http://www.youtube.com/watch?v=tdF4Ks6Mewk&feature=related; http://www.youtube.com/watch?v=g0yyr6M_c9s&feature=player_embedded#!; http://www.youtube.com/watch?v=aO119CA6Tj8&feature=player_embedded#!; http://www.youtube.com/watch?v=bnGOcHaBbHY&feature=player_embedded; http://www.youtube.com/watch?v=g0yyr6M_c9s&NR=1; http://www.youtube.com/watch?v=TqF_Osbutbs&feature=player_embedded#!; http://readrussia.com/magazine/Winter2010/00061/

23. Chechenskie bandyuki pod prikrytiem prodazhnykh mentov proizveli reiderskij zakhvat ZAO "Polad-Avto" [Chechen gangsters took over Polad-Avto car sales center under the cover of corrupt cops]. *Youtube*, May 18, 2017. Retrieved May 14, 2018, from https://www.youtube.com/watch?v=gsJULpFMvjw
24. This is a series of videos of a dispute over a TV company in Tula, which turns into a criminal investigation. A group of armed people is storming the premises of the company in an apartment building. There are around 50 stormtroopers involved in the storming. Police does not interfere but calls for backup support. More police arrives later and stops the storming, arresting 35 perpetrators. 81 Gogolevskaya Street, Tula, Russia, July 31, 2008. Retrieved May 30, 2010, from http://mreporter.ru/ReporterMessages!viewReport.do?reportid=14308; http://www.youtube.com/watch?v=K0Zf1nN-3m0&feature=related; http://www.youtube.com/watch?v=n2qAMmHDMuA

    See also: V tsentre Moskvy proizoshel reiderskij zakhvat kompanii izvestnoj televedushchej Ksenii Merts [Hostile takeover of a company that belongs to a famous TV anchor Kseniya Merts took place in downtown Moscow]. *Youtube*, September 4, 2015. Retrieved May 14, 2018, from https://www.youtube.com/watch?v=ttWJc4c41iE
25. This video shows police storming a private bank "Guta-kapital," using axes and sledge hummers, braking in through the bullet proof glass, and arresting private security guards. The police is also attempting to get through armored doors. It is unclear why the police are performing locksmith functions. Moscow, Russia, April 15, 2007. Retrieved May 30, 2010, from http://www.ochevidets.ru/rolik/7551/
26. This video shows the central market in Izhevsk, Russia. Retrieved September 24, 2010, from http://rutube.ru/tracks/2915664.html?v=684c60f05dc23be5b92c1d33f65eddf0

    A swift change of the director in Izhevsk's central market, Izhevsk, Russia. Retrieved September 24, 2010, from http://rutube.ru/tracks/2915664.html
27. This is a hostile takeover of a large public utilities enterprise Teplokommunenergo in Rostovskaya oblast, Russia, on May 27, 2010. Retrieved May 30, 2010, from http://www.youtube.com/watch?v=yi22U4-pXOk
28. Somewhere in Russia, stormtroopers on two buses arrive at a porcelain factory and move in, August 2006. Retrieved September 24, 2010, from http://rutube.ru/tracks/1448362.html?v=de86dfd56af302f2e5d8b6ddb87f8a29
29. These two videos show hostile takeovers of intercity public transportation businesses in Moscow. Komu na Rusi otzhimat' biznes khorosho [Who in Russia has advantages in taking over businesses]. *Youtube*, May 29, 2016.

Retrieved May 14, 2018, from https://www.youtube.com/watch?v=-GEqtVzWt7s; See also: Ublyudki Rossii, reiderskij zakhvat, mentovski bespredel [Bastards of Russia, hostile takeover, police abuse]. *YouTube*, February 13, 2016. Retrieved May 14, 2018, from https://www.youtube.com/watch?v=dN2yEih23iw

30. This video shows a massive storming and fight in the market in Severnoe Butovo, Moscow, on August 4, 2008. Raiders occupy administrative premises of the market and later the salesmen attempt to storm the second floor to regain control of the market. Retrieved September 24, 2010, from http://www.youtube.com/watch?v=_1MruOJOWkM&feature=related
31. This video shows a storming and fight for a café in Moscow. Reiderskij zakhvat kafe "Khachapuri" na Paveletskoj [Hostile takeover of Khachapuri on Paveletska]. *Youtube*, August 9, 2013. Retrieved May 14, 2018, from https://www.youtube.com/watch?v=P2O-Fz13edY; See also Reidery zakhvatili "Khachapuri" na Paveletskoj vmeste s baranom Tolej. Video [Raiders took over Khachapuri on Paveletska along with ram Tolya]. *Vesti*, August 9, 2013. Retrieved May 14, 2018, from https://www.vesti.ru/doc.html?id=1116002&cid=520

References

Abrams, N. (2014). *Political Thugs: Criminal Corporate Raiding and Property Rights in Early-Capitalist Eastern Europe*. Ph.D. Dissertation, University of California, Berkeley.

Adachi, Y. (2010). *Building Big Business in Russia: The Impact of Informal Corporate Governance Practices*. New York: Routledge.

Alexeev, M. (1988). Market vs. Rationing: The Case of Soviet Housing. *Review of Economics and Statistics, 70*(3), 414–420.

Bernstam, M., & Rabushka, A. (2003). *From Predation to Prosperity: Breaking UP Enterprise Network Socialism in Russia*. Washington, DC: Hoover Institution.

Birdsall, K. (2000). "Everyday Crime" at the Workplace: Covert Earning Schemes in Russia's New Commercial Sector. In S. Lovell, A. Ledeneva, & A. Rogachevskii (Eds.), *Bribery and Blat in Russia*. London: Macmillan.

Duhamel, L. (2010). *The KGB Campaign Against Corruption in Moscow, 1982–1987*. Pittsburgh: University of Pittsburgh Press.

Feige, E. (1997). Underground Activity and Institutional Change: Productive, Protective, and Predatory Behavior in Transition Economies. In J. Nelson, C. Tilly, & L. Walker (Eds.), *Transforming Post-Communist Political Economies* (pp. 21–34). Washington, DC: National Academies Press.

Firestone, T. (2010). Armed Injustice: Abuse of the Law and Complex Crime in Post-Soviet Russia. *Denver International Law & Policy Review, 38*(4), 555–580.

Fitzpatrick, S., Rabinowitch, A., & Stites, R. (1991). *Russia in the Era of NEP: Explorations in Soviet Society and Culture.* Bloomington: Indiana University Press.

Glaz'ev, S. (1997). *Genotsid: Rossiya i novyj mirovoj poryadok* [Genocide: Russia and the New World Order]. Moscow: Erga.

Goland, I. (1998). *Krizisy, Razrushivshie NEP: Valiutnoe Regulirovanie v Period NEPa* [Crises That Destructed NEP: Currency Regulation During NEP]. Moscow: Nachala.

Karatuev, A. (1998). *Sotsial'no-ekonomicheskie osnovy gospodstva byurokratii v SSSR i v sovremennoj Rossii* [Socio-Economic Foundations of Domination of Bureaucracy in the USSR and in Modern Russia]. Dissertation, DSc Economics, Volgograd, 08.00.01 Political Economy, 268 p. Retrieved July 22, 2012, from http://www.dissercat.com/content/sotsialno-ekonomicheskie-osnovy-gospodstva-byurokratii-v-sssr-i-v-sovremennoi-rossii

Kireev, A. (2007). Raiding and the Market for Corporate Control: The Evolution of Strong-Arm Entrepreneurship. *Problems of Economic Transition, 50*(8), 29–45.

Kondrat'eva, T. S., & Sokolov, A. K. (Eds.). (2009). *Rezhimnye lyudi v SSSR* [Regime People in the USSR]. Moscow: ROSSPEN.

Kornai, J. (1980). *The Shortage Economy.* Amsterdam: North-Holland Press.

Kudriavtsev, V. (1991). *NEP: Vzgliad so Storony* [NEP: View from Aside]. Moscow: Moskovsky Rabochy.

Latov, Y. (2001). *Ekonomika vne zakona: ocherki po teorii i istroii tenevoj ekonomiki* [Economy Outlaw: Essays on Theory and History of the Shadow Economy]. Moscow: Moskovski obshchestvenny nauchny fond.

Ledeneva, A. (2008a). Blat and Guanxi: Informal Practices in Russia and China. *Comparative Studies in Society and History, 50*(1), 118–144.

Ledeneva, A. (2008b). Telephone Justice in Russia. *Post-Soviet Affairs, 24*(4), 324–350.

Osipian, A. (2010). Corrupt Organizational Hierarchies in the Former Soviet Bloc. *Transition Studies Review, 17*(4), 822–836.

Pleines, H. (2000). Large-Scale Corruption and Rent-Seeking in the Russian Banking Sector. In S. Lovell, A. Ledeneva, & A. Rogachevskii (Eds.), *Bribery and Blat in Russia.* London: Macmillan.

Rivman, D. (2002). *Kriminal'naya viktimologiya* [Criminal Victimology]. Saint Petersburg: Piter.

Rojansky, M. (2014). Corporate Raiding in Ukraine: Causes, Methods and Consequences. *Demokratizatsiya: The Journal of Post-Soviet Democratization, 22*(4), 411–443.

Sakwa, R. (2011, December 5). Raiding in Russia. *Russian Analytical Digest: State-Business Relations and Modernization* (105), 9–13.

Shlapentokh, V. (2007). *Contemporary Russia as a Feudal Society: A New Perspective on the Post-Soviet Era*. New York: Palgrave Macmillan.

Shlapentokh, V., & Arutunyan, A. (2013). *Freedom, Repression, and Private Property in Russia*. New York: Cambridge University Press.

Simis, K. (1982). *USSR: The Corrupt Society: The Secret World of Soviet Capitalism*. New York: Simon & Schuster.

Social Darwinism. Encyclopædia Britannica. Retrieved August 12, 2017, from https://www.britannica.com/topic/social-Darwinism

Spiridonov, V. (2000). Attitudes to Bribery and Blat in Contemporary Russian Society: The Psychologist's View. In S. Lovell, A. Ledeneva, & A. Rogachevskii (Eds.), *Bribery and Blat in Russia*. London: Macmillan.

Vaksberg, A. (1991). *The Soviet Mafia*. New York: St. Martin's Press.

Varchuk, T., & Vishnevetsky, K. (2002). *Viktimologiya*. Moscow: UNITY-DANA: Zakon i pravo.

Voslensky, M. (1984). *Nomenklatura: The Soviet Ruling Class*. Garden City, NY: Doubleday.

Yakovlev, A. (2001). *Sotsiologiya prestupnosti (kriminologiya): osnovy obshchej teorii*. Moscow: Sodejstvie novy vek.

CHAPTER 4

Mass Privatization: Virtual Reality, Volatile Rights, and Violent Raiding

Chronology of Raiding and Privatization

In the best traditions of state-bred parasites, Russian nouveau riches created organizations that similar to black holes in space sucked in public property without any benefit to economic development, state, or society. Hanley (2000, p. 143) calls this process "'*nomenklatura* privatization'—the surreptitious seizure of state-owned property by communist era officials." Hanley (2000) is certainly not alone in his less-than-flattering characterization of mass privatization in Russia. Havrylyshyn and McGettigan (1999) delineate five main types of different privatization techniques, including restitution, case-by-case direct sales and equity offerings, management buyouts, employee buyouts, and mass privatization. The authors point out that transition economies applied a wide variety of privatization techniques and their combinations. With this variety in applied techniques combined with the country's specific initial economic conditions and background, "radically different outcomes have resulted, both in terms of ownership structure and overall efficiency gains. … [m]anagement and employee buyouts accounted for more than half the firms privatized in Russia" (Havrylyshyn & McGettigan, 1999, p. 16).

Corruption may have also played a key role in the results of the post-socialist privatization. Barnes (2003, p. 533) researches the Hungarian, Czech, and Russian post-Communist transformations and suggests that "some post-communist political economies were burdened by impenetrable cross-ownership groups, money-laundering banks, and captured states,

A. L. Osipian, *Political and Economic Transition in Russia*,
https://doi.org/10.1007/978-3-030-03831-1_4

while others had effectively limited corruption and laid the groundwork for long-term development." The author further suggests that these varying outcomes resulted from differences in the context of state-economy relations on the eve of the socialist system collapse and the mode of transfer of state property into private hands, also known as the mass privatization of the early 1990s.

The outcomes of Russia's mass privatization—both immediate and long-run—can hardly be regarded as a success. The emergence of a small group of oligarchs as a result of the mass privatization would not qualify as a major achievement in terms of the declared goals of privatization. Instead of creating a middle class as a base for democratic reforms, the mass privatization brought to life numerous criminal groups and criminal-like businesses. Barnes (2003) clearly considers the mass privatization a theft of public property, titling his comparative study "Comparative Theft." The author categorizes Russian economic transition as asset destruction, pointing out the dominant role of conglomerates and saying that banks served the function of facilitators of asset shifting, while the state was captured by major economic actors (Barnes, 2003, p. 538). As the market reforms have proceeded, post-socialist states had experienced a parade of state captors (Barnes, 2007a, p. 71). These state captors may be regarded as predatory raiders of the highest level, occupying top echelons of power and exploiting the state apparatus in their personal interests.

It is interesting that, along with the process of mass privatization, there was also privatization of state functions, including that of resolving commercial disputes. With a multitude of new businesses emerging every day through privatizing state assets and the state stepping aside from the regulatory process due to both its incompetency in new matters and its irresponsibility toward its citizens, a partial lawlessness is born overnight in a strictly regulated Stalinist society. A new type of private mediators and arbiters emerge, many with criminal backgrounds and reputations in criminal circles. As Frye (2000, p. 17) puts it, "In countries with weak judicial systems, disorganized bureaucracies, or ineffective regional governments, the state often lacks the capacity to be a neutral third-party enforcer of many disputes." And that is when private arbitrage comes into play. Private arbitrage in this case includes criminal enforcers and threat of violence, not sanctioned by the state.

Directors of Soviet plants and factories become involved in what Barnes (2006) calls "destructive entrepreneurship," by siphoning off state assets. Paradoxically, while Soviet enterprises finally received their lawful private owners, no capital investment has been made in these production facilities for many years and even decades. One would expect it to be the other way around: publicly owned enterprises would be of little interest to any particular individual, while privatized enterprises would become well-managed and elicit strong investment from their new owners. But the post-Soviet reality indicated the opposite. Not only large industrial enterprises and collective farms, but even small service enterprises, such as Soviet-type cafeterias, laundries, and shoe repair shops, were run down by new owners.

State capture is another characteristic of the Russian polity related to mass privatization and its aftermath. In the course of privatization, Russian predators capture the state and exploit the state apparatus for their goals of unlawful hostile takeovers, property accumulation, and personal enrichment. According to Hellman, Jones, and Kaufmann (2003, p. 751), state capture may be defined as "the efforts of firms to shape the very institutional environment in which they operate." In the highly corrupt environment of transition economies, this capture implies big businesses, the oligarchs, rather than just firms.

When it comes to any significant and long-lasting socioeconomic or cultural phenomenon, the task of periodization becomes practically imminent. The same may be true in the case of corporate predatory raiding in post-Soviet Russia. Despite some attempts by a few scholars to present some kind of chronology of predatory raiding in Russia, or its periodization, such a periodization might be premature. Three decades of dramatic property redistribution and predatory raiding in Russia have not produced enough material to introduce a well-grounded periodization of predatory raiding.

Starting from the violent racket of the second half of the 1980s and up to the new incoming wave of privatization to be held in 2019, there was little time in terms of a major politico-economic transformation, such as the one that has taken place in Russia. Of course, it is possible to highlight certain stages or rather even benchmarks in the development of the predatory raiding movement in Russia by marking such significant economic events as the voucher privatization of the early and mid-1990s and the crisis raiding of 2008. However, the question is whether such a periodization will be complete and scientifically grounded, and to what extent?

Barnes (2007b) delineates six phases of struggle for property in Russia. This study summarizes these phases and their major characteristics in Table 4.1.

It is possible to extend the periodization of predatory raiding in Russia beyond Barnes (2007b), that is, beyond 2006 to 2018. The 2008 financial

Table 4.1 Periodization of property redistribution in Russia

Stage	*Time frame*	*Period*	*Major characteristics*
1	1987–1990	Late Gorbachev era, Perestroika	Disillusioned, cynical, and ambitious Communist Party functioneers created new private enterprises from nothing.
2	1991–1994	Post-Soviet mass privatization	Soviet-era industrial managers used their positions in firms, control over information, access to capital (including workers' bonus funds), and reformers' insistence on leaving enterprise valuations fixed—despite rapid inflation—to transfer ownership to themselves.
3	1995–1997	Post mass privatization	Rigged loans-for-shares auctions extended the empires of some of the national-level "oligarchs."
4	1998–1999	Collecting shares as debt payments, debt roll-up	New bankruptcy law allowed companies to force debtors to sell off assets at a large discount, even if the debt owed was small.
5	2000–2003	Putin strengthens federal government	The federal government began to affect the competition over assets, both directly and indirectly.
6	2004–2006	The Yukos affair	The takeover of Yuganskneftegaz revealed both the intent of the federal state to reassert control over property, especially in the oil sector, and the constraints it faced in doing so.

Source: Completed by the author based on: Barnes, Andrew. (2007b). Industrial Property in Russia: The Return of the State and a Focus on Oil. *SAIS Review*, 27(2), pp. 47–62. Retrieved July 22, 2012, from http://muse.jhu.edu/journals/sais_review/v027/27.2barnes.pdf

crisis and post-crisis period changed little in terms of bankruptcy raiding (Osipian, 2012). In 2010, Mayor of Moscow, Yuri Luzhkov, was removed from office. Nevertheless, nothing changes in Moscow, including in terms of property protection and raiding. In 2014, financial crisis resulted in many foreign investors and large corporations, including car manufacturers and retailers, withdrawing from Russia. These companies and investors sold their assets. Finally, in 2018, President Putin extended his rule for another six years, until 2024. Thus, no change should be expected, including in much needed land reform. Land issue is moved to the future at least for another several years. Predatory raiding in land on a massive scale will come inevitably.

Corporate governance and its transformations along the line of economic transition may also give an idea about the periodization of corporate predatory raiding in Russia. Dolgopyatova (2007) says that the rapid redistribution of property rights on already privatized state economic assets started in the mid-1990s. The author also points out to the specifics of corporate governance in Russia, so unusual for foreign investors. Issues of corporate governance were first addressed in the mid-1990s, when voucher privatization was over, triggering the dynamic redistribution of property rights: "At that time, attention was focused on predominance of employee ownership and on the managers, which had enough power to discriminate against outside owners (including foreign investors who were shocked by the habits of Russian corporate governance)" (Dolgopyatova, 2007, p. 250). Economic growth, which followed the financial crisis of 1998, sparked off a new wave of redistribution of property rights and revealed the problems in Russian corporations that were caused by loopholes in corporate legislation and enforcement. A variety of aspects of corporate governance in Russia is also presented in Iwasaki (2007), and Yakovlev (2007), where the authors point out to skepticism regarding the reforms that came to replace optimism of the early 1990s.[1]

It may also be possible to mark the chronology of predatory raiding based on major symbolic cases of hostile takeovers, such as the case of TogliattiAzot and other large enterprises and joint-stock companies, but this approach would not be perfectly correct. Moreover, the question that emerges here is the one of choice between the optimal criteria for conducting a periodization. The redistribution of property continues, and so the criteria for estimating the changes in the predatory raiding phenomenon are hard to formulate clearly. There is no doubt that Russian raiding has its prehistory and history and that the chronology of predatory raiding can be presented as a sequence of stages, but only in the future. Simply put, the phenomenon of predatory raiding should reach its high point in the stage of development.

Despite the criticism of the possibility of giving a precise and complete periodization to the phenomenon of predatory raiding at present, this study will nevertheless offer what may be seen as the most successful attempt of such a periodization, presented by other scholars. The history of business hostile takeovers in Russia received its periodization in the report presented by the Center of Political Technologies. Experts who expressed their opinions in this report thought that there have been three waves of predatory raiding in Russia. The first wave started with the disintegration of the Soviet Union and ended by the mid-1990s. Hostile takeovers were occurring as early as in 1992 and 1993, when holders of only 3 percent of the stock were conducting meetings of shareholders and re-electing the general manager, and then were claiming the managerial rights over the entire company through the court. The second wave, which took place in the second half of the 1990s, is broadly known to the general public: this is the wave of privatization of major enterprises, the famous loans-for-shares auctions. It is exactly at that time that a number of financiers emerged in Russia, who held certain financial resources and tried their best to acquire by any means as much of production facilities and other material assets as possible. The start of the third wave was signified with the Yukos case, which opened the new era, the era of state raiding in addition to private raiding.[2]

State institutions may be more successful predatory raiders than private businesses. This is especially true in authoritarian, predatory regimes. Yakovlev, Sobolev, and Kazun (2014) use the term predatory policing to investigate the clash between Russian business and predatory state, pointing to violence and the ways to resist it. Commenting on the Yukos case and its meaning for the Russian business environment, the authors suggest that bureaucratic elites at the federal level relied on the existing law enforcement system and demonstrated their power to bring big business under its control. According to the authors, the Yukos case led to changing the balance between the business and state bureaucracy: "The consequence of the YUKOS case was a change in the balance of forces within the 'ruling coalition,' and as a result, big business became a 'junior partner' of the federal bureaucratic elite" (Yakovlev et al., 2014, p. 175). This dramatic change, when big business's role diminishes in lieu of the dominance of the federal bureaucratic elite may appear less dramatic if one is to recall that big businesses grew from the Soviet party and state apparatus. Nevertheless, the Yukos case and its outcome—bad for business and good for predatory state bureaucrats—signify a new stage in the history of predatory raiding movement in Russia.

Waves of predatory raiding—if such exist at all—may not necessarily coincide with waves of mass privatization, major economic and financial crises, or other major shifts that affect the national economy. Waves of Russian M&A are studied by Musatova (2011), including with quantitative methodology that follows the dynamics of M&A of Russian companies. Tarkhanova (2008, p. 8) points out that the functioning of the Russian institute of raiding is characterized by a clearly manifested asynchrony of the raiding waves between the center and the regions, different motives of raiding. In the center, it is the investment raiding, and in the regions it is the liquidation raiding. Waves of raiding attacks move from the center to the regions with a certain delay, bringing a variety of diversified technologies of hostile takeovers of enterprises, and cultivating and preparing the grounds for large business players to enter new markets.

Overall, scholars point out that the process of privatization was nothing but de facto raiding or at least a necessary basis for predatory raiding. Skidanova (2010, p. 15) holds a similar view. The period of privatization, in essence, has become the first wave of raiding in Russia, the global redistribution of the communal or mutual property, its redistribution into the domain of private interest, which further led to formation of the business ethics in the country. Raiding emerged within the limits of the spontaneous distributive model and later acquired forms of illegal distributive model, that is, the model that uses abuse, violence, and so on. Here, apparently, the author points to public office abuse by the state bureaucrats and violence that comes from the side of stormtroopers hired by the predatory raiders.

Large-scale privatization in Russia is to continue, and so is predatory raiding. The Chairman of the Accounts Chamber and former Minister of Finance Alexei Kudrin says that the presence of the state in the Russian economy is unreasonably high and hopes that the government will continue the process of privatization: "But I know, how moderate is today's position of the government in regards to reducing the share of public sector in the economy. Perhaps, during the last year or two, we had certain steps undertaken toward increasing the state's share in the economy, including through buying large state companies."[3] Kudrin expects further privatization of large state companies to be part of economic restructuring and basis for strengthening the competitive environment in the national economy.

It is not as easy to follow the evolution of predatory raiding in Russia and to divide it into meaningful stages or periods, as it may appear at first glance. What terms would be applicable to fulfill this task: evolution, genesis, chronology, stages, phases, periods, major marks, or benchmarks? Chronology relates to the timing of a certain process, stages are those of a certain program realization, and major marks are marks on the way to achieving a certain goal. These terms do not apply to predatory raiding very well. Predatory raiding is a phenomenon, a relation, but not a system, even if predatory raiding acquires a systemic character and certain elements of raiding become institutionalized. It is hard to answer the question of whether predatory raiding can be characterized by the presence of clearly demarcated stages of its emergence, formation, and development.

One more key question relates to criteria to be used in a likely periodization of predatory raiding. This study suggests a preliminary periodization of predatory raiding in Russia with the use of the following major criterion: the form of ownership of the targeted company or property, attacked by predatory raiders. Accordingly, this study arrives to the following stages of predatory raiding: first stage—conflicts around the cooperative property of the late 1980s; second stage—raiding of state property, starting from the large-scale voucher privatization of the early 1990s; third stage—raiding of private property starting in the late 1990s and through the 2000s, when the struggle for assets goes on between private companies; fourth stage—struggle over land, which continues since the early 1990s, but will achieve its peak only in the near future; and fifth stage—raiding companies raid other raiding companies and do so not in the course of competition, but in order to take over their property. Overall, such a periodization has a right to exist, but this study has to point out that the stages in this periodization are not clearly demarcated; instead, they overlap. For instance, privatization continues, and thus it would not be fair to limit its time to the 1990s only. Here, this study emphasizes dominance, prevalence of some forms of raided property over others rather than their exclusivity.

Predatory raiding as a form of redistribution of property is certainly not the first wave of property redistribution in modern Russia. Privatization conducted in the early 1990s was the first wave of distribution of state property. Accordingly, the phenomenon of predatory raiding cannot be considered without first looking into the earlier forms of property distribution, including, first of all, privatization. It is necessary to briefly characterize the earlier process of property distribution, including the processes of moving property away from under the state and its further privatization.

The exploitation of humans by humans became possible thanks to a surplus in households back in the era of natural production, also called subsistence farming. Similarly, predatory raiding is possible only in the presence of significant assets, including production capacities and other economic assets; otherwise, predatory raiders would have nothing to take over. However, predatory raiders are not interested in any economic assets per se, but only in those assets that are in demand and promise a high margin.

The USSR was a self-sufficient and a relatively closed system, while the socialist production was not limited by the production plan; instead, it was aimed at a continuous increase of the gross national product. Producing more of everything was always encouraged by the system. If there was a plan, then it was always a good idea to overproduce, to exceed the plan, and it was always rewarded by the authorities. The post-Soviet society, formally divided into former Soviet republics and a few quasi-independent territorial and ethnic enclaves, is no longer a self-sufficient system. The production in Russia is limited by the unclear perspectives of future sales of the produced product, depending on the fluctuation of prices, supply, demand, and other variables.

The major advantages of the Soviet socialist system were guarantees, including social guarantees and full employment, and the prioritization of material production, growth in tangible assets, prevalence of production capacities, and consumer goods over consumer services. The major deficiencies included a slow pace of economic growth, underdeveloped services industry, and corruption, including primarily parasitic forms of existence in many segments of the economy and state bureaucracy. The major advantages of the new market-oriented Russian system include a relatively quick response to changing consumer demand. Major disadvantages include a lower level of social guarantees, fluctuations at the level of production of material assets, reorientation on proprietary values, ownership, and a much higher level of corruption at all levels of state bureaucratic hierarchy.

Privatization as Unequal Distribution of Property

This work is not intended to offer a detailed description of post-Soviet privatization, or its analysis, since privatization is already presented in a significant block of literature on the economics of transition and market reforms. Moreover, works that cover privatization, corporate governance in the emerging markets, and institutional change in transition economies are not in short supply (see, for instance, Federowicz & Aguilera, 2003; Rosenbaum, Bönker, & Wagener, 2000; Tridico, 2011). Instead, this study presents a few major points of privatization as they relate directly to the economic roots of predatory raiding.

Privatization naturally implies unequal distribution of property, no matter what the criteria for distribution would be. Historically, privatization denotes not just a process of changing owners and transition from more smooth to less smooth distribution of property among economic agents, but the externally forced transition of public property into private ownership. In this case, economic agents are thought to be economically rational individuals or households. A distinct feature of the Russian privatization is that there was not merely a change of owners, but a change in the dominating forms of ownership, transition from the monopoly of the state property to private property, including property rights on the means of production. This is explained by the massive scale of the Russian privatization, conducted by the state order in a matter of just a few years. The history of humanity perhaps has not seen such a massive privatization in just one country as that occurred in Russia in the 1990s.

It is also expected that unequal distribution of property and results of business activities will increase the effectiveness of each economic unit, firm, or enterprise and the national economy overall. Apart from property distribution, the major issue in the justification of privatization is the effectiveness. A relatively equal distribution of property that anticipates equal distribution of the product of labor, often referred to as *uravnilovka* during the Soviet era, is being sacrificed in the name of higher effectiveness of production and an increase in the total social welfare, which would positively affect the disposable income of the entire population or at least the majority of the population. The question is: are privatized enterprises more effective? Does privatization make a typical Soviet enterprise more effective? The literature shows that privatization brings higher levels of effectiveness, but there are significant challenges to this conclusion as well.

Mass privatization of the 1990s in Russia took place under the condition of a weak state, says Barnes (2003, pp. 543–544):

> The Russian state, for its part, seemed so incapable of influencing events and actors by the end of the 1990s that scholars began to call it "weak," "privatized," and even "feudal" in the way its authority had been "parcelized."[4] Several patterns reinforced this impression: President Yeltsin frequently reshuffled his government to prevent a palace coup, the Central Bank was unable to develop or implement a plan for consolidating the banking sector in the wake of the financial crisis of 1998, the central government could not collect enough taxes to fund a shrinking budget, and even the relatively powerful regional governments seemed unable to control natural resource exporters on their territory. With its dominating conglomerates, uncontrolled banks, and incoherent state, the Russian political economy at the end of the 1990s was better structured for capital flight than for capital investment....

Havrylyshyn and McGettigan (1999) review a selection of studies on privatization experiences in transition countries. The authors report that the empirical studies almost invariably show that privatized enterprises outperform state enterprises. Moreover, the existing scholarly literature identifies de novo or startup firms as being the best performers, followed by outsider-dominated firms, while insider-dominated firms are the least efficient among those newly privatized. However, one should keep in mind that the enterprises that were most effective during the Soviet period were also the most likely candidates for privatization. Indeed, both collectives of workers and the administration were eager to privatize their enterprises if they were effective and produced profit. Such an incentive seems to be obvious. Accordingly, the correlation between performance and the form of property may be path dependent. Path dependency in this case diminishes the role of privatization in increasing the effectiveness of an enterprise.

Another example of path dependency is the wish of newly emerged entrepreneurs, which in most of the instances were directors of Soviet enterprises or their immediate relatives and family members, were interested in privatizing those plants that worked for export. If an enterprise sold a significant portion of its product abroad, the management tried to make the revenue remain abroad in order to avoid taxation and, most importantly, move it to personal bank accounts. Many of these managers later escaped to foreign countries, following their unreturned revenues.

The interest in privatizing the most effective Soviet enterprises from the side of the workers' collective, management, and outside investors is well understood. However, the interest of the state to privatize these enterprises is hard to explain. If the state thought that privatization would lead to an increase in the effectiveness of enterprises, then it would be quite logical to assume that the state would start privatization from the least effective enterprises, and certainly not from the most effective ones. If the state thought that its services and consumer goods sector did not work effectively, the state should have privatized existing services and consumer goods enterprises instead of privatizing industrial giants, such as machine-building plants and steel mills.

The level of concentration also plays a role in the economic effectiveness of enterprises. Pivovarsky (2001) researches the links between ownership concentration and enterprise performance in the former Soviet republic. He investigates this relationship by using the data on 376 medium and large enterprises. The author reports that ownership concentration is positively correlated with the economic performance of enterprises.

The findings also point to the higher effectiveness of enterprises, if they are owned by foreign banks and companies, ceteris paribus. Another interesting finding is that ownership by domestic investment funds and holding companies does not have a positive effect on performance.

The social or human factor that was involved in the socialist production has to be accounted for during the massive privatization. The real new owners of enterprises sometimes preferred to stay in the shade. According to Pivovarsky (2001, p. 16), "Given the equity considerations traditional in the socialist society, outright concentration of ownership by the insiders was not politically acceptable. Enterprise managers often had to disguise themselves as outsiders by establishing proxy legal entities that would participate in the privatization auctions." Owners come to the enterprise as an outside force, be it predatory raiders or an enterprise's very own leaders. Since the real participation of workers in the management of enterprises was and still is traditionally insignificant, workers are indifferent to the "regime change" as long as their workplaces and employment prospects are preserved.

The change of the owner, or even the change of the form of property per se, does not bring an increase in effectiveness. The idea of privatization, or at least the way it was presented and sold to the public, implies an increase in effectiveness due to two major factors. First, it is expected that privatization creates necessary legal and proprietary grounds for private investment in formerly state enterprises. Second, privatization expects to bring incentives for workers to work better by making them shareholders. Both of these factors have little to do with privatization the way it was conducted in the transition economies. The investment argument for privatization did not work for a very simple reason: the state property was simply divided by the number of people in the country through the voucher system.

People brought their paper vouchers to enterprises and in exchange received a share of the enterprise. As a result of this transaction, no real investment took place. On the contrary, enterprises that exported their products, lost part of their revenue, because the new owners, that is, the old management, obtained the opportunity to defraud the government, to avoid taxation, and to collect the revenue abroad in the country of export, transferring it to personal accounts. Later, the situation became even more criminalized. New owners not only siphoned off the revenues, but also sold many marketable assets overseas, such as new equipment, and then left the country to enjoy their life abroad. All these negative features of privatization of the 1990s point to divestment; it denotes a process in finance opposite to investment. Capital outflow in all the forms became one of the major characteristics of the early post-Soviet transition period. As a result, enterprises lost their funds instead of attracting some additional funding, as was initially intended.

The second component, that is, the incentives, did not materialize as well. Workers did not have many incentives to work better due to privatization for three obvious reasons. First, dividends on their shares in the enterprise were either absolutely insignificant or in most of the instances absent. The culture of profit sharing did not develop in Russian enterprises, since the management had complete control over the enterprise's revenues and profits. Second, the system of worker participation in the process of decision making was undeveloped and still is undeveloped. Third and most important, open joint-stock companies did not anticipate the distribution of shares among their employees only. Anyone could buy stocks of enterprises with which they had nothing to do. This would be a normal practice in the economies with developed stock markets and necessary regulatory institutions. In the former Soviet republics, however, such markets and institutions were absent. As a result, minor holders of shares had no control over the enterprises. Vouchers were issued by the state and then bought by those who intended to privatize the enterprises. In a situation with rapidly declining real wages, raising unemployment, and no clear prospects for the future, people were eager to sell their vouchers at a nominal price.

Initially, people paid a great deal of attention to their vouchers. A few years later, however, they realized that they were deceived by the state. In 1999, I asked about 300 or so of my students in Ukraine if they knew how their parents invested their vouchers: did they sell them, did they invest them, and did they receive any dividends? No students were able to respond to this question. Very few students even knew of the privatization vouchers and their meaning, despite the fact that many of them majored in Economics. This was only five years after the launch of the voucher privatization. This simple fact of young people being unaware of the destiny of their vouchers points to the low interest in their families to the process of privatization and their part in it.

Simply put, the state enterprises were hijacked by their directors or by outside financial groups. In the first case, there was virtually no resistance. In the second case, the resistance was almost entirely from the side of the directors, not the workers. A few years later, Russian oligarchs will say that while Rothschild, Rockefeller, DuPont, and Ford created and accumulated, they preserved from complete destruction. While the system in its present form is ineffective, the new owners block further reforms and try to stabilize their present position. In this sense, they are absolutely interested in preserving the status of private property in order to preserve their ownership over the former state enterprises and other assets.

The major object of the conflict, as it is in most of the predatory raiding attacks, is a typical Soviet enterprise, by now fully or partially privatized. This is of no surprise, since the Soviet economy was based on large industrial enterprises. These were not US-type corporations. Each Soviet enterprise was a separate entity, even though all of them were closely linked economically. This means that one enterprise cannot be located in two different cities, or is least likely to have smaller branches outside its main industrial "campus." Some enterprises were so-called full-cycle enterprises, when the production line included everything from metal production to the final consumer product. The number of employees varied from a few dozens to tens of thousands. Each enterprise had its own budget, even though all of them belonged to the state. Some enterprises were profitable while others were not. Profitability here has socialist specifics: the more profit an enterprise was making, the more it was paying to the state budget, but also had some funds left for development.

A typical large Soviet enterprise consisted of three distinct parts. The first part produced military products, the second part produced civil products, and the third part produced consumer products. For instance, a large machine-building plant would produce missile carriers, mining machines, and frying pans, all in different departments and workshops. In addition, all the plants were interconnected, especially if located in one city. The entire social infrastructure was built around large enterprises and was largely funded by them. Plants owned everything from kindergartens to apartment complexes to resort hotels. They also administered waiting lists for cars, apartments, kindergarten placements, tourist vacations, and performed numerous other social functions. Workers were attached to plants and factories in many ways, not just through their work. It was always better to work on a large plant than to be a teacher, doctor, or civil servant.

Perhaps a philosophical question of fairness would not be entirely out of place during the process of mass privatization. Maybe the fairness in distribution is not in giving everyone equally, but in awarding everyone according to one's merits. However, this question was not on the agenda in the early 1990s. The major task was privatization itself, while the new owners were predetermined. Accordingly, during the process of privatization and from the standpoint of pure economics, it does not matter who will eventually concentrate the ownership rights over former state enterprises. At the same time, from the standpoint of fairness, it would be interesting to know exactly for what kind of merits certain individuals obtain major economic assets created by the country's population over several decades of labor.

Solzhenitsyn calls privatization a "frenzy of thieving" (Pearce, 2011). It can hardly be said better than this. Privatization in Russia is oftentimes mixed or even confused with the process of primary accumulation of capital. This process, in its turn, is frequently mentioned during the characterization of Russian predatory raiding along with privatization. According to some observations presented by the Center of Political Technologies, some respondents suggest that raiding exists everywhere in the world, and it cannot be viewed as a social, economic, or political phenomenon. However, in the world practice, raiding either received a criminal status, described in a Criminal Code of a certain country, or a legal status of M&A, which occurs throughout the world. For instance, in the US and Europe, this is a legal business. Each country in its history had to go through the stage of primary accumulation of capital, which accounted for raiding as well. However, in countries, where the process of the primary accumulation of capital had been completed, one would no longer find methods used by Russian raiders. In Russia, there is a process of forming a biased and twisted mentality of the business community.[5] Here, respondents apparently refer to Wild-West or so-called cowboy capitalism, especially popular in the 1990s.

Concluding Remarks

The phenomenon of predatory raiding cannot be considered without first looking into the earlier forms of property distribution, including first of all the mass privatization. The processes of moving property away from under the state and its further privatization have been highly controversial. The exploitation of humans by humans became possible thanks to a surplus of produce created by households in the era of subsistence farming. This surplus made the partial expropriation possible. Similarly, predatory raiding is possible only in the presence of significant economic assets, including production capacities and other objects of property. If there would be no valuable material assets, predatory raiders would have nothing to take over. The abundance of natural resources with high market value adds significantly to the list of objects targeted by predatory raiders in Russia.

Following the evolution of predatory raiding in Russia and dividing this process into meaningful stages or phases is not an easy task. What terms and criteria would be applicable to fulfill this task? Chronology relates to the timing of a certain process, stages are those of a certain program realization, major marks are marks on the way to achieving a certain goal. These terms do not apply to predatory raiding very well. Predatory raiding is a phenomenon, a relation, but not a system, even if raiding acquires a systemic character and certain elements of raiding become institutionalized. Even though specialized raiding organizations and companies use elaborate schemes for hostile takeovers, they themselves do not constitute a unified and completed system. It is hard to answer the question of whether predatory raiding in Russia can be characterized by the presence of clearly demarcated stages of its emergence, formation, development, and decline.

Notes

1. Dallago, Bruno, & Iwasaki, Ichiro (Eds.). (2007). *Corporate Restructuring and Governance in Transition Economies*. New York: Palgrave Macmillan.
2. Reiderstvo kak sotsial'no-ekonomicheskij i politicheskij fenomen sovremennoj Rossii: otchet o kachestvennom sotsiologicheskom issledovanii. Issledovanie "Tsentra politicheskih tehnologij" pod rukovodstvom Bunina. Moskva, 2008. [Raiding as a socioeconomic and political phenomenon of the modern Russia: A report on the qualitative sociological investigation. An investigation conducted by the Center of Political Technologies led by Bunin]. Moscow, May 2008. Retrieved June 12, 2009, from http://www.politcom.ru/; http://www.compromat.ru/main/mix1/raiderycpt.htm
3. Kudrin nadeetsya, chto pravitel'stvo vskore perejdet k "proryvnym reformam" [Kudrin hopes that the government will soon move to implementing break-through reforms]. *Newsru.com*, May 25, 2018. Retrieved May 25, 2018, from https://www.newsru.com/finance/25may2018/kudrinsbrbreakfst.html
4. Stephen Holmes, "What Russia Teaches Us Now: How Weak States Threaten Freedom," *American Prospect*, no. 33 (July–August 1997): 30–39; Michael McFaul, "Russia's 'Privatized' State as an Impediment to Democratic Consolidation," parts I and II, *Security Dialogue* 29:2(1998): 191–99 and 29:3(1998): 315–32; Richard E. Ericson, "Is Russia in Transition to a Market Economy?" *Post-Soviet Affairs* 16:1(2000): 18–25; and Katherine Verdery, *What Was Socialism, and What Comes Next?* (Princeton, NJ: Princeton University Press, 1996), 204–28. Both Ericson and Verdery take the term "parcelization of sovereignty" from Perry Anderson, *Lineages of the Absolutist State* (London: NLB, 1974).

5. Reiderstvo kak sotsial'no-ekonomicheskij i politicheskij fenomen sovremennoj Rossii: otchet o kachestvennom sotsiologicheskom issledovanii. Issledovanie "Tsentra politicheskih tehnologij" pod rukovodstvom Bunina. Moskva, 2008. [Raiding as a socio-economic and political phenomenon of the modern Russia: A report on the qualitative sociological investigation. An investigation conducted by the Center of Political Technologies led by Bunin]. Moscow, May 2008. Retrieved June 12, 2009, from http://www.politcom.ru/; http://www.compromat.ru/main/mix1/raiderycpt.htm

References

Barnes, A. (2003). Comparative Theft: Context and choice in the Hungarian, Czech, and Russian Transformations, 1989–2000. *East European Politics and Societies, 17*(3), 533–565.

Barnes, A. (2006). *Owning Russia: The Struggle over Factories, Farms, and Power*. Ithaca, NY: Cornell University Press.

Barnes, A. (2007a). Extricating the State: The Move to Competitive Capture in Post-Communist Bulgaria. *Europe-Asia Studies, 59*(1), 71–95.

Barnes, A. (2007b). Industrial Property in Russia: The Return of the State and a Focus on Oil. *SAIS Review, 27*(2), 47–62. Retrieved July 22, 2012, from http://muse.jhu.edu/journals/sais_review/v027/27.2barnes.pdf

Dolgopyatova, T. (2007). Corporate Ownership and Control in Russian Companies: Trends and Patterns. In B. Dallago & I. Iwasaki (Eds.), *Corporate Restructuring and Governance in Transition Economies* (pp. 250–274). New York: Palgrave Macmillan.

Federowicz, M., & Aguilera, R. (Eds.). (2003). *Corporate Governance in a Changing Economic and Political Environment: Trajectories of Institutional Change*. London: Palgrave Macmillan.

Frye, T. (2000). *Brokers and Bureaucrats: Building Market Institutions in Russia*. Ann Arbor: University of Michigan Press.

Hanley, E. (2000). Cadre Capitalism in Hungary and Poland: Property Accumulation among Communist-Era Elites. *East European Politics and Societies, 14*(1), 143–178.

Havrylyshyn, O., & McGettigan, D. (1999). *Privatization in Transition Countries: A Sampling of the Literature*. Washington, DC: The International Monetary Fund. *IMF Working Paper Series, 99*(6), 1–45.

Hellman, J., Jones, G., & Kaufmann, D. (2003). Seize the State, Seize the Day: An Empirical Analysis of State Capture and Corruption in Transition Economies. *Journal of Comparative Economics, 31*(4), 751–773.

Iwasaki, I. (2007). Corporate Law and Governance Mechanism in Russia. In B. Dallago & I. Iwasaki (Eds.), *Corporate Restructuring and Governance in Transition Economies* (pp. 213–249). New York: Palgrave Macmillan.

Musatova, M. (2011). Empiricheskij analiz dinamiki sliyanij i pogloshchenij rossijskikh kampanij [Empirical Analysis of Mergers & Acquisitions Dynamics of Russian Companies]. *Mir ekonomiki i upravleniya, 11*(2), 118–128. Retrieved June 18, 2017, from https://cyberleninka.ru/article/v/empiricheskiy-analiz-dinamiki-sliyaniy-i-pogloscheniy-rossiyskih-kompaniy

Osipian, A. (2012). Predatory Raiding in Russia: Institutions and Property Rights After the Crisis. *Journal of Economic Issues, 46*(2), 469–479.

Pearce, J. (2011). *Solzhenitsyn: A Soul in Exile.* San Francisco: Ignatius Press.

Pivovarsky, A. (2001). *How Does Privatization Work? Ownership Concentration and Enterprise Performance in Ukraine.* IMF Working Paper Series WP/01/42 (pp. 1–45). Washington, DC: The International Monetary Fund. Retrieved January 10, 2012, from http://www.imf.org/external/pubs/ft/wp/2001/wp0142.pdf

Rosenbaum, E., Bönker, F., & Wagener, H.-J. (Eds.). (2000). *Privatization, Corporate Governance and the Emergence of Markets.* London: Palgrave Macmillan.

Skidanova, L. (2010). *Reiderstvo kak sotsial'no-ekonomicheskij fenomen* [Raiding as a Socio-Economic Phenomenon]. Doctoral Dissertation (Manuscript), Moscow State University, Moscow.

Tarkhanova, Z. (2008). *Funktsionirovanie instituta reiderstva v RF* [Functioning of the Institute of Raiding in the RF]. Dissertation, Severo-Osetinsky State University, Vladikavkaz.

Tridico, P. (2011). *Institutions, Human Development and Economic Growth in Transition Economies.* London: Palgrave Macmillan.

Yakovlev, A. (2007). Evolution of Corporate Governance in Russia: Governmental Policy vs Real Incentives of Economic Agents. In B. Dallago & I. Iwasaki (Eds.), *Corporate Restructuring and Governance in Transition Economies* (pp. 275–296). New York: Palgrave Macmillan.

Yakovlev, A., Sobolev, A., & Kazun, A. (2014). Means of Production Versus Means of Coercion: Can Russian Business Limit the Violence of a Predatory State? *Post-Soviet Affairs, 30*(2–3), 171–194.

CHAPTER 5

Prospects of Raiding Evolution: Prognosis Is Optimistic

Perspectives of Raiding Movement

State officials like to speculate that the wave of predatory raiding that once took over the entire Russia is now receding, slowly but steadily. Such is the official position of the Russian authorities, and it is of little surprise, as the country needs foreign investment and technologies. In reality, however, predatory raiding has quite a promising future and good perspectives in the short run and in the long run. At this point, the predatory raiding movement continues focusing mainly on enterprises, but soon, predatory raiders can start targeting individuals as well. So far, there is not even an urgent need for the predatory raiding movement to change or transform, even though there are already suggestions that predatory raiding is converting into a white-collar crime.[1] It is also surprising that while the state authorities recognize the overwhelming problem of corruption and acknowledge that the problem of bureaucratic corruption is not disappearing or even diminishing despite all the proclaimed state anti-corruption efforts, they see the predatory raiding phenomenon being on the declining trajectory.

A gradual decline in predatory raiding activities may sound promising to Russian entrepreneurs. However, not everyone shares in the optimism of Russian bureaucrats. Barnes (2006) suggests that the situation with property rights in Russia is unlikely to stabilize in the foreseen future. The author points out to the changing forms of predatory raiding depending on the stage of politico-economic transition and particular laws enacted in the country. These changes signify the transition from one stage or phase

A. L. Osipian, *Political and Economic Transition in Russia*,
https://doi.org/10.1007/978-3-030-03831-1_5

to the other, but not the stability with guaranteeing enforcing owners' rights over their property. "Perhaps the best observers can hope for, then, is an analysis that helps explain why the Russian struggle for property moves from phase to phase rather than to a stable system of regularized capitalist competition" (Barnes, 2006, p. 230). Apparently, the lawlessness in regard to property rights is here to stay, and predatory raiders certainly contribute to its longevity.

Despite some assurances that the wild 1990s [likhie devyanostye] are left behind and that modern Russia is distinct with more civilized business practices, numerous media reports show a different picture. In fact, not only are the aggressive and violent practices same, but the spheres in which they occur are same as well. Moreover, these practices move to other sectors of economic and social life, advanced by predatory raiders. Below are a few selected vignettes of predatory raiding from 2016 and 2017, reported in the Russian media.

On December 27, 2017, there were shots fired on the territory of a Moscow confectionary factory Menshevik. The panic ensued. According to witnesses, people were jumping from windows on the second floor in an attempt to escape premises. Police special force team moved to the factory, where the shootout took place, and they have yet to find the shooter.[2] The perpetrator turned out to be the factory's former director, Ilia Averianov, who was tired of filing complaints against predatory raiders and appealing to different law enforcement agencies. Averianov, armed with a rifle, gunned down a security guard during the dispute with the new owners of the factory. The shooter alleges intentional staged bankruptcy as a classical scheme of hostile takeover and says that it is an ethnic Ossetia mafia that includes two Moscow prosecutors that takes away his factory.[3] This is a typical scene from the 1990s with guns, violence, and dead bodies. A clear lack of fortification on the factory allowed one armed man to cause chaos and interrupt production.

A similar picture is seen in Russia's regions. Violence in battle for all kinds of property may be observed throughout the country. In Ekaterinburg, one of Russia's largest regional centers, unknown individuals threaten to kill dwellers of the building who refused to pay for parking.[4] In February of 2017, a group of around 15 stormtroopers armed with knives and clubs tried to occupy a parking lot and force locals to pay a monthly fee. The battle ensued, involving around a hundred men. The raiders retreated but said that they would shoot the most active participants of the local resistance and the rest would pay anyway. The police refused to investigate the conflict. Collective action employed by the locals as a strategy to resist predatory raiders is well seen in this example.

Large-scale predatory raiding that has little to do with business may be on the rise as well. In December of 2017, the Jehovah's Witnesses lost real estate in St Petersburg valued at 880 million rubles, that is, approximately $25 million.[5] A few months earlier, the church of Jehovah's Witnesses was outlawed in Russia. The Russian government does not tolerate churches that come from the West and exert influence over the local population. The city authorities promise that the building taken away from the Jehovah's Witnesses in St Petersburg would be handed to scientists, namely, to a medical research institute.[6] Jehovah's Witnesses had 395 branches around Russia, and its branch in St Petersburg owned property—mostly real estate—estimated at 2.1 billion rubles, that is, $35 million. The market value of the 55 real estate objects that belonged to the church in the city may be much higher.

Despite the constitutional separation of church and state, the Russian government clearly favors its traditional church—Russian Orthodox Church. Russian Orthodox Church uses its favored status and now claims its rights over about a thousand buildings in Moscow.[7] These buildings belonged to the church before the Bolshevik revolution of 1917. Russia enacted the law on restitution in 2010, at which point the church received the right to claim its property back. The problem is that most of these objects are used by other organizations. Many of these organizations are not private enterprises, but public ones, including museums and educational institutions, and they have nowhere to go.

Medvedev's famous *koshmarit' biznes*, that is, "causing nightmares for business," continues as usual.[8] The situation with the interference of law enforcement agencies in private business operations has become so bad that President Putin had to interfere personally. As Schreck (2018) points out, during the state-of-the-nation address, delivered at the height of the electoral campaign on March 1, 2018, Putin said that Russia must "get rid of everything that enables corrupt officials and law enforcement officers to pressure businesses." President Putin and Prime Minister Medvedev have made similar calls numerous times in the past.

Siloviki continues to play a major role in all aspects of Russian politics (see, for instance, Soldatov & Rochlitz, 2018). In June of 2016, Putin suggested introducing criminal responsibility for law enforcement officers for violations of entrepreneurs' rights[9]: "It is necessary to critically lower possibilities of unlawful criminal prosecution (of business). Moreover, law enforcement officers should carry personal responsibility for unjustified actions that lead to destruction of business. I think that this responsibility may also be criminal." President Putin also pointed out the need to have a well-balanced policy in this regard and create a barrier for possible abuse of authority by law enforcement agencies.

Rochlitz (2014, p. 89) describes a charismatic situation of how a usual hostile takeover in Russia works:

> Imagine being a young innovative entrepreneur in Russia. A couple of years ago, you had a brilliant idea, you were able to get some money, which permitted you to start a business. The business began to grow, with your company eventually becoming one of the leaders in its field. Until one morning, access to your office is denied by a group of armed people in black uniforms. A sleek lawyer presents you with a document stating that you no longer own your business. The document is evidently a forgery, but it contains the official seal of a local judge. You call the police, but after viewing the document an officer confirms that the document is legal. The officer then asks you to kindly leave the company premises as you no longer own the firm.

It is precisely about this hypothetical young innovative entrepreneur that Russia's opposition politician, Irina Khakamada, spoke in the Kremlin during the meeting with President Putin. She spoke highly critical of Russia's business environment, attacking Putin for not doing enough in this regard. Khakamada says that creative entrepreneurial people are needed to form the middle class, but regional leaders do not necessarily support small- and medium-sized businesses, and Putin agrees that more can and should be done in this direction.[10] Krylova (2018, p. 1) calls entrepreneurs in contemporary Russia as "endangered species." Apparently, legally registered entrepreneurs in Russia are located quite low in the food pyramid, much lower than predatory raiders. The reaction to Putin's most recent statement of March 1, 2018, was swift. Media reports titled "Entrepreneurs are rescued from jail: what financial crimes may be decriminalized,"[11] "Businessmen can get their sentences monetized: some of their crimes may be decriminalized,"[12] and "Punished, but not jailed"[13] filled the media space. However, this media frenzy, which is not new, may result in nothing, as the system does not change.

Will the situation with predatory raiding in Russia change for the better thanks to bringing new blood into the political establishment? After inauguration on May 18, 2018, President Putin signed orders on new government.[14] The complete list of ministers in the new government, confirmed by Putin and published on that day, shows that not much has changed, and the new government essentially equates to the old one, with all familiar faces.[15] Shuffling and reshuffling the old deck of all-too-familiar play cards is Putin's favorite occupation. In May of 2018, the media reported that the Russian stock market has been losing foreign investors for five weeks.[16] This decline did not prevent Igor Shuvalov, Russia's first deputy prime minister, responsible, among other things, for attracting foreign investments in the country, to receive an offer from Putin. The president offered Shuvalov the leadership of Vneshekonombank (VEB), and Shuvalov promised to do a good job in this new position.[17] After all, this position is also directly related to foreign economic activities.

The newly appointed Chairman of the Accounts Chamber, Alexei Kudrin, hopes that the government will soon move to breakthrough reforms, pointing to support of competition and small businesses.[18] Kudrin is by no means a new face in the Russian political establishment. He previously served in the Russian government as the minister of Finance, from May 2000 to September 2011, surviving even the financial crisis of 2008. His long-term colleague, Anton Siluanov, is a newly appointed minister of Finance and first deputy prime minister. Siluanov also named main directions for economic reforms, among which are state support for funding infrastructure, reforming social expenditures, tax breaks, and liberalizing hard currencies control.[19] Clearly, dealing with widespread corruption and predatory raiding is not among the priorities.

Shuvalov, Kudrin, Siluanov, and other mutually replaceable functioneers of the Russian political establishment continue the rhetoric of economic restructuring, much needed future economic growth, and development. However, their former colleagues may have a somewhat different view on the economic perspectives for Russia. The former deputy chairman of the Central Bank of Russia, Sergey Aleksashenko, does not share in their cautious optimism. To the contrary, Aleksashenko (2018, p. 1) suggests that, "In the economic realm, Putin effectively undermined Russia's still-emerging and very fragile system for protecting property rights—the basis of all economic activity. This in turn caused a sharp decline in private investment and thus contributed to the long-term economic slowdown." Having a poor system for protecting property rights guarantees good perspectives for predatory raiding.

State support in funding infrastructure, reforming social expenditures, tax breaks, liberalizing hard currencies control, and foreign investment may be important for economic restructuring and modernization, but there are more fundamental things, such as land. Land remains the magnet for predatory raiders, with raiding activities in agriculture, construction and development, and extraction industries expected to increase. In April of 2016, around 1000 people showed up for the protesting action against a takeover of land that belongs to Timiryazev Agricultural Academy.[20] In the authoritarian Russia that does not tolerate protests, 1000 participants in any protesting action is an unusually high number and points to the significance of the problem. Finally, that unites in itself issues of predatory raiding, land, church, and the state. Patriarch Kirill wrote a letter to President Putin, expressing concern about the redistribution of church lands.[21]

Both old and new forms of predatory raiding have a lot of potential, as areas for predatory raiders are plenty. There are numerous undiscovered and undeveloped territories and spaces for the raiding movement. They include everything from defense industry enterprises to such exotic businesses as dolphinariums. Media outlets flash out reports with titles from "Raiders can attempt to take over 200 defense enterprises in Russia"[22] to "Moscow dolphinarium was taken over by predatory raiders on Monday."[23] Not *only* humans and dolphins suffer from predatory raiders. Raiders have reached such distant regions as Yakutiya and such exotic businesses as gathering of mammoth tusks. In May of 2018, in Yakutsk, gatherers of mammoth tusks protested a documentary shown by the *Russia 24* channel.[24] The reason for the protest that gathered a few dozen people was a fear that after the documentary, raiders would come and take over the business. The locals state that gathering the tusks of mammoths fallen during the Ice Age, over 10,000 years ago, along with crafts made from the tusks, keeps them afloat financially and rescues them from unemployment. These forms of self-employment may now be threatened by predatory raiders.

Contrary to the assurances of state bureaucrats about the decline in raiding activities and its move from the center to the regions, the media reports that in 2008, the number of raiding attempts on enterprises has increased significantly.[25] Apparently, the standard explanation that everything that could be raided in Moscow was already raided a long time ago and that predatory raiders simply have nothing else to raid in Moscow does not correspond to the reality. The raiding movement does not limit itself to hostile takeovers of objects, including industrial, trade, business, administrative, housing, research, educational, social, cultural, and other objects. Bureaucratic resources are actively involved in predatory raiding, thus creating additional opportunities for state-based raiding. Confiscation of goods, including from retail networks, is yet another form of predatory raiding.

> Stores that sold mobile phones or microwave ovens were raided under the pretext that these commodities were counterfactual. These events showed that raiding, which had previously been concentrated on big industries, had entered a new sphere of the economy. The goods confiscated during the raids created a tremendous source of illegal income for officials. They would sell the goods illegally on the open market or buy them at very low prices. Customs officers often confiscated imported goods using the most ridiculous pretexts (for instance, any type of mistake in documentation). The criminal activity of Russian customs officials was acknowledged by the highest officials, including the president. Confiscated goods would be sold at auction to a chosen firm at a minimal price. (Shlapentokh, 2007, p. 146)[26]

Prospects for predatory raiding in Russia are rather good. In ecology, predation is considered as a mechanism of population control. Thus, when the number of predators is scarce, the number of preys should rise. When this happens, the predators would be able to reproduce more and possibly change their hunting habits. As the number of predators rises, the number of preys decline. This results in food scarcity for predators that can eventually lead to the death of many predators.[27] This kind of fluctuation is expected in nature. But Russian predatory raiding may be unnatural. Economically speaking, predatory raiding in Russia is only capable of exogenous growth, expansion based on involving additional resources and targets of raiding attacks. The breeding ground of predatory raiding in Russia remains intact as corruption continues to grow, crossing imaginary lines of possibility.

Expansion strategies of the predatory raiding movement do not recognize geographic or sectoral boundaries. From Moscow to regions, from large corporations to street vendors, from private sector to state customs control, from stocks and bonds to agricultural land, from criminal underworld to state bureaucracies, predatory raiders discover new niches and new opportunities for their enrichment. Everything that could be raided is raided or will be raided. Russian predatory raiding is not creative; predatory raiders do not produce or create anything. There is no added value as a result of predatory raiders' actions. Thus, the only way predatory raiding in Russia can continue is by expansion.

As the wave of Russia's mass privatization has receded, the fight of private entities for state assets is far from over. In addition, private entities now fight among themselves for already privatized state assets. Barnes (2006) points to a likely continuous character of the struggle over property in Russia, as the state-private axis of the fight switches to private-private axis. Similarly, Hellman (2002) also predicts the potential for long-term fights for property and ownership in Russia. The continuous fight for property with the use of noneconomic tools of influence may result in a permanent lawlessness in ownership rights.

A Revolutionary Theory of Permanent Lawlessness

Similar to Lev Trotsky, who was exporting permanent revolution from Russia with a changing success, western investors try to export their capitals to Russia, or, to be more precise, to successfully invest them there. They bring ideas of western corporate managerialism along with the capital. However, ideas are not that easy to take away, so the major concern of western investors is about their capitals. It is quite clear then that they worry about the future trends in the predatory raiding movement in Russia. The position of the Russian authorities in this regard is unequivocal: predatory raiding is declining. Such a position is easy to explain, since foreign investors have to be convinced in stability of property rights in Russia. However, there are other opinions as well (See, for instance, Sonin, 2003, 2005). The evolutionary way from the institutional theory of permanent distribution to the practice of endless or permanent lawlessness is not as long as it may appear at a first glance. So, the question is: Will predatory raiding disappear? In order to address this question, one has to think of whether the bases and components of this phenomenon will disappear, or will they survive, remain, strengthen, or transform.

Corruption is oftentimes referred to as being fundamental to predatory raiding or one of its most significant components. If predatory raiding is unlikely to go away through the disappearance of vulnerable objects, territories, and spheres of raiding, then, perhaps predatory raiding may be eliminated through combating and eliminating corruption. This brings to the fore the question on the current state of corruption in Russia and future prospects. Simply put, how is Russia doing in terms of corruption?

Given the high level of corruptness in state organs, national media further propels public perceptions about corruption. Litvinova (2011) reports in Russia's popular media outlet *RBK Daily* that only 9 out of every 100 people have not learned how to give bribes.[28] This implies that over 90 percent of Russians have experiences of giving bribes to state bureaucrats, educators, health providers, or police officers. Another media report states that the average bribe in Russia exceeds $10,000.[29] According to the press release of the Ministry of the Interior, issued in 2011, bribes Russian citizens pay average 250,000 rubles.[30] From 2008 to 2012, the average size of bribe increased 33 times, reaching 300,000 rubles or $12,000.[31] Figures vary, however. The Economic Crimes Prevention Unit within the Ministry of the Interior reports the average bribe of around $2000.[32] In 2013, the average bribe was reported at 145,000 rubles, that is, around $5000, more than double as compared to 2012.[33] Human rights activists reported that average bribe in Russia in 2014 has tripled, reaching $10,000.[34] In 2017, the Ministry of the Interior reported that average bribe indicated a 75 percent increase as compared to 2016 and exceeded $5000.[35] In Moscow, average bribe increased by two-and-a-half times over 2016, reaching $35,000.[36] These are large bribes, paid by entrepreneurs, corporations, and other large and wealthy property owners. Petty bribes and gifts, given to street level bureaucrats, remain unaccounted for.

Russia's Minister of the Interior Vladimir Kolokol'tsev pointed out that from 2012 to 2013, the number of bribery incidences increased by 18 percent.[37] Similarly, in Moscow, cases of bribery increased by 17 percent from 2016 to 2017. But Russia's Ministry of the Interior itself is not free of corruption. The allegations of corruption in law enforcement agencies and courts, including their involvement in predatory raiding, are numerous. One out of every five Russians believe that corruption in law enforcement and courts is not only present, but widespread.[38] Corruption damage in the first ten months of 2013 was estimated at 21 billion rubles.[39] According to another report, in 2013, corruption damage in the energy industry alone was estimated at 21 billion rubles, with 2500 economic crimes reported in the energy sector.[40] The Ministry of the Interior investigated 16,000 cases of embezzlement and gross waste in that year.[41]

If one of the bases or necessary conditions for predatory raiding—corruption—is not likely to disappear from the face of Russian reality in the next few decades, then what is the situation with the other base or condition, high crime rates? Can one expect the decline in the army of predatory raiding stormtroopers, professional fraudsters, corrupt bureaucrats, and other agents of raiding? Some researchers were overly optimistic about the anti-crime prospects in modern Russia. For instance, in 1997, Aslund

(1997) concluded that the level of crime in Russia would eventually fall. The author stated that there are many reasons why this should happen. Aslund (1997, p. 91) grounded his positive expectations regarding crime levels in Russia in that, "Overwhelmingly, the most important economic roots of crime have dwindled—price controls, export controls, subsidized credits and multiple exchange rates. In addition, the whole Russian society is mobilizing against crime. It would be surprising if such an onslaught would not reduce crime for a long time."

Surprising as it may be, as of 2018, the crime rate in Russia is not likely to decline either in the short run or in the long run. On the contrary, crime as one of the bases for aggressive predatory raiding proliferates. Aslund (1997, pp. 91–92) offered the following reasons for crime in Russia to decrease:

> [l]iberalization and stabilization have removed most of the mechanisms of rent-seeking and corruption; far-reaching privatization has transferred most state property to the private sector; the Russian legislation is being improved; the Russian media report professionally and extensively on crime; government allocations to law enforcement have risen considerably; the number of prisoners is increasing fast; social order is improving; the legal education has become very prestigious and attractive; the Russian market is gaining strength, but crime implies high transaction costs, which impede the effective functioning of the market.

The practice shows, however, that these factors may be insufficient to reduce crime, to say the least.

Corruption and crime remain on the agenda. Russia continues to face constant challenges of corruption and high crime rates, including murders and armed robberies. Hence, the state with its law enforcement apparatus also remains on the scene with its anti-raiding campaign. As the President of Chechnya, Ramzan Kadyrov, rightly points out,

> The claims should not be addressed to us. The claims of dissatisfaction should be addressed to the leadership of the country. Why do they let us do whatever we want? Is there no prosecutor's office? Did you forget the Investigations Committee? Where is the State Audit Chamber, the FSB, all those organizations? This question is not for us. If we are such corrupt bureaucrats, then why are we not in prison yet?[42]

Kadyrov critically points to state organs and officials responsible for fighting corruption.

While surveys address predominantly street level or petty corruption, with which some Russians have to deal on a regular basis, grand-scale corruption continues in Russia as well. In March 2017, the Anti-Corruption Foundation [Fond bor'by s korruptsiej, FBK], founded by Alexei Naval'ny in 2011, published its largest investigation about mansions, yachts, and vineyards that allegedly belonged to Premier Minister Dmitry Medvedev.[43] The Anti-Corruption Foundation issued a report titled *How oligarch gives a bribe to vice premier. Decomposing the mechanics*, about the grand bribe given to a top-ranked state official by Mikhail Prokhorov, Russian oligarch with an otherwise reasonably good reputation.[44] The bribe was allegedly given to Alexander Khloponin, deputy prime minister of the Russian Federation, through the purchase of his Italian villa at a grossly inflated price. A piece of real estate that could hardly bring its owner $10 million, if placed on the market, was suddenly acquired by the oligarch for around $40 million. Naval'ny called Prokhorov's buying Khloponin's villa in Italy a classic bribe to the vice premier.[45] In response to these accusations, Prokhorov filed a lawsuit against Naval'ny.[46]

Problems also remain in the court system, which plays key roles in both predatory raiding and anti-raiding. Independence of judges and courts, and thus the independence of court decisions, remains a serious problem. The objectivity and lawfulness of court decisions is sometimes dubious. Independence of judges, courts, and hence court decisions remains at stake, while their decisions are often questionable. Ledeneva (2004, p. 86) offers a fragment of an interview with an ex-judge:

> Question: We hear a lot about political pressure put on judges.
>
> Answer: The mechanism is traditional—distributing favors and privileges. Let's say you are the chairman of a court, and you want to become a member of the Supreme Court. Are you going to refuse to take the advice of the chairman of the Supreme Court? No, you're not. Or for example, the mayor calls you up and says you're really in debt. But I'll pretend not to see it, he says, and by the way, I have a libel case in your court tomorrow. For some reason, the mayor always wins.

While commenting on economic or property conflicts, Moscow's now ex-mayor Yuri Luzhkov is constantly referring to a proper court decision.[47] There is an opinion, however, that when it comes to the interests of the Moscow city authorities, or to the mayor himself, Moscow courts become rather subjective. The reasons for this loyalty are understandable—for several years, the Moscow courts are, as a matter of fact, financed by the city authorities. This practice is against the law. For example, on February 3, 1999, Yuri Luzhkov proposed a joint agreement with the city courts including additional financing from the municipal budget. The amount of financing will depend on actual results of the court system activity. The mayor mentioned that in 1998, 42 million rubles were allocated from the municipal budget for court development; during the last six years, the judges were given 121 apartments. On January 25, 2001, he had announced that in 2001 the city authorities were ready to "financially support" the court system, specifically, to "solve the problem" of computerization of Moscow courts.[48]

Even the European Court for Human Rights in Strasburg continues to suspect that there is something wrong: the offended Mayor Luzhkov always wins in Moscow courts.[49] Luzhkov, who served as the Mayor of Moscow from 1992 to 2010, has over 50 victories in defamation lawsuits under his belt buckle. Ironically, one of these lawsuits was against Eduard Limonov for his libelous phrase "Moscow courts are controlled by Luzhkov." Both Limonov and Radio Svoboda were ordered to pay Luzhkov 500,000 rubles each in compensation for moral damages.[50]

The legislative process, improvement of laws, law amendments, increasing the level of executed court orders, and law enforcement are insufficient in the anti-raiding campaign. Volkov (2005) offers comments on the role of law and the loopholes in Russia. Volkov (2004, p. 143) states that,

> Although legal codes and their loopholes and omissions are important, a full account of enterprise takeovers compels one to look at extra-legal realities to explain the way laws work in post-Soviet Russia. No law contains the rules of its application. No law defines the legal facts that it is supposed to regulate. It would be an oversimplification to assume that the legal 'rules of the game' determine and therefore contain exhaustive explanations of the practices to which they refer. A reference to some 'informal rules' or 'informal culture' responsible for the discordance between the written laws and their working in practice only obscures reality and explains little, for it leads to a multiplication ad infinitum of various tacit rules allegedly governing the application of formal rules.

The balance of formal and informal rules denotes the prevalence of either law obeying behavior or legal nihilism.

Pistor and Xu (2004, p. 172) point out that the incompleteness of law and the information problems distinguish transition economies from developed market economies in a negative way: "Given the scale and scope of economic and legal reforms that are taking place concurrently, law in transition countries is bound to be highly incomplete, that is, its meaning and application to specific cases are largely untested, and the scope of liability is therefore uncertain." As a result, court decisions and law enforcement cannot effectively deter violators. The application of laws to specific cases of predatory raiding is complicated by different interpretations of law as well as the influence of the outside forces on the judiciary process. Courts and judges in Russia are not independent. At the same time, the external assessment recognizes that the legislation of Russia is highly compliant with the Model Law on International Commercial Arbitration (Chapaev, 2007, p. 13).

Corruption, high crime rates, and state authoritarianism with its repressive apparatus form a necessary basis for the predatory raiding movement to grow and develop. At the same time, waves of privatization, re-privatization, and ideas of windfall tax may play a most significant role in the chronology of predatory raiding and peaks of raiding activity. As the process of privatization continues, predatory raiding companies may be certain that their services will be in high demand. Major predatory raiders have always welcomed news on yet another wave of privatizing state property. And the perspectives of privatization, given the remaining total of state-owned assets, are almost limitless. According to Shlapentokh and Arutunyan (2013, p. 21), Russian liberals of the Perestroika era "spearheaded a host of authors who demanded the privatization of everything in society: not only mines and factories but also institutions in education and science, as well as police and corrections." Given the political and economic trends observed in modern Russia, predatory raiding is unlikely to experience a sharp decline in the near future.

Concluding Remarks

Given the state of affairs in contemporary Russia, predatory raiding has a promising future in the country. Russian business ecosystem is not ready to weed out predatory raiders, and the state has no interest in doing this either. Predatory raiding gains in popularity and becomes a widespread practice that targets both enterprises and individual property owners. As many hostile takeovers are done by state agencies, the government is unable to offer a viable solution for the problem of predatory raiding formulated as a short-run or long-run state policy. On the one hand, predatory raiding in Russia is getting converted into a white-collar crime. This is explained by the strengthening of corporations in the country. On the other hand, there are still plenty of examples of violent criminal raiding similar to that of the 1990s. Both old and new forms of predatory raiding have a lot of potential in Russia. Areas and targets for predatory raiding are still plenty.

Contrary to the assurances of top state bureaucrats about the steady and significant decline in predatory raiding, the media reports point to the opposite. A suggestion that everything that could be raided in Moscow was already raided in the 1990s and 2000s and that raiders simply have nothing else to raid in Moscow does not correspond to the reality. It is true that predatory raiders stage their attacks on enterprises, land, and private owners in Russia's regions, but that does not imply that raiders had abandoned Moscow and St Petersburg. Corruption as a fundamental base for predatory raiding continues to flourish throughout Russia, including in its largest and most developed cities. Only a dramatic reduction in corruption can put an end to predatory raiding.

Notes

1. Reiderstvo v Rossii prevratilos' v "belovorotnichkovyj" ugolovny promysel [Raiding in Russia turned into a "white collar" criminal business]. *Newsru.com*, May 20, 2008. Retrieved May 9, 2009, from http://www.newsru.com/finance/20may2008/togliattiazot.html
2. Spetspodrazdeleniya voshli na fabriku, gde proizoshla strel'ba, no najti strelka poka ne udalos' [Police special forces moved to the factory, where the shootout took place, but they have yet to find the shooter]. *Newsru.com*, December 27, 2017. Retrieved December 27, 2017, from https://msk.newsru.com/article/27dec2017/menshevik.html
3. Prokuror Moskvy vzyal pod lichnyj kontrol' situatsiyu na fabrike "Men'shevik" [Moscow city prosecutor personally controls the situation on Menshevik factory]. *Govorit Moskva*, December 27, 2017. Retrieved December 27, 2017, from https://govoritmoskva.ru/news/146124/
4. V Ekaterinburge neizvestnye ugrozhayut ubijstvom zhitelyam doma, otkazavshimsya platit' za stoyanku [In Ekaterinburg, unknown individuals threaten to kill dwellers of the building who refused to pay for parking]. *Newsru.com*, February 4, 2017. Retrieved February 4, 2017, from http://www.newsru.com/russia/04feb2017/eburgaction.html
5. U "Svidetelej Iegovy" otobrali nedvizhimost' pod Peterburgom na 880 mln rublej [Jehovah's Witnesses lost real estate in Petersburg valued at 880 million rubles]. *Newsru.com*, December 8, 2017. Retrieved December 8, 2017, from https://realty.newsru.com/article/08dec2017/iegov_realty

6. Otobrannoe u "Svidetelej Iegovy" zdanie v Peterburge otdadut uchenym [Building taken away from Jehovah's Witnesses in Petersburg will be handed to scientists]. *Newsru.com*, December 26, 2017. Retrieved December 26, 2017, from https://realty.newsru.com/article/26dec2017/iegov_med
7. RPC pretenduet na tysyachu zdanij v Moskve [Russian Orthodox Church claims a thousand buildings in Moscow]. *Newsru.com*, December 22, 2017. Retrieved December 22, 2017, from http://www.newsru.com/religy/22dec2017/rest.html?utm_source=tema-main
8. Directly translated, ***koshmarit' biznes*** means causing nightmares for business. Clifford Levy. Medvedev says Russia should end business 'nightmares.' *The New York Times*, August 1, 2008. Retrieved from http://www.nytimes.com/2008/08/01/world/europe/01iht-01russia.14927480.html Khvatit koshmarit' biznes. *Forbes*, Retrieved from http://www.forbes.ru/ekonomika/vlast/32096-hvatit-koshmarit-biznes
9. Putin predlozhil vvesti ugolovnuyu otvetstvennost' dlya silovikov za narushenie prav predprinimatelej [Putin suggested introducing criminal responsibility for law enforcement officers for violations of entrepreneurs' rights]. *Newsru.com*, June 17, 2016. Retrieved June 17, 2016, from http://www.newsru.com/russia/17jun2016/siloviki.html
10. Khakamada v Kremle opustila Putina i zastavila zaikat'sya [Khakamada in Kremlin attacked Putin and made him mumble]. *YouTube*, Apr 10, 2018. Retrieved May 14, 2018, from https://www.youtube.com/watch?v=wQvO9gFwrSQ
11. Predprinimateley spasayut ot otsidki: kakie finansovye prestupleniya mogut stat' neugolovnymi [Entrepreneurs are rescued from jail: what financial crimes may be decriminalized]. *Zagolovki*, May 23, 2018. Retrieved May 23, 2018, from http://zagolovki.ru/daytheme/bisnes/23May2018
12. Biznesmenam monetiziruyut sroki: nekotorye ikh prestupleniya mogut stat' neugolovnymi [Businessmen can get their sentences monetized: some of their crimes may be decriminalized]. *Kommersant*, May 23, 2018. Retrieved May 23, 2018, from https://www.kommersant.ru/doc/3636585
13. Kulikov, Vladislav. (2018). Nakazhut, no ne posadyat [Punished, but not jailed]. *Rossijskaya Gazeta*, May 23, 2018. Retrieved May 23, 2018, from https://rg.ru/2018/05/22/verhovnyj-sud-predlozhil-dekriminalizovat-neskolko-statej-uk.html
14. Prezident podpisal ukazy o sostave novogo pravitel'stva [Putin signed orders on new government]. *Kremlin.ru*, May 18, 2018. Retrieved May 18, 2018, from http://www.kremlin.ru/events/president/news/57495
15. Opublikovan polny spisok ministrov novogo pravitel'stva Rossii, utverzhdennyj Putinym [Complete list of ministers in the new government con-

firmed by Putin is published]. *Strana.ua*, May 18, 2018. Retrieved May 18, 2018, from https://strana.ua/news/141896-polnyj-spisok-vitse-premerov-i-federalnykh-ministrov-rossii-utverzhdennykh-putinym.html

16. Rossijsky fondovy rynok teryaet zarubezhnykh investorov uzhe pyat' nedel' [Russian stock market has been losing foreign investors for five weeks]. *Newsru.com*, May 25, 2018. Retrieved May 25, 2018, from https://www.newsru.com/finance/25may2018/ruinvest.html
17. Putin predlozhil Shuvalovu vozglavit' VEB, Shuvalov poobeshchal "ne podvesti" [Putin offered Shuvalov to lead VEB, and Shuvalov promised "not to let him down"]. *Newsru.com*, May 23, 2018. Retrieved May 23, 2018, from https://www.newsru.com/finance/24may2018/shuvalov.html
18. Kudrin nadeetsya, chto pravitel'stvo vskore perejdet k "proryvnym reformam" [Kudrin hopes that the government will soon move to breakthrough reforms]. *Newsru.com*, May 25, 2018. Retrieved May 25, 2018, from https://www.newsru.com/finance/25may2018/kudrinsbrbreakfst.html
19. Siluanov nazval osnovnye napravleniya reform v ekonomike [Siluanov named main directions for economic reforms]. *Newsru.com*, May 25, 2018. Retrieved May 25, 2018, from https://www.newsru.com/finance/25may2018/siluanovsbrbreakfast.html
20. Okolo tysyachi chelovek prishli na miting protiv iz'yatiya zemel' u Timiryazevskoj sel'khozakademii [Around a thousand people showed up for the protest against a takeover of land that belongs to Timiryazev Agricultural Academy]. *Newsru.com*, April 11, 2016. Retrieved April 11, 2016, from http://www.newsru.com/russia/11apr2016/timiryazevskaya.html
21. Patriarch Kirill is a de facto top-ranked politician, as the Russian Orthodox Church enjoys a very high status in the Russian state. See: Patriarkh Kirill napisal pis'mo Putinu: RPC opasaetsya peredela rynka tserkovnoj zemli [Patriarch Kirill wrote a letter to Putin: he worries about the redistribution of church lands]. *Newsru.com*, September 9, 2012. Retrieved September 9, 2012, from http://www.newsru.com/religy/11sep2012/lord_landlord.html
22. Reidery mogut zahvatit' 200 oboronnyh predpriyatij v Rossii [Raiders can attempt to take over 200 defense firms in Russia]. *Newsru.com*, April 10, 2008. Retrieved May 9, 2009, from http://realty.newsru.com/article/10Apr2008/military
23. V ponedel'nik byl sovershen reiderskij zahvat moskovskogo del'finariya [Moscow dolphinarium was taken over by raiders on Monday]. *Newsmsk*, April 7, 2009. Retrieved June 23, 2009, from http://www.newsmsk.com/article/07Apr2009/delfin.html

24. V Yakutske proshel miting sborshchikov bivney mamonta, vozmushchennykh fil'mom "Rossii 24" [In Yakutsk, gatherers of mammoth tusk protested a documentary shown by *Russia 24* channel]. *Newsru.com*, May 26, 2018. Retrieved May 26, 2018, from https://www.newsru.com/russia/26may2018/bivni.html
25. V Moskve za proshedshij god sushchestvenno uvelichilos' kolichestvo popytok reiderskih zahvatov predpriyatij [The number of attempts of raiding takeovers in Moscow over the last year has increased significantly]. *Notheft.ru*, January 21, 2009. Retrieved July 22, 2009, from http://www.notheft.ru/v-moskve-za-proshedshij-god-sushhestvenno-uvelichilos-kolichestvo-popytok-rejderskih-zahvatov-predpr
26. Shlapentokh (2007) clearly refers to the widely publicized case of Euroset-Motorola, also described by Yakovlev, Sobolev, and Kazun (2014): "The … case involved the illegal seizure of 167,000 Motorola cell phones (with an approximate value of $17 million) on 29 March 2006 by the customs authorities, supplied to Euroset on the basis of an official import contract (Kryazhev and Levitskiy 2006). The investigating authorities have changed the reasons for the seizure of the phones several times (including the allegation that 'they were harmful to consumer health'), but in the end, the criminal case was closed on 24 August 2006 due to a lack of evidence and 117,500 cell phones were returned to Euroset. This case was widely reported in the media (and included an informal conversation between George W. Bush and Vladimir Putin at the G-8 Summit in St. Petersburg in July 2006) and had serious political implications – in the form of dismissal of the head of the Federal Tax Service Aleksandr Zherikhov and Prosecutor General Vladimir Ustinov (Myers 2006)." Yakovlev, Sobolev, and Kazun (2014) suggest that when businesses face violent pressure from state agents, they prefer to cooperate with the authorities. Nevertheless, some businesses resist such a pressure and attract the attention of the general public with their complaints of abuse of authority committed by the law enforcement agencies. The authors consider the case of Euroset-Motorola a typical example of a "public defense" of property rights. Yakovlev, Andrei, Sobolev, Anton, & Kazun, Anton. (2014). Means of production versus means of coercion: can Russian business limit the violence of a predatory state? *Post-Soviet Affairs*, 30(2–3), pp. 175–176. See also: Kryazhev, D., & Levitskiy, R. (2006). Oplata po kontrafaktu: MVD nashlo novyy predlog dlya iz'yatiya sotovykh telefonov [Payment for a Counterfactual: MVD has a New Pretext for Seizing Cell Phones]. *Kommersant*, April 4. http://www.kommersant.ru/doc/662801; Myers, S. L. (2006). Putin Fires Prosecutor, Providing Grist for Kremlinologists. *The New York Times*, June 3.
27. Predation. Biology Online Dictionary. Retrieved May 6, 2017, from http://www.biology-online.org/dictionary/Predation

28. Litvinova, Anastasiya. (2011). Tol'ko devyat' chelovek iz sta eshche ne nauchilis' davat' vzyatki [Only nine out of every hundred people have not learned how to give bribes]. *RBK Daily*, June 15, 2011. Retrieved June 15, 2011, from http://www.rbcdaily.ru/2011/06/15/focus/562949980430428
29. Sredni razmer vzyatki v Rossii prevysil 10 tysyach dollarov [Average bribe in Russia exceeds $10,000]. *Newsru.com*, July 24, 2011. Retrieved July 24, 2011, from http://www.newsru.com/finance/22jul2011/vziatka.html
30. Rossiyane dayut "na lapu" v srednem po 250 tysyach rublej, rasskazali v MVD [Average bribes Russians pay are 250 thousand rubles, says MVD]. *Newsru.com*, October 18, 2011. Retrieved October 18, 2011, from http://www.newsru.com/russia/18oct2011/corruption.html
31. Srednij razmer vzyatki v Rossii vyros v 33 raza za chetyre goda [Size of average bribe increased 33 times over the last four years]. *Newsru.com*, August 22, 2012. Retrieved August 22, 2012, from http://www.newsru.com/russia/22aug2012/vziatko.html
32. V politsii vychislili razmer sredney vzyatki – ona bol'she sredney zarplaty [Police named the size of an average bribe; it exceeds average salary]. *Newsru.com*, October 25, 2012. Retrieved October 25, 2012, from http://www.newsru.com/russia/25oct2012/bribes.html
33. MVD: srednij razmer vzyatki v Rossii za god udvoilsya [MVD: the size of an average bribe in Russia over the last year has doubled]. *Newsru.com*, March 21, 2014. Retrieved March 21, 2014, from http://www.newsru.com/finance/21mar2014/rubrbery.html
34. Pravozashchitniki zayavili ob uvelichenii vtroe srednego razmera vzyatki v Rossii [Human rights activists reported that average bribe in Russia has tripled]. *Newsru.com*, September 3, 2015. Retrieved October 18, 2015, from http://www.newsru.com/russia/03sep2015/corrup.html
35. V MVD nazvali srednij razmer vzyatki v Rossii – za god on vyros na 75% [Ministry of the Interior reports that the average bribe in Russia increased 75 percent over the last year]. *Newsru.com*, March 16, 2017. Retrieved March 16, 2017, from http://www.newsru.com/russia/16mar2017/mvd.html
36. Srednyaya summa vzyatki v Moskve za proshlyj god vyrosla v 2,5 raza [Average bribe in Moscow increased 2.5 times in the past year]. *Newsru.com*, January 26, 2017. Retrieved January 26, 2017, from http://newsmsk.com/article/26jan2017/bolshedeneg2.html
37. MVD: srednij razmer vzyatki v Rossii za god udvoilsya [MVD: the size of an average bribe in Russia over the last year has doubled]. *Newsru.com*, March 21, 2014. Retrieved March 21, 2014, from http://www.newsru.com/finance/21mar2014/rubrbery.html
38. Rossiyane otsenili razgul korruptsii: mestnuyu vlast' obvinyayut vse chashche, GIBDD – rezhe [Russians gave their thoughts on the scope of

corruption: local authorities are alleged more frequently, while traffic patrol less frequently]. *Newsru.com*, October 23, 2013. Retrieved October 23, 2013, from http://www.newsru.com/russia/23oct2013/opros_2.html

39. Ushcherb ot korruptsii za 10 mesyatsev 2013 goda sostavil 21 milliard rublej [Corruption damage in first ten months of 2013 is estimated at 21 billion rubles]. *Newsru.com*, December 9, 2013. Retrieved December 9, 2013, from http://www.newsru.com/russia/09dec2013/21.html
40. MVD: srednij razmer vzyatki v Rossii za god udvoilsya [MVD: the size of an average bribe in Russia over the last year has doubled]. *Newsru.com*, March 21, 2014. Retrieved March 21, 2014, from http://www.newsru.com/finance/21mar2014/rubrbery.html
41. MVD: srednij razmer vzyatki v Rossii za god udvoilsya [MVD: the size of an average bribe in Russia over the last year has doubled]. *Newsru.com*, March 21, 2014. Retrieved March 21, 2014, from http://www.newsru.com/finance/21mar2014/rubrbery.html
42. Kadyrov v interv'ju: "Esli podumat', mozhno zabolet'... No my staraemsya voobshche ne dumat'" [Kadyrov in an interview: "One can fall ill because of thinking... We try not to think at all"]. *Newsru.com*, June 18, 2010. Retrieved June 18, 2010, from http://www.newsru.com/russia/18jun2010/kadyrov.html
43. FBK opublikoval samoe masshtabnoe rassledovanie – ob usad'bakh, yakhtakh i vinogradnikakh, kotorye yakoby prinadlezhat prem'eru Medvedevu [FBK published its largest investigation about mansions, yachts and vineyards that would be belong to premier Medvedev]. *Newsru.com*, March 2, 2017. Retrieved May 21, 2018, from https://www.newsru.com/russia/02mar2017/dimon.html
44. Kak oligarkh platit vzyatku vitse-prem'eru. Razbiraem mekhaniku [How oligarch gives a bribe to vice premier. Decomposing the mechanics]. Fond bor'by s korruptsiej, April 26, 2018. Retrieved May 21, 2018, from https://navalny.com/p/5852/
45. Naval'ny nazval pokupku Prokhorovym villy Khloponina v Italii klassicheskoj vzyatkoj vitse-prem'eru [Naval'ny called Prokhorov's buying Khloponin's villa in Italy a classical bribe to vice premier]. *Newsru.com*, April 26, 2018. Retrieved May 21, 2018, from https://realty.newsru.com/article/26apr2018/bribe
46. Prokhorov podal v sud na Naval'nogo iz-za obvinenij v dache "vzyatki villoj" byvshemu vitse-prem'eru Khloponinu [Prokhorov filed a lawsuit against Naval'ny in response to accusations of giving bribe by villa to ex-premier Khloponin]. *Newsru.com*, May 21, 2018. Retrieved May 21, 2018, from https://www.newsru.com/russia/21may2018/prohorov.html
47. Yury Mikhaylovich Luzhkov is a well-known Russian politician who served as the Mayor of Moscow from 1992 to 2010. He was also vice-chairman

and one of the founders of the ruling United Russia party. Yury Luzhkov was dismissed from the Mayor's office by the then president Dmitry Medvedev in 2010, with the offensively formulated official reason, "as the one who lost trust."

48. Conflict over lands in South Butovo. *Barometer of democracy*, No. 56, June 19, 2006. Retrieved June 18, 2010, from http://www.demos-center.ru/projects/649C353/6AF8CAF/1155543103#2
49. Strasburg zapodozril neladnoe: oskorblennyj mer Luzhkov vsegda vyigryvaet v moskovskih sudah [Strasburg suspects something wrong: the offended Mayor Luzhkov always wins in Moscow courts]. *Newsru.com*, June 18, 2010. Retrieved June 18, 2010, from http://www.newsru.com/russia/18jun2010/limonov.html
50. Gerasimenko, Olesia. (2007). Luzhkov otzhal pol-Limonova [Luzhkov took over half-Lemonov]. *Gazeta.ru*, November 14, 2007. Retrieved November 14, 2007, from https://www.gazeta.ru/social/2007/11/14/2311487.shtml

References

Aleksashenko, S. (2018). *Putin's Counterrevolution*. Washington, DC: Brookings Institution Press.

Aslund, A. (1997). Economic Causes of Crime in Russia. In J. Sachs & K. Pistor (Eds.), *The Rule of Law and Economic Reform in Russia* (pp. 79–94). Boulder, CO: Westview Press.

Barnes, A. (2006). *Owning Russia: The Struggle over Factories, Farms, and Power*. Ithaca: Cornell University Press.

Chapaev, R. (2007). *International Commercial Arbitration: Assessment Report on the Results of the Assessment in the CIS (Armenia, Azerbaijan, Georgia, Kazakhstan, Kyrgyz Republic, Moldova, Russia, Tajikistan, Turkmenistan, Ukraine, Uzbekistan) and Mongolia*. Washington, DC: EBRD-World Bank Retrieved May 9, 2009, from http://www.ebrd.com/country/sector/law/judicial/arbitrat/arbitration.pdf

Hellman, J. (2002). Russia's Transition to a Market Economy: A Permanent Redistribution? In A. Kuchins (Ed.), *Russia After the Fall* (pp. 93–109). Washington, DC: Carnegie Endowment for International Peace.

Krylova, Y. (2018). *Corruption and the Russian Economy: How Administrative Corruption Undermines Entrepreneurship and Economic Opportunities*. New York and London: Routledge.

Ledeneva, A. (2004). Underground Financing in Russia. In J. Kornai, B. Rothstein, & S. Rose-Ackerman (Eds.), *Creating Social Trust in Post-Socialist Transition* (pp. 71–90). New York: Palgrave Macmillan.

Pistor, K., & Xu, C. (2004). Beyond Law Enforcement: Governing Financial Markets in China and Russia. In J. Kornai, B. Rothstein, & S. Rose-Ackerman (Eds.), *Creating Social Trust in Post-Socialist Transition* (pp. 167–189). New York: Palgrave Macmillan.

Rochlitz, M. (2014). Corporate Raiding and the Role of the State in Russia. *Post-Soviet Affairs, 30*(2–3), 89–114.

Schreck, Carl. (2018). Russian Asylum Applications in U.S. Hit 24-Year Record. *Radio Free Europe/Radio Liberty*, May 2. Retrieved May 14, 2018, from https://www.rferl.org/a/russian-asylum-applications-in-u-s-hit-24-year-record/29204843.html

Shlapentokh, V. (2007). *Contemporary Russia as a Feudal Society: A New Perspective on the Post-Soviet Era*. New York: Palgrave Macmillan.

Shlapentokh, V., & Arutunyan, A. (2013). *Freedom, Repression, and Private Property in Russia*. New York: Cambridge University Press.

Soldatov, A., & Rochlitz, M. (2018). The Siloviki in Russian Politics. In D. Treisman (Ed.), *The New Autocracy: Information, Politics, and Policy in Putin's Russia* (pp. 83–108). Washington, DC: Brookings Institution Press.

Sonin, K. (2003). Why the Rich May Favor Poor Protection of Property Rights. *Journal of Comparative Economics, 31*(4), 715–731.

Sonin, K. (2005). Institutsional'naya teoriya beskonechnogo peredela [Institutional Theory of Endless Redistribution]. *Voprosy ekonomiki, 7*, 1–15. Retrieved May 9, 2009, from http://fir.nes.ru/~ksonin/VESonin.pdf

Volkov, V. (2004). The Selective Use of State Capacity in Russia's Economy: Property Disputes and Enterprise Takeovers, 1998–2002. In J. Kornai, B. Rothstein, & S. Rose-Ackerman (Eds.), *Creating Social Trust in Post-Socialist Transition* (pp. 126–147). New York: Palgrave Macmillan.

Volkov, V. (2005). Po tu storonu sudebnoj sistemy, ili Pochemu zakony rabotayut ne tak, kak dolzhny [On the Other Side of the Justice System or Why Don't Laws Work as They Should]. *Neprikosnovennyj zapas, 4*(42). Retrieved May 9, 2009, from http://magazines.russ.ru/nz/2005/42/vv6.html

CHAPTER 6

The Invisible Hand of the Market and Indivisible Hand of the State

State as an Instrument of Legitimization and Raiding

Along with the emerging Adam Smith's classical notion of invisible hand of the market, in Russia, there is also indivisible hand of the state. The notion of indivisible in the context of the modern Russian state means duality: the state gives away its property through privatization and at the same time wants to preserve its power. In the case of the state giving away its property through privatization, state bureaucrats de facto give it away to themselves. The process when state bureaucrats give the state property away to themselves in the course of the mass privatization corresponds directly with the notion of captured state. Referring to post-socialist states, Barnes discloses the notion of captured state, having this process "eventually leading to a system where no single group owns the state, but where it is still not insulated. Instead, several competing groups fight with each other to raid it for their own benefits" (Barnes, 2007, p. 71). Political clans of state captors raid the state property in a highly competitive process using their political power instead of market power.

When the issue of power preservation comes to the fore, this meant to be not only political, or broader state power, but economic power as well. The state is not satisfied with retaining its controlling authority. It needs much more than that. Thus, the limits of potential privatization will never be reached. The state prefers to hold on to some of the assets, and sometimes these are the most valuable assets. The controversy comes into play

A. L. Osipian, *Political and Economic Transition in Russia*,
https://doi.org/10.1007/978-3-030-03831-1_6

when those who captured the state re-assign state property to themselves as private owners while maintaining that they are, indeed, the state.

The notion of the grabbing hand of the state has already found its way into the scholarly literature, including as combined with the notion of invisible hand of the market (See, for instance, Shleifer & Vishny, 2002). The authors describe government pathologies faced by transition societies, such as that of Russia, and offer some cures for these pathologies. The giving hand of the Kremlin counterbalances the notion of the grabbing hand of the state. The Russian political establishment is so much involved in country's business that it is sometimes referred to as the Kremlin Corporation.

In the spirit of Alfred Kokh's formula of "state as the seller,"[1] one can certainly add a formula "state as an instrument" regarding the post-Soviet Russia. A de facto takeover of state offices with the goal of using state authority in predatory raiding and hostile takeovers converts bureaucratic offices into effective instruments of predatory raiding. A famous phrase about the conversion of authority into property [pereplavit' vlast' v sobstvennost'] finds its application not only in characterizing the process of mass privatization in the 1990s, but equally so in describing the predatory raiding phenomenon in the 2000s and 2010s. The former head of Yukos is even more critical when it comes to the issue of using the state authority and spreading raiding practices in the regions: "He [Sechin] is an organizer and inspirer of the bacchanalia of state raiding that destroyed Yukos and moved on spreading around the entire country."[2] Thus, Khodorkovsky unequivocally accuses the state apparatus of raiding his company and other companies as well.

Illegal activities of state bureaucrats aimed primarily at self-enrichment negatively impact business environment in the country. This point on the detriment of bureaucratic corruption has been raised in the scholarly literature continuously. Markus (2015) emphasizes that in Russia such actions of civil servants undermine not only the flow of income that a given private business enjoys, but also the fundamentals of private ownership. Indeed, it is them, the corrupt bureaucrats, who create comfortable conditions for predatory raiders, allowing them to act without punishment and supporting their illegal actions in exchange for a bribe or share in the proceeds.

Private predatory raiders collude with state organs. This is perhaps the only way raiders can be successful in modern Russia. As Sakwa (2011, p. 9) puts it, "Raiders rely on their positions of authority and typically act with government approval, and often in concert with governmental authorities, to exert an improper influence on the prosecution process, in particular with the courts and the police." This way of understanding maintains the duality of state approach and points to the unholy alliance between raiders, including outright criminals, and the state. But the synergy between the state and raiders, or rather even raiding as a phenomenon, is much more complex. In many instances, state officials do not wait on raiders to come and make an offer of cooperation, or to collude. Instead, they can make offers of raiding a certain business or appropriating a certain piece of state property or a parcel of land to professional raiding companies or to a final consumer. Furthermore, state bureaucrats also act on their own, utilizing their power and resources in order to appropriate valuable property, especially when it comes to alienation-appropriation of public property.

Accusations against the state authorities and particular state officials in hostile takeovers become a routine.[3] Both state-controlling organs and law enforcers, including court bailiffs' services, are being blamed by property owners and businessmen for taking active part in hostile takeovers.[4] State offices also fall victim to political raiding.[5] A state office becomes a value in itself, a source of rent, and an instrument of raiders to be used in hostile takeovers. There are also quite good and creative ideas among those expressed by the statesmen. For instance, Luzhkov came out with a much better use of the ban on leaving the country. Moscow's mayor suggests holding the owners of those enterprises that do not pay their employees in a timely manner responsible: "According to the Labor Code, if the owner does not pay money to his worker, this situation qualifies as forced labor. Forced labor in this country is illegal and prosecuted under the law. If you own an enterprise, you should pay your workers."[6] Unfortunately, this idea is not likely to be implemented. Also, Russian oligarchs leave the country and travel abroad freely, despite their lawsuits with the state tax authorities and numerous commercial disputes with creditors.

As this study has already pointed out, predatory raiders will need to become inventive in developing old sectors and discovering new territories for potential raiding. The state would have to become more inventive too, especially those of its representatives who are actively involved in predatory raiding. Citizens and the state becoming separate entities created a need for a new system of relations between them and the new mechanisms for the realization of such a system. The separation of citizens and the state leads to modification of the mechanisms with which the state influences its citizens. Earlier, the state could simply withdraw a certain sum of money from the salary of the debtor; however, today, this mechanism is nowhere near as effective. First, all adults were employed, and there was an article in the administrative code and even a legal provision in the criminal code for not being employed. Second, everyone received a salary, and the salaries were paid in a timely fashion, with no arrears and delays. Third, all employees worked at the state enterprises, for there were no other enterprises but the state ones. Fourth, the level of execution of court orders was quite high.

In contemporary Russia, it is not that easy for the state to take away money from its citizens, even by a court decision. It is easier to make the decision than to execute it. Not everyone works these days, as unemployment rates fluctuate widely and may be on average 10 percent or so in Russia. Moreover, not all of those employed, including civil servants, receive their salary in a timely fashion. Wage arrears have fallen since the 1990s, but the irregularity in payment of wages is not rare. Also, less than half of all working adults are employed in state enterprises. Finally, the level of execution of court orders is quite low. Ledeneva (2006, p. 182) refers to official statistics, pointing out that in Russia in 1997 the level of execution of court orders was 56 percent.

Laws are generally perceived as rules and regulations backed by sanctions. Such an understanding of laws assumes the existence of effective law enforcement tools and mechanisms. This function is traditionally retained by the state. If the law enforcement tools and mechanisms, provided and indeed monopolized by the state, are not in place or simply ineffective, the "backed by sanctions" part of the formula loses it meaning. Naturally, there is little respect for the law in a society where laws, no matter how sophisticated and fair they might be, are not backed by effectively enforced sanctions.

The situation with the execution of court orders is improving, but not to the extent that all the payments to the state would be enforced though the simple withholdings mechanism. That is why court bailiffs continue proposing innovations and inventions, demanding Russian cell phone operators surrender money from cell phone prepaid accounts of debtors.[7] This practice sounds somewhat naïve, because no one would want to lose business and clients. Also, the state itself protects the confidentiality of clients. Of course, Russian court bailiffs collect in cats, cows, and bananas, but bananas have to be sold and cats need care.[8] There is something from the Middle Ages and medieval tax collection in taking away livestock—kettle, poultry, and other domestic animals.

Debtors, attacked by the state, do not give up. They are now independent subjects or legal entities, forcefully separated from the state by the state itself. Because of this separation, they use courts and the judiciary branch of authority more and more actively in their property disputes with the state. In this regard, they are similar to Russian businesses that more and more frequently turn to courts in search of resolving their commercial disputes with other businesses and the state as well (Gans-Morse, 2017). There are even precedents of such a struggle being successful for citizens. For instance, in St. Petersburg, the court ordered bailiffs to compensate an alimony debtor for a spoiled vacation, because he was not allowed to leave the country.[9] Citizens use courts and other means in their fight against state raiding. For instance, a businessman, who defaulted on payments, hired gangsters to prevent court bailiffs from taking away his Hummer SUV.[10] Perhaps, he was right, because seized vehicles sometimes get dismantled on police parking lots and sold in spare parts. The owners then have a hard time claiming their cars.

It is no news that customs officers are noted for "selling" expropriated imported cars and other goods to themselves at "fair auctions" at significantly reduced prices. According to media reports, such practices occur not only in customs, but in courts as well. For instance, court bailiffs gave a Maserati belonging to a debtor to someone they knew. A Maserati costs 8 million rubles ($260,000), and the case is being investigated by the prosecutor's office.[11] Mistrust in law and order quite naturally brings to life an urge for self-defense. People no longer expect to see any social justice and fairness from the state, but they hope that the state and those who represent the state would act by the law.

The Federal Services of Court Bailiffs [Federal'naya sluzhba sudebnykh pristavov, FSSP] suggests taking away cars, and hunting and fishing licenses from the debtors. If a person defaults on payments, the state can deprive him/her of the car. Sometimes, a person who does not know or intentionally violates traffic rules accumulates fines of $2000–$3000. One wonders why such a person should be deprived of a car and not the license. But the state is more concerned with the collection of fines than with the safety of its citizens. Everything moves to the proprietary dimension with alienation, expropriation, and appropriation of private property. In addition, seizure, and even more so the sale of personal property without a court order, is illegal in Russia. It is also unclear why the police stop the car. Does this mean that if the car is not used, there is no need to collect a fine? Some people avoid paying debts by simply not using their cars. Again, the principle of "do not get caught" is dominant in this kind of interactions between the citizen and the state.

Russian society is not progressing, but is regressing in many ways. Unlike in the Soviet period, in the 1990s and 2000s, private cottages are being built instead of hospitals and schools. The very architecture of new buildings points to the regression: massively built brick mansions are distinct with turrets, tasteless, onion-domed, and pointed spires. Instead of high-tech industries, modern medicine, and education, the society creates assets that were designed many decades ago.

Privatization of the state powers takes place in Russia. Takeover of the function of power is being realized through political raiding. The state in any country serves a certain class, not the entire society, and in this sense it is privatized. This is normal, because historically the state was created by the ruling top strata of the society, the power-holding minority. The power thus was de-personified evolutionarily, but nevertheless always represented the interests of the ruling class. In this case, the state is privatized not by a separate class, but by families and clans. These families and clans represent a narrower range of people than is the case with the ruling class. During the Yeltsin era, the term "the family" emerged. Clanship, a sign of the Middle Ages, now develops in modern Russia. Clans in power and clans opposing them constitute the political picture of today's North Caucasus region. The ruling dynasties emerge. The function of power, initially taken over by the clan, begins to actually be inherited, although the legal transfer of power by right of succession is not institutionalized. This volatility in the inheritance rights also creates conflict between the clans.

In the Middle Ages, family clans that existed throughout Europe, from Italy in the south to Scotland in the north, were defined within their territorial domains. With the development of state power, clans began usurping particular power structures. Similar processes are observed in Russia. The authoritative clans control regions, areas, and territories. Family clans also began controlling ministries and agencies, including law enforcement agencies. The appointment of a new senior-level officer, if an outsider, leads to the displacement and replacement of all the subordinate staff. The new director brings in his/her own team, which are members of his/her clan. The state is being privatized based on regional and functional principles. In the regions, leading positions in government are being distributed between family members and close relatives. In offices and departments, including police and prosecutors' offices, similar processes take place. Professionalism is no longer used as a primary or at least an essential criterion for appointments and promotions.

Clans compete among themselves, which is expressed on the surface in such phenomena as the animosity and struggle between the regions and the center, as well as competition, internal wars, and feuds between the agencies that have similar or overlapping functions. The courts now have come into conflict with the court bailiffs' service. The prosecutor's office has its own investigations committee, and the most important things are entrusted to the state security services, the Russian FSB [Federal Security Services, FSB], because the authorities do not rely 100 percent on the police. Multiplication and division of law enforcement agencies on separate groups or "offices" does not lead to increased efficiency in combating crime, including corporate predatory raiding, but instead strengthens internal feuds. Russian population is already completely confused by the variety of stripes and insignias on the uniforms of law enforcement officers. It is hard to distinguish between a policeman, a private security guard, and a predatory raider.

Volkov (2005b) offers the following view on the "privatization" of government functions and strengthening of state bodies:

> The weakness of the Russian state is not determined by the lack of personnel, equipment, organizational or financial resources. It comes from the fact that its individual units, especially those which may exercise the administrative or physical coercion, have considerable autonomy and, therefore, in conditions of market demand follow private commercial interests of the informal groups within these units, rather than formal rules and goals of the organization, determined by the public interest. Accordingly, in the context of privatization of the state, its consolidation and strengthening leads to contradictory effects and consequences, because the arbitrary influence of its individual segments strengthens instead of strengthening legal and administrative environment in general. If the state becomes a business, the strengthening of its resources and power only strengthens the entrepreneurial capabilities of civil servants.

Apparently, the legal and administrative environment is not strengthened as much, or even weakened. The state transforms from the major institution into a tool or an instrument. Those who have access to the state power use it themselves or rent it out to others. That is why claims about the state-building do not have an objective basis. The state is not developing as an institution, but only as a tool for improving the implementation of governmental functions of authority, used in the interests of certain clans. These interests do not always coincide with the interests of the masses.

Revision of Privatization Results as a Gift to the Raiding Movement

Privatization plays a key role in understanding the process of creating market economy and building democracy in Russia. The presence of remaining questions means that the results of privatization in terms of prices paid and ownerships bought may be placed into doubt, at least potentially. Referring to Volkov (2005a), Zon (2008) divides the era of Russian privatization into four major stages. The first stage took place at the end of the Soviet era, between 1988 and 1991. This period of late Perestroika was characterized by the hidden privatization, when directors of Soviet enterprises created cooperatives through which they acquired enterprises' most valuable assets. The second stage lasted from 1992 to 1995. This phase went under the sign of voucher privatization that helped transfer all small and medium-sized enterprises into private hands. During this stage, the state maintained rights over 30 percent of the shares, workers' collectives and management received 60 percent of shares, and the remaining 10 percent of the shares were allocated to external investors. According to Zon (2008, p. 50), "In many cases these state shares were bought by outsiders who could often use their leverage to capture the privatized firms." And that was not the end of privatization.

The third stage of Russian privatization occurred during 1996 and 1997, marked by the privatization of many large enterprises, including first of all those in the sphere of natural resources. These industrial giants were acquired by individuals close to Yeltsin's presidential administration, at very low prices. The fourth stage of privatization, which started in 1998, became distinct by a wave of predatory raiding attacks. These attacks were usually done with the help of state agencies, including law enforcement agencies. As a result, there was a change in the ownership of many thousands of enterprises. This change led to the creation of vertically integrated holdings, with many becoming de facto monopolies in certain sectors of the economy or exercising monopolistic control over certain territories. These four stages of privatization, presented by Volkov (2005a) and Zon (2008), convey the genesis of property redistribution in Russia.

The head of the Russian Union of Industrialists and Entrepreneurs [Rossijskij soyuz promyshlennikov i predprinimatelej, RSPP], Alexander Shokhin, stated in 2007 that Russian business considers the possibility of reviewing the results of some privatization cases of the 1990s as acceptable. At the same time, Shokhin pointed out that in general the discussion over the results of privatization is already in the past. He said, "It would be a very good thing if the government would serve as an example. If the government would explain why it buys certain assets when it buys them."[12] Overall, the revision of the results of privatization can be considered as a gift to the predatory raiding movement. If the idea of revising the results of privatization is legitimate, then the action of redistributing property can also gain legitimacy. Predatory raiders can name such actions as a "velvet re-privatization."

State officials are still not decided on the issue of a possible revision of privatization results, or at least its legal aspects. In fact, such a process takes place from the very beginning of privatization. The process of distribution and redistribution of property, including state property, continues. By revising the results of privatization, the state provides predatory raiders with the opportunity for raiding attacks based on legal documents. These legal documents would confirm the legal violations that took place during the initial privatization of targeted firms. Accordingly, even the claims about possible revision of privatization results may be viewed as a gift to predatory raiders. The possible slogan of predatory raiders, "Give us the revision of privatization results!" may be similar to the Anarchists' "Steal the stolen!" slogan that dates back to the times of the October Socialist Revolution.

Similar to participants of the first wave of privatization of the early 1990s, modern predatory raiders are very interested in the instability of the system of state-guaranteed property rights. Moreover, similar to participants of the first wave of privatization, predatory raiders are only interested in such instability continuing until they take over others' properties. After that, predatory raiders would be absolutely interested in the rock-solid stability of the system of property rights and institutional rigidity of the institutions of property. Unfortunately, modern Russian predatory raiders do not read the works of Mikhail Bakunin and Pierre-Joseph Proudhon. Therefore, they have to satisfy their ambitions of building an ideologically charged concept of "property redistribution" with such cornerstones as the publicly recognized dubiousness of the results of initial privatization of the 1990s and the low level of legitimacy of the current lawful owners.

The authorities do not have an unequivocal position on the possibility of revision of privatization results and legitimacy of swiftly accumulated fortunes. On June 28, 2000, President Vladimir Putin met in the Kremlin with 21 leading Russian businessmen and some ministers. During the meeting, Putin stated that there would be no revision of privatization results. The public interpreted this statement as a promise of amnesty for all leading businessmen and their capitals. At the same time, Putin did not promise amnesty for fortunes accumulated illegally during the privatization of the 1990s. Accordingly, the issue of legitimacy of property, including legitimacy of capital and results of privatization, remains open. In this case, such openness means openness to interpretation, when legitimacy can always be questioned by different socioeconomic and political groups.

Dubiousness of the results of initial privatization is obvious. Even such founding fathers and ideological leaders of privatization as Anatoly Chubais and Egor Gaidar have no doubt regarding the imperfections of the results of initial privatization of the 1990s, especially when it comes to social justice. There is no doubt that businessmen will use the state apparatus as the legitimized violence machine in order to strengthen the system of property rights as well as for redistribution of property, including by the means of violence and coercion. In this context, the calls for revision of privatization results remain of high interest, including to predatory raiders. The key question here is "Revision in whose favor?"

According to a poll conducted by the Russian Public Opinion Research Center [Vserossijsky tsentr issledovanij obshchestvennogo mneniya, VCIOM], privatization is not the major cause of the public's negative views of business. The real cause of such negative views is the high level of social inequality. At the same time, creation of new jobs is considered a major responsibility of business. Shokhin says,

> Perhaps, the new redistribution of property is not the most important thing for the population. If the old oligarchs will be replaced with the new ones, either through state corporations or 'violet re-privatization', this will not cause the sudden appearance of social justice and social equality.[13]

But the people's views are no longer the major concern of the authorities. The state worries about preserving business.

While watching the reports about hostile takeovers and impunity of the clients and organizers of predatory raiding in the media, enterprises have no choice but to organize the self-defense detachments with militia formed of worker collectives. Such precedents already exist. Moreover, they are perfectly legal and comply with the state legislature. The law that allows large companies to form their own militarized security services already exists in Russia.[14] In August 2007, Putin signed the law that allows the country's largest oil and gas companies, Transneft and Gazprom, to create corporate armies.[15] The state corporation Gazprom is already using this law and creating its own army.[16]

Predatory raiding exists because there are material values to fight for. The Soviet economy was a system oriented predominantly on the production of material values, and much less so on the provision of services. Production capacities represented a significant part of the national economy. Today, these production capacities are called "the real sector of the economy." If the sector of consumer services was more developed to the same extent as material production, as is the case in modern market economies, then the target for potential hostile takeovers would not be as large. Over three decades of market reforms, Russia has built a sprawling services sector, which adds to potential targets for predatory raiders. Russians have accumulated significant personal wealth, also targeted by predatory raiders. This personal wealth appreciates and thus becomes more attractive to raiders. The dynamics of personal wealth in Russia for the period of 1995–2015 is presented in Fig. 6.1. Data on personal wealth in Russia for the period of 1995–2015 is presented in Table 6.1.

From the current oligarchs to those who are in firm opposition to the existing ruling political regime, everyone is aware that a small group of wealthy individuals attempts further strengthening of property rights through the legislation and by further reforming the society. This group of individuals owns a significant part of the national wealth. Glaz'ev (1997, p. 88) in his quite radical work notes, "At present, the task of the ruling elite is to secure the achieved results." Such a task is well understood by the public, especially taking into consideration the growing predatory raiding movement. Glaz'ev (1997, p. 88) points to this process in his utter critique of the current state of the affairs:

> The best guarantee to secure the achieved results and security for the ruling elite in Russia is a complete liquidation of Russian statehood and elimination of the national self-consciousness of the Russian people. These tasks are fulfilled with the help of economic policy of the federal executive power, the ideology of the ruling regime, distinct by Russophobe, moral decay and fear imposed through television, as well as the policy of the state reform in Russia.

The author points to ideological and psychological pressure on the population and creation of an atmosphere of fear and uncertainty. The cultural component in this process is clear. Of course, there is no reason to overestimate

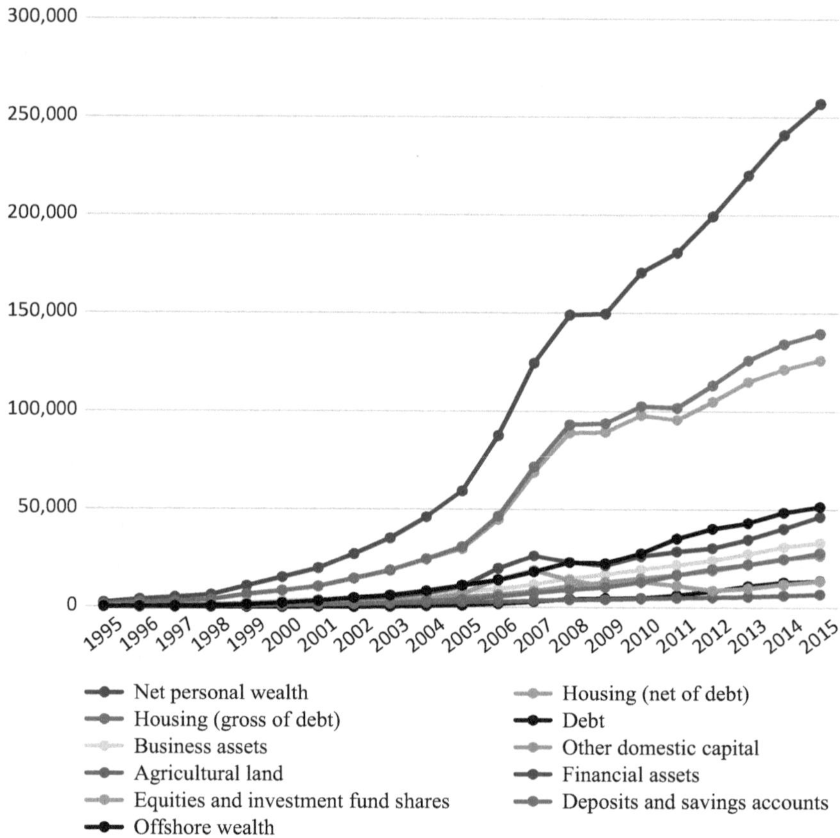

Fig. 6.1 The dynamics of personal wealth in Russia, 1995–2015

and dramatize the situation, but it is obvious that the predatory raiding phenomenon is something more than a bold storming of firms.

The growing anti-corruption campaign in Russia, propelled by the state authorities, indicates that the ruling elites want to legalize and secure their wealth from a possible new wave of predatory raiding, storming, and assaults. The director of the Center of Anti-Corruption Research and Initiatives of Transparency International Russia, Elena Panfilova, says, "There are people among the elites who have something to lose, and now they would like to get exactly that piece of history where there is an independent court, no new raiders attacking them, and no need to buy scores

Table 6.1 Personal wealth in Russia, 1995–2015, (as average end-of-year values; current prices; billion Russian rubles)

	Net personal wealth	*Housing (net of debt)*	*Housing (gross of debt)*	*Debt*	*Business assets*	*Other domestic capital*	*Agricultural land*	*Financial assets*	*Equities and investment fund shares*	*Deposits and savings accounts*	*Offshore wealth*
1995	2255	1440	1445	5	410	350	60	297	191	105	109
1996	3837	2392	2400	8	729	567	162	482	293	185	235
1997	4943	2886	2901	15	900	670	229	822	559	258	335
1998	6087	3637	3659	21	1070	737	332	901	555	340	479
1999	10,665	6398	6424	27	1751	1109	642	1375	893	472	1142
2000	15,182	8265	8307	42	2808	1781	1027	2054	1341	699	2055
2001	19,807	10,438	10,518	80	3712	2364	1349	2501	1446	1034	3156
2002	27,081	14,473	14,608	134	4448	2881	1567	3513	2003	1481	4647
2003	35,206	18,586	18,834	248	5275	3441	1834	5355	3171	2142	5990
2004	45,997	24,209	24,722	513	6465	4211	2253	7112	4099	2954	8211
2005	59,317	29,875	30,876	1001	7763	5248	2515	10,555	6512	3964	11,125
2006	87,525	44,667	46,472	1805	9196	6465	2731	19,787	14,244	5435	13,874
2007	124,574	68,659	71,556	2897	11,573	8216	3356	26,239	18,695	7396	18,104
2008	149,104	88,899	93,083	4183	14,542	10,639	3903	22,876	13,791	8907	22,786
2009	149,672	89,267	93,888	4621	16,789	12,811	3979	21,302	10,877	10,221	22,314
2010	170,720	97,973	102,675	4702	19,239	14,757	4482	25,978	12,976	12,747	27,530
2011	180,858	95,607	101,683	6077	21,535	16,636	4899	28,613	11,030	16,456	35,103
2012	199,444	104,955	113,306	8351	23,948	18,839	5109	30,388	8534	19,545	40,153
2013	220,331	115,060	125,926	10,866	27,373	21,848	5525	34,736	9815	21,898	43,162
2014	241,112	121,442	134,285	12,843	30,977	24,891	6085	40,258	11,744	24,666	48,435
2015	257,051	126,116	139,661	13,544	33,170	26,362	6808	46,334	13,490	27,965	51,430

Source: Composed by the author from the data presented in Novokmet, Piketty, & Zucman (2017)

of Faberge eggs." Panfilova points out that the wealthy elites are most of all afraid of "the young generation of scary managers and lawyers, which have an interest in robbing these elites." This urges modern millionaires, including numerous state bureaucrats, to demand the rule of law and order. The new rich men are less afraid of possible responsibility for their past actions in the 1990s and 2000s, when they made their fortunes.[17]

Predatory raiding is associated with redistribution, but the socialist system was often referred to as the redistribution system as well. Socialism never had clear guidelines of practice. Bolsheviks and their leader, Vladimir Lenin, had a very vague idea of what the new socialist society was going to be like. Karl Marx and Frederick Engels did not offer much direction either. They were focused on describing capitalism and proving its demise. As a result, Bolsheviks had clear theoretical principles, but did not have a clear course of action. Lenin suggested the order of civilized cooperators; Nikolai Bukharin suggested some reforms for agriculture, since Russia at the time of the October Revolution was largely an agrarian society; Lev Trotsky was ultra-left, and therefore preoccupied with the red terror and transformation of the Bolshevik revolution into world revolution.

The concept of civilized cooperators did not comply with the idea of large machine-based production, industries, branches, trusts, cartels, and monopolies. The solution that Russian Marxists had offered was as follows. In capitalist Russia, when there is a given factory or plant, or even a monopoly, the profit received goes into the pocket of its owner, the capitalist. The capitalist expropriates profit from his workers. When the socialist revolution came, as Marx put it, expropriators are expropriated. The practical application of this was that the owner of a factory was removed, and the profit went to the people through the state budget. In theory, of course, there could be no profit under socialism, because profit is a derivative of the supply value, obtained through the exploitation of a human by another human. This exploitation is possible because of the existence of private property on the means of production, that is, machines, equipment, land, and so on. Communism and even socialism preclude exploitation, and thus there could be no profit. It is exactly for this reason the private property on the means of production was eliminated in Soviet Russia.

What privatization of the early 1990s meant in theory was the introduction of private property on the means of production. This automatically implied the return of exploitation, although at that time the focus was on an increase in economic effectiveness and efficiency, instead of exploitation in a class-based society. However, that was only in theory. In practice, this change meant giving the factory back to a single private owner and channeling profits not into the state budget but into the new owner's private pocket. This study is not considering the delusion of voucher privatization and dispersion of property rights among the many, because this was nothing but a deceptive way of getting to the ultimate ends. What was wrong with this situation was that the factory, the plant, or the natural monopoly was not the same older version of the factory, but the new one, built under socialism and that the owner was new as well. In the case of Russian privatization, a Soviet manager or a state bureaucrat was in power when the privatization started.

Borisov (2006) suggests that Russian history has four massive, revolutionary redistributions of property, and the top authorities initiated all of these four redistributions. The first stage was in the era of Ivan the Terrible. The second one was organized by Peter the Great. The third stage was done by the Bolsheviks after the Great Russian revolution of 1917–1921. The fourth one we lived through from 1990. In the 1990s, the state authorities simply initiated the process of redistribution and then stepped aside:

> The process went on 'horizontally' in accordance with the laws of social-Darwinism: only the strongest, deepest, and greediest were able to survive. This was predetermined by the very scheme of privatization, when each enterprise with broken technological and economic ties was atomized and thrown to the market, as a puppy in ice water, in the form of public joint-stock companies, and the absence of market infrastructure. (Borisov, 2006, p. 1)

As one can see from this periodization, all of the great redistributions of property were quite violent, and thus there is no reason to think that the current redistribution should be peaceful and nonviolent. Oprichniks of Ivan the Terrible or stormtroopers of modern corporate predatory raiders are just the soldiers of state-organized redistribution. In contrast to the freelance soldiers of fortune, these soldiers are on a fixed pay rate.

In this regard, the statement of the then President Medvedev on the predatory raiding problem sounds especially good: "The still massive illegal hostile takeovers of firms, also known as raiding, manifest disrespect for property and the work of many people."[18] President Medvedev suggests that it is absolutely necessary to approve the anti-raiding package of laws in such a form that it would not be yet another declaration, but would include real instruments that can be used against predatory raiding. This suggestion calls to memory a famous slogan of the 17th meeting of the KPSS, saying: "October and Perestroika: the revolution goes on!" And so does predatory raiding that came with Perestroika.

Concluding Remarks

A few points may be underlined in conclusion of this chapter. Privatization of the state powers takes place in Russia. Takeover of the function of power is being realized through political raiding. In any country, the state as a dominant political superstructure serves almost entirely or in some cases exclusively a certain class, not the entire society. In this sense, the state is de facto privatized by this ruling class. Historically, the state was created by the ruling top stratum of the society, the power-holding minority. In case of transitional societies, including post-Soviet states, the state is privatized by extended families and clans. These may be Communist elites or clans based on regional affiliation or kinship. Both are characteristic for Russia. These families and clans represent a narrower range of people than the ruling class would normally be. Their interests usually do not coincide with the interests of the masses, and the results of the mass privatization of the 1990s in Russia are a good example of such a divergence in interests.

The state transforms from the institution into a tool or an instrument, used by those who have access to the state power in their personal, family, and clan interests. That is why claims about the process of state-building in Russia do not have an objective basis. Institutions in the market economy are called upon to minimize transaction costs. Minimization of transaction costs under the optimization of societal production is the major function of state and nonstate institutions in the mixed market-type economies. While the state loses its credibility, legitimization of the exercised authority, as well as property rights on the country's wealth, becomes problematic.

At this point, it is undeniable that the results of initial mass privatization of state assets that took place in the turbulent 1990s are very dubious in terms of their legitimacy, economic effectiveness, and social justice. Nevertheless, a substantial number of businessmen, both small and large, attempt to use the state machine in order to substantiate and protect their property rights. At the same time, other businessmen, including oligarchs, have somewhat different ideas about the possible use of the state. They use the state as the legitimized violence machine for redistribution of property, including by the means of violence and coercion. These two diverging views, ideas, and actions naturally lead to divergence of functions and thus the duality of the state itself. On the one hand, the state is to guarantee the protection of property rights. Yet, on the other hand, the state is used to break the status quo in order to proceed with redistribution of assets. This redistribution means the denial of legitimization of the current property and its owners.

The growing anti-corruption campaign in Russia is propelled by the federal authorities in both Moscow and throughout the regions. The anti-corruption campaign conducted in the regions signifies the attempt of the capital that comes from Moscow to secure property and investments from raiding attempts of local corrupt elites and predatory raiders. In a more general sense, this campaign indicates that the ruling elites want to legalize and secure their wealth from a possible new wave of predatory raiding, storming, and assaults. Predatory raiding is based in part on overwhelming corruption, and thus fighting corruption, restricting it, keeping it within certain controllable limits allows for limiting or restricting the threat of predatory raiding. Balancing corruption and impunity with anti-corruption efforts becomes a new task of the ruling political regime aimed at strengthening the system of property rights and protecting property of those loyal to the regime.

Notes

1. See: Kokh, Alfred. (2001). Gosudarstvo prodavets [State as the Seller]. In Anatoly Chubais (Ed.). *Privatization Russian Style*. Moscow: Vagrius.
2. Vlast' davit na menya postoyanno. Tyur'moj. Interv'yu Reuters s Mikhailom Khodorkovskim (original'naya russkaya versiya) [State Authorities put pressure on me all time. By prison. Reuter's interview with Mikhail Khodorkovsky (the original Russian version)]. *Khodorkovsky.ru*, September 18, 2011. Retrieved September 18, 2011, from http://khodorkovsky.ru/mbk/articles_and_interview/2011/09/18/16606.html

   Khodorkovsky v interv'yu Reuters predrek Rossii novy krizis i porassuzhdal o mesti [Khodorkovsky predicted a new crisis for Russia and talked about a revenge in an interview given to Reuters]. *Newsru.com*, September 18, 2011. Retrieved September 18, 2011, from http://www.newsru.com/russia/18sep2011/hodorkovsky.html

   Forget reform if Putin stays in power – Khodorkovsky. *Reuters*, September 18, 2011. Retrieved September 18, 2011, from http://uk.reuters.com/article/2011/09/18/uk-russia-politics-khodorkovsky-idUKTRE78H0RD20110918
3. Administratsiyu Pskovskoj oblasti obvinili v popytke sovershit' reiderskij zahvat [Administration of Pskovskaya oblast' was accused of an attempt of raiding takeover]. *Notheft.ru*, November 25, 2008. Retrieved July 22, 2009, from http://www.notheft.ru/administraciju-pskovskoj-oblasti-obvinili-v-popytke-sovershit-rejderskij-zahvat

4. This is a video of a market being closed by court bailiffs. Market "Druzhba" in Surgut, Siberia, Russia, has been closed by the court bailiffs three times due to violations of fire safety requirements in some of its warehouses. Tenants of the market and its management consider it an act of predatory raiding. Surgut, HMAO, Russia, August 2009, December 2009. Retrieved September 24, 2010, from http://www.youtube.com/watch?v=vVU53bOTrhI&feature=related http://www.youtube.com/watch?v=vVU53bOTrhI
5. Sviridenko, Aleksandr. (2009). Konstitutsionnyj sud poshel na printsip [Constitutional Court took the stand]. *Kommersant' Ukraina*, No. 128, July 30, 2009. Retrieved July 30, 2009, from http://www.kommersant.ua/doc.html?docId=1212705
6. Luzhkov predlagaet ne vypuskat' za granitsu tekh, kto zaderzhivaet zarplatu [Luzhkov suggests to ban from living the country those who has wage arrears before their employees]. *Newsru.com*, August 1, 2009. Retrieved August 1, 2009, from http://www.newsru.com/russia/01aug2009/lu.html
7. Pristavy trebuyut ot rossijskikh sotovykh operatorov den'gi so schetov abonentov-dolzhnikov [Bailiffs demand from cell phone companies money from the accounts of their clients-debtors]. *Newsru.com*, August 27, 2009. Retrieved August 27, 2009, from http://www.newsru.com/finance/27aug2009/mobil.html
8. Rossijskie pristavy sobirayut dolgi kotami, korovami i bananami [Russian bailiffs collect debts through cats, cows, and bananas]. *Newsru.com*, August 31, 2009. Retrieved August 31, 2009, from http://www.newsru.com/finance/31aug2009/cats.html
9. Pretsedent: v Peterburge sud vzyskal s sudebnyh pristavov kompensatsiyu za sorvannyj otpusk alimentshchika [A precedent: in Petersburg, the court ordered bailiffs to compensate an alimony debtor for a spoiled vacation]. *Newsru.com*, July 29, 2009. Retrieved August 27, 2009, from http://www.newsru.com/russia/29jul2009/court2.html
10. Zadolzhavshij biznesmen nanyal banditov, chtoby te pomeshali uvezti ego Hummer na shtrafstoyanku [A businessman in debt hired gangsters to prevent bailiffs from taking his Hummer away to the towing parking lot]. *Newsru.com*, August 27, 2009. Retrieved August 27, 2009, from http://auto.newsru.com/article/26Aug2009/hummer-vernyt
11. Sud'i otdali znakomomu Maserati za 8 mln rublej, prinadlezhashchij dolzhniku [Court bailiffs gave an 8-million-ruble Maserati that belonged to a debtor to someone they knew]. *Newsru.com*, August 20, 2009. Retrieved August 20, 2009, from http://auto.newsru.com/article/20Aug2009/maser
12. RSPP gotov peresmotret' nekotorye privatizatsionnye sdelki 90-h godov [RSPP is ready to revise some privatization deals of the 1990s]. *Newsru.com*,

December 6, 2007. Retrieved May 9, 2009, from http://www.newsru.com/russia/06dec2007/shohin.html

13. RSPP gotov peresmotret' nekotorye privatizatsionnye sdelki 90-h godov [RSPP is ready to revise some privatization deals of the 1990s]. *Newsru.com*, December 6, 2007. Retrieved May 9, 2009, from http://www.newsru.com/russia/06dec2007/shohin.html
14. Gazprom i Transneft' poluchat pravo imet' sobstvennye vooruzhennye sily [Gazprom i Transneft' will be granted the right to have their own military forces]. *Babr.ru*, March 27, 2007. Retrieved June 10, 2009, from http://news.babr.ru/?IDE=36823
15. Putin podpisal zakon, pozvoliayushchij "Transnefti" i "Gazpromu" sozdat' korporativnye armii [Putin signed the law that allows "Transneft" and "Gazprom" to create corporate armies]. *Newsru.com*, August 1, 2007. Retrieved May 9, 2009, from http://palm.newsru.com/russia/01aug2007/gazpromarmy.html
16. Vpervye v Rossii sozdayutsya korporativnye armii [First time in Russia corporate armies are created]. *Evangelie.ru*, July 16, 2007. Retrieved June 10, 2009, from http://www.evangelie.ru/forum/t35744.html
17. Panfilova: Rossijskaya elita hochet obezopasit' sebya ot novykh reiderov [Panfilova: Russian elites want to secure themselves from new raiders]. *Rosbalt*, July 7, 2008. Retrieved July 22, 2009, from http://www.rosbalt.ru/2008/07/07/501362.html
18. Krajnov, Yaroslav. (2008). Istoriya reiderstva: osobennosti natsional'nogo peredela [History of raiding: specifics of national raiding]. *Notheft.ru*, July 17, 2008. Retrieved July 26, 2009, from http://www.notheft.ru/istorija-rejderstva-osobennosti-nacionalnogo-peredela

References

Barnes, A. (2007). Extricating the State: The Move to Competitive Capture in Post-Communist Bulgaria. *Europe-Asia Studies, 59*(1), 71–95.

Borisov, Y. (2006). *Igry v russky M&A* [Russian M&A Games]. Moskva. Retrieved June 10, 2017, from https://coollib.com/b/346433/read

Gans-Morse, J. (2017). *Property Rights in Post-Soviet Russia: Violence, Corruption, and the Demand for Law*. New York: Cambridge University Press.

Glaz'ev, S. (1997). *Genotsid: Rossiya i novyj mirovoj poryadok* [Genocide: Russia and the New World Order]. Moscow: Erga.

Ledeneva, A. (2006). *How Russia Really Works*. Ithaca, NY: Cornell University Press.

Markus, S. (2015). *Property, Predation, and Protection: Piranha Capitalism in Russia and Ukraine*. New York: Cambridge University Press.

Novokmet, F., Piketty, T., & Zucman, G. (2017). From Soviets to Oligarchs: Inequality and Property in Russia 1905–2016. WID.world Working Paper No. 2017/09, NBER Working Paper No. 23712. Retrieved June 1, 2017, from http://www.nber.org/papers/w23712

Sakwa, R. (2011). Raiding in Russia. *Russian Analytical Digest: State-Business Relations and Modernization*. No. 105, December 5, 2011, pp. 9–13.

Shleifer, A., & Vishny, R. (2002). *The Grabbing Hand: Government Pathologies and Their Cures*. Cambridge, MA: Harvard University Press.

Volkov, V. (2005a). Transformation of Russian State after 2000. *Public Lecture*, April 2, 2009. Retrieved June 10, 2009, from http://www.polit.ru/lectures/2009/04/02/estado.html

Volkov, V. (2005b). Po tu storonu sudebnoj sistemy, ili Pochemu zakony rabotayut ne tak, kak dolzhny [On the Other Side of the Justice System or Why Don't Laws Work as They Should]. *Neprikosnovennyj zapas, 4*(42). Retrieved June 10, 2012, from http://magazines.russ.ru/nz/2005/42/vv6.html

van Zon, H. (2008). *Russia's Development Problem: The Cult of Power*. New York: Palgrave Macmillan.

CHAPTER 7

The Invisible Hand of the Market and Invincible Hand of the Raider

Transaction Costs and Forest Wolves

In addition to the indivisible hand of the Russian state, there is also the invincible hand of the predatory raider. Invincible means incapable of being overcome or defeated: unconquerable. The term invincible comes from Latin *invincibilis*: *in-*, not; *vincibilis-*, conquerable. Russian raiders are unnatural predators. In nature, predators attack the easiest prey, the weakest; they attack the smallest, youngest, oldest, or sick animals. By attacking the weakest, they serve the function of population control. By attacking the oldest, they serve the function of population control in reverse, leaving more food for the youngest. By attacking the sick, they save the rest from the possible spread of the disease. For those reasons, wolves are considered forest cleaners. But the function of "forest" cleaners or forest wolves can hardly be ascribed to Russian predatory raiders.

The market is Russian predatory raiders' ecosystem or forest, but they clean it not from the weakest, the newly emerged, unsustainable, near bankrupt, the ineffective and inefficient, distinct with poor management, and thus most vulnerable. Instead, predatory raiders attack Russia's most lucrative businesses and public assets. By doing so, they create obstacles for entrepreneurship development and market reforms. The natural questions would be: How can Russian predatory raiders be so distinct from natural predators? Why are they capable of staging successful attacks on most successful businesses? How can they catch, overpower, and plunder the strongest animals in the pack, instead of the weakest ones?

A. L. Osipian, *Political and Economic Transition in Russia*,
https://doi.org/10.1007/978-3-030-03831-1_7

The answer to this set of questions lies in the fact that Russian predatory raiders use the state or so-called *administrativny resurs* [administrative resource], or they represent the state and are part of state apparatus. Given their involvement with the state and the type of prey they aim at, Russian predatory raiders can hardly be regarded as "cleaners" of business ecosystem from the weakest, and thus their usefulness for the national economy is dubious, to say the least. Predatory raiders function to the detriment of business.

Russian predatory raiders—both private raiding companies and corrupt state bureaucrats—demonstrate gain seeking that can hardly result in achieving the public good. Danner's (1996, p. 49) description of Adam Smith's invisible hand of the market matches Russian predatory raiders in one sense, that of rejection of moral principles:

> Smith's Invisible Hand emancipated gain-seeking from both the other appetites and moral control. Because economic interest requires mutuality, reciprocity, and harmonizing economic goals, personal gain-seeking can effectively achieve the public good (Smith, 1952: Books 1 and 2), Smith in effect denying the need for moral principles and tutelage.

As far as tutelage, and political tutelage in particular, is concerned, Russian predatory raiders need it critically, otherwise they will not be able to continue their predation with current success, if at all.

Whether useful for the market reconfiguration or harmful to it, Russian predatory raiders appear to be not only liberated from moral control, but also unconquerable, invincible, indeed. The growth of predatory raiding points to the fact that so far the state has not been able to overcome or defeat predatory raiders. Even if some predatory raiders end up behind bars, the phenomenon itself does not disappear or even decline. Maybe one of the reasons is that predatory raiding is becoming more and more entrenched and institutionalized.

The institutions in the market economy are called upon to minimize transaction costs. Minimization of transaction costs under the optimization of societal production is the major function of state and nonstate institutions in the mixed and predominantly market-type economies. This section intends to clarify whether predatory raiders can be considered as positive and useful market agents, with the phenomenon of predatory raiding considered as a useful institution to the market-type transition economy. Is it true that raiders act not only in their own best interests, but also to the benefit of the economic system overall, as follows from the "invisible hand of the market" of Adam Smith? Do raiders strengthen the national economy? Simply put, is it true that raiders serve as "market cleaners"? This study also clarifies institutional aspects of raiding by considering such issues as legitimacy of property and property rights, and illegality of predatory raiding.

Countries of the former Socialist Bloc undergo transition from a relatively simple societal organization and an average level of productivity to a complex society with low levels of productivity. Socially complex societies are characterized by low levels of productivity. Such societies are not less productive by nature, but rather due to their organizational characteristics. Each productive unit or worker in particular can be highly productive, but the complexity of the societal organization necessitates the existence of a large number of specialists in unproductive sectors of the economy, such as lawyers in the legal services sector. It is true that institutions facilitate the decline in transaction costs. This is the fundamental reason for the institutionalization of any process. However, in societies with a complex organizational structure of socioeconomic relations, a significant part of the qualified workforce and capital is being channeled to regulatory functions. Moreover, the share of transaction costs in the total volume of societal production increases.

Perhaps the most illustrative evidence of the complexity of modern Russian society as compared to the Soviet era society is the fact that there are more bureaucrats in Russia now than there were in the entire Soviet Union in 1990.[1] Russia's current population is only 142 million people versus the 285 million people in the USSR. The complexity of the system of socioeconomic relations as a result of the inverted type of transformation leads to an increase in the complexity of regulatory systems and expansion of the bureaucratic apparatus. The powerful Narkomfin [Narodny komissariat finansov SSSR, i.e. the People's Commissariat of Finance of the USSR], with its army of financial inspectors watching the revenues of small entrepreneurs during the NEP era, was later transformed into a centralized structure which stopped dealing with the small entrepreneurs because they no longer existed in the era of developed socialism. The struggle of the state authorities against supplemental incomes of the population, including individual entrepreneurialism, led to little need for financial inspectors and financial oversight. All finances moved to the level of state enterprises, be it metallurgic giants or enterprises of Soviet retail trade.

Development of private property and entrepreneurialism brought to life the Colossus of "Tax Inspection," born overnight on the ruins of the Soviet system. This Colossus could change its name to Tax Administration, be divided into the Administration and Inspection, or undergo other organizational metamorphoses, but its major function remains the same—to collect taxes from nonstate entities. Property relations became the major determinant of the transition period. The Tax Inspection, despite changes in its name, in essence is a part of the huge apparatus brought to life by the rapidly increased complexity of socioeconomic relations and complex organizations, which were discussed in previous paragraphs.

Sonin (2005, p. 15) suggests that, "A low level of protection of property rights in the economy not only forms a favorable environment for property redistribution, but also leads to real costs, one has to hire guards and lawyers, support politicians and pay state bureaucrats in order to take away from others and in order to protect one's own property." As a result, transaction costs of each individual producer or owner increase. At the same time, there is not any serious initiative for collective action in creating a less threatening and dangerous environment and decreasing the transaction costs that can be observed in Russia. High transaction costs equate to low economic effectiveness.

The threat of predatory raiding is a source of additional transaction costs. Companies bear the cost of organizing and monitoring financial security as well as maintaining the physical security of property and territory of their enterprises. Companies establish a position referred to as the director of the Department of Economic or Corporate Security. The task of the department is to oversee the defense strategies of the firm and watch for potential risks of predatory raiding. Such kinds of expenses, from hiring specialists and lawyers to installing extra locks and iron doors, cannot be categorized as productive expenses. As a result, the effectiveness of each particular enterprise decreases. The effectiveness of the national economy overall also declines. This creates the paradox of having a less productive society which consists of highly productive individual working units. Increasing the productivity of a single worker by increasing professional qualifications and introducing technical improvements does not necessarily lead to the expected increase in the level of productivity of the entire system.

The lack of law enforcement leads to an increase in transaction costs. The loss of capital in Russia upsets foreign investors, forcing them to revise their optimistic prognoses. George Soros expresses his disappointment regarding problematic investments in Sviaz'Invest. In 1998, Soros' funds announced a $2 billion loss in Russia. Soros refers to it as the worst investment in his career: "I have grave regrets as an investor" (O'Brien, 1998). Foreign investors claim that their primary concern is the supremacy of law and that there is a lack of law enforcement in Russia, but what they really want is for the law to be convenient for them. This supremacy of convenient laws is the number one condition, advanced by the potential investors and presented to Russia and other former Soviet republics.

Western companies expected high profits on their capital invested in Russia and other former Soviet states. Several qualities made Russia a most attractive endeavor for foreign investors, including the existence of a highly qualified workforce available at a price ten times lower than that of the West in terms of nominal US dollars, the richest natural resources in the world already researched and developed, excellent currency exchange rates, and the opportunity to dictate the course of the reform. Foreign investors, however, failed to consider the imminent instability of transition systems. At the start, foreign investors were acquiring the most valuable Soviet enterprises for a petty price and signing the long-term leasing contracts with unbelievably good terms. Only later did they start facing the problems of "making business" in Russia. They soon found out that the institutional market infrastructure is virtually absent, while high levels of corruption and bureaucratic dictatorial practices do not allow for working normally; "normally" in this case meant as defined by Western standards.

Western companies, including large corporations and other investors, want both the high rate of return on their investment in the former Soviet republics while only experiencing a low risk on their investments. They expect the state to safeguard their investments from predatory raiders. Such expectations are hard to deem as rational. Rational economic agents in the classical sense of this term act in a market environment, regulated by the state, and consider such an environment as normal and, indeed, the only possible type of environment. But the objective reality in developing countries and transition economies differs significantly from that in the developed and well-established market economies.

Western investors expected not only equal conditions or standards typical for western markets. They expected most favorable regimes, best possible treatment, and all kinds of preferences, as compared to national investors. They wanted tax breaks and state support. Moreover, many long-term contracts were signed on the wave of economic romanticism of the early 1990s, when local bureaucrats were very welcoming of their western investors in an attempt to gain some attention from their state supervisors. The Russian economy still pays the price for such enthusiasm.

Here is one good example of how poorly calculated actions of state bureaucrats can cause high economic losses. The Moscow city authorities filed a lawsuit in the Moscow Commercial Arbitrage Court against McDonalds, demanding an increase in the leasing rates for some of the company's restaurants. These restaurants use the premises in downtown Moscow, which belong to the city. The leasing contract on two premises in downtown Moscow between the Moscow city government and McDonalds were signed in the early 1990s for the term of 49 years at a symbolic rate of $1 per square meter (approximately ten square feet) per year. It seemed normal at the time when Soviet bureaucrats wanted this symbol of the West to come to the Soviet capital. Now, however, this deal represents a pure economic loss for the city where square meters, be it housing or businesses, are among the most expensive in the world.

The city government has already turned to court with the request of setting a market rate for the leased premises, but the court denied the request. Now the city government is asking to set the rate that would be in compliance with the newly introduced law, according to which the minimum rate of leasing in Moscow should be no less than 1000 rubles ($35).[2] There are some opposite actions as well. For instance, the Moscow Mayor's Office calls on investors to rent dilapidated mansions for a symbolic rent of only one ruble per year.[3] Who knows, maybe in the future these mansions will cost millions and the Mayor's Office will try to take over them again, removing the renting companies.

The main point of the example with the dispute between the Moscow Mayor's Office and McDonalds, as well as of the problem overall, is a critique of a certain concept of "supremacy of law," actively advanced by western businessmen and politicians representing interests of the business, that is, western investors. On the one hand, western investors would like to enjoy all kinds of preferences and benefits. Oftentimes, they not only ask for such benefits, but indeed demand them. On the other hand, they demand stable market laws, which would again facilitate their business according to western standards. Woodruff (2005, p. 1) points to this problem, saying that,

> Normally countries, which are of interest to foreign investors, have to listen to lectures on exceptional importance of the supremacy of law and property rights for economic development. Russia is no exception in this sense. Such lectures or morals can be given by economic scholars, representatives of investment funds, statesmen and even political scientists, but they are very similar in their content.

Woodruff (2005) offers an excerpt from the interview given to the media by Condoleezza Rice, after her visit to Moscow in 2005, in order to support his point. This study will also present a brief point regarding her comments. The US Secretary of State Condoleezza Rice said on April 20, 2005, that she "pretty pointedly" told Russian officials that the outcome of the criminal case against former oil tycoon Mikhail Khodorkovsky would affect prospects for business investment in Russia. Rice said the Russian government's handling of the case "shook people's confidence" and that it was important for officials to demonstrate that laws and regulations are fair and applied "consistently over time, applied consistently over various cases." Secretary Rice said she tried to remind Russian officials that their country is in transition toward a government based on the rule of law, "so people are looking for signals, and perhaps reading signals more fully than if this were a fully formed state."[4] Condoleezza Rice made the comments following a two-day visit to Moscow, where she met with President Vladimir Putin and other Russian senior officials.

At the time of Rice's visit, Khodorkovsky, who was Russia's wealthiest man when he headed Yukos, was awaiting a verdict after a trial on charges of tax evasion, fraud and embezzlement. His company, once Russia's largest oil producer, has been largely dismantled in a parallel tax case. As Barnes (2007, p. 53) characterizes the whole operation, "The government, acting in just as predatory a manner as had the oligarchs in the past, made unreasonable demands, tried to prevent Yukos from meeting them, and then used the courts to justify an asset grab regardless of progress toward repayment." One may call this event emblematic of the government return, but the major point is that this is no longer just the government, but the predatory state.

Legitimacy of Property and Renationalization

Similar to the filtration of the topic of market transition into a more focused topic of privatization, the topic of privatization is being converted into a more specific topic of property rights. Such a trend is characteristic not only for Russian scholars, but may be traced through western publications as well (See, for instance: Blasi, Kroumova, & Kruse, 1997; Denisova, Eller, Frye, & Zhuravskaya, 2012; Hedlund, 2008; Rosefielde, 2008; Smallbone & Welter, 2009). The topic of property rights finds its further development in the topics focused on the relationship between the state authorities and state power and owners, as well as in the topic of corporate relations and conflicts (See, for instance: Frye, 2010a, 2010b; Gould, 2011; Pirani, 2010; Radygin & Arkhipov, 2000; Semenov & Sizov, 2002; Zon, 2008). For all these authors, the starting point is the market transition of the 1990s and the main line of discovery is mass privatization. Privatization, and the way it was conducted, is the key to understanding the legitimacy of owners and the results of privatization.

Considering the causes of predatory raiding requires an understanding of the degree of legitimacy of property rights over enterprises, be it private property rights or collective property rights. This study will not venture into the well-developed theme of privatization. Instead, this study will resort to a hypothetical example and more specifically a proof from the opposite. Let us imagine that due to some extraordinary socioeconomic and political changes, the state decides to conduct renationalization and has all the necessary resources for such a conflicting and contradictory process. The key question will be as follows: will the government compensate current owners for the value of the renationalized property? The answer is obvious. No state in the post-Soviet space would compensate current owners for the value of the renationalized property. First, it is not in the tradition of the Russian state. Second, it is quite obvious that all the wealth accumulated in private hands, and first of all means of production was "stolen" from the state. To be more precise, it was "stolen" from the people, because most of the socialist property formally belonged to the people rather than the state and collective farms. Indeed, in most of the instances, such a "theft" was organized with the help of the state itself.

Alienation of property and its handing over to private hands was done not at the initiative of the masses, but at the initiative of the state, with the active use of the state apparatus, and in order to serve the interests of private entities and individuals. This handling of people's wealth was presented as compensable, but in fact it was handed over to a few private faces for free. Thus, the legitimacy of virtually any Russian business and owners of property is, mathematically speaking, approximating or moving toward zero.

It remains unclear to the general public how former employees of Research Institutes [Nauchno-issledovatel'sky institute, NII], Komsomol leaders, appraisers and suppliers of wholesale bases, producers of rubber toys, and graduates of culinary vocational schools managed to have a sufficient amount of money in order to acquire industrial giants at the time of mass privatization of the 1990s. Accordingly, the redistribution of property, including by force, often called predatory raiding, is regarded as such technically, because the legitimacy of the present owners is equal to that of the predatory raiders; that is, equal to zero. Here, the famous French political economist Proudhon comes to mind with his very famous expression that "property is a theft" (Proudhon, 1994). The only exception in terms of legitimacy would be small entrepreneurs who worked long hours for many years in order to establish and sustain their small businesses. But these people are not among those who acquired the industrial giants right after the fall of the socialist system. Moreover, and unfortunately, they are among those who may suffer from predatory raiding the most.

The mass privatization of the 1990s and beyond is frequently referred to as *prikhvatization*, from the Russian *prikhvatizatsiya*, that is, the semi-criminal appropriation of state property by those in power. What would the state do if a present owner would say that he was not the initial owner after the privatization and that he deserves compensation for his/her enterprise which is about to be renationalized by the state because he/she paid the market price for it? The response of the state would be the same as in the first case, because the nature of money, with which a given enterprise was bought from the previous owner, let us say, in 1999 or 2005, would still be dubious. It would not be clear where an honest entrepreneur managed to earn millions of dollars for buying an enterprise during the financial crisis of 1998–1999. It is very doubtful that this money was earned with hard labor. It is more likely that there were manipulations with stocks and bonds, restructuring, and numerous other fraudulent activities in order to appropriate enterprises and changing owners. If there is no legitimacy, then there is no compensation. This hypothetical example of renationalization and legitimacy of property on the means of production, concentrated in the hands of just a handful of individuals, leads to the next section, devoted to the possibility of revising the results of mass privatization and its impact on the predatory raiding movement.

It is highly unlikely that anyone would seriously consider a possibility of renationalizing apartments, even though the vast majority of apartments are privatized, while in the Soviet era all of them belonged to the state, except a relatively small number of cooperative apartments. There were not too many apartments built by private companies during the post-Soviet period. Most of the privatized apartments are the former state apartments built in the Soviet period. Why then cannot the state renationalize these apartments even hypothetically, without compensating their present owners? These apartments were privatized at a petty nominal price, as were large industrial enterprises. The answer this study can offer is as follows: these apartments were privatized not by the outsiders or by directors of local housing projects (*ZhEKs*) by analogy with directors of Soviet enterprises, but by the tenants themselves. These tenants worked for these apartments for many years in the Soviet era and clearly deserved them. In fact, they passed these apartments to their children and other family members through the institution of registration, known as *prop-iska*.[5] Those who bought apartments in the post-Soviet period paid the full market price for them, which make their property rights legitimate.

But all of this applies to the main body of former state housing and remains in reasonable limits of use. As far as large newly built mansions and penthouses are concerned, including those built in natural preserves and without proper permissions, the situation is quite different. The state could easily expropriate these expensive housing units without any compensation, even though the term renationalization would not fit well here, because these luxury living units were not built by the state. To the contrary, they were built by private construction companies in the post-Soviet period. It would be possible because the situation here is somewhat reminiscent of the privatization of Soviet industrial giants. The money needed to acquire luxury living units, mansions, and castles have dubious origins. As the Russian proverb goes, "one cannot build a stone palace by righteous labor." Accordingly, legitimacy of property rights on such luxury housing is shady and dubious. The legitimacy of property is defined not by the fact of who owns what, but by the fact of who deserved what, and how this right of property is earned by its present owner.

Volkov (2005b) is being somewhat unclear when he states that legitimacy can only be applied to the authority (legitimate or illegitimate), and that the concept of legitimacy may not be applied to property. In fact, the opposite is true. The concept of legitimacy may be applied to property and quite possibly to other categories. Legitimacy is determined by the people, not by the law. The state authority is legitimate if it is supported by the people. If the state power is a tyranny, directed against its own people, then it is illegitimate simply because it is anti-people and is not supported by the people. The tyrannical political regime can, of course, tailor a set of laws specifically for itself to make the tyranny appear legitimate, but that would be pseudo-legitimacy.

The legitimacy of property is determined in a manner similar to the legitimacy of the state authority. What counts is not the origin of the object, but the origin of the property right on this object. Property is a relationship regarding certain objects. Such a relationship can exist between individuals, economic agents, the state and individuals, and so on. When it comes to the legitimacy of property, this is the relationship between the people and the property owner. This is not the relationship between the state that sets the laws and the property owner. If the people in its mass think that the owner deserves the property, then this property is legitimate, that is, his/her right over this piece of property is legitimate.

The state can take away the property by force, even though the people will disapprove of it, considering the property owner as a legitimate owner. But who was opposing the Yukos affair and taking it away from Khodorkovsky? The people were indifferent because the aspect of legality was of little interest to them in this case. Facing the question "You became one of the richest men in the 1990s by buying assets of the superpower for cheap. Maybe that was the reason for Putin to assault such oligarchs as you are?" Khodorkovsky offers the following response:

> There is no doubt that Putin played on such feelings of former Soviet people. However, it is even sadder that people who were born in the era of capitalism repeat the myth about 'the assets bought for cheap.' Some respectable foreign investors were buying assets much cheaper, including in Russia, East Germany, and Latin America. I can offer quite a few examples. An asset costs exactly as much as one is ready to pay for it in this particular place in this particular time. Let me note that some investors received shares of Yukos and Yukos' branches cheaper than we did. I don't even mention a shameful story of buying the stolen after the company's destruction.[6]

Khodorkovsky's answer does not sound very convincing, especially when it comes to the acquisitions done by foreign investors. There is no developed capital market in Russia even today, not to mention the early 1990s. In the early 1990s, the whole notion of the market, let alone capital market, was very vague, at best. Indeed, according to market-based economic laws, an economic asset costs exactly as much as one is ready to pay for it in this particular place at this particular time. In this sense, a commodity exchange or a stock exchange for that matter is the best expression of such logic of asset valuation. However, when it comes to privatization "for cheap," everything becomes more complicated. The acquisition or a buyout for any price, even the "market" price, is unlikely to add to the legitimacy of the new owners. This suggestion especially applies to the notion of legitimacy given by the people rather than that given by the law. That is why the alleged manipulation with public opinion is quite logical in such contested cases.

The people were indifferent, because it is understood that even if a former Komsomol functioneer had an entrepreneurial talent, it would still be impossible to accumulate a fortune of $18 billion at a reasonably young age, especially when the country was in a lengthy economic stagnation. Thus, the legitimacy of this fortune was approximating zero. The legitimacy as a company's manager is a different issue, especially if it is an effective manager. The former head of Yukos pointed out that, "As a businessman, I feel sorry that the most effective oil company in post-Soviet Russia was destroyed. Not just changed the owner, but precisely destroyed as a well-functioning mechanism."[7] It appears that the young and hard-working manager of a huge company, formed out of the pieces of large Soviet enterprises did not get a chance to convert it into something completed and effective under the new market conditions. Indeed, Khodorkovsky was deprived of this chance.

As far as the concerns of the US State Secretary go, they are focused not on the legitimacy borne by the people, but on the legitimacy set by the law. And this is quite natural, because she represents the interests of western investors. An attempt to determine the rules of the game and to obey these rules within the established legal limits misses the most important determinant. The legitimacy of any business or property is determined primarily by the people, and only then by the state. In the case of foreign investors, this legitimacy is determined by the people of the host country.

Even though Volkov's thesis regarding the application of legitimacy is somewhat arguable, his merit is obvious and lies in the way that he raises the issue of the applicability of legitimacy to categories, phenomena, and institutions other than the state authority or state power. On the surface, legitimacy is normally expressed through the legitimacy of the state authority. That is why the impression emerges that the concept of legitimacy may be applied to the state authority and may not be applied to property and property rights. Ruling political regimes often speculate on the issue of the concept and possibility of significant and earlier privatized economic assets as well as the legitimacy of the property rights of these assets' current owners. In this way, the ruling political regimes hope to achieve certain goals and gain popularity with the masses.

Do the hints about possible renationalization have a chance to be considered as indications of Russian patriotism? The question addressed to Khodorkovsky was as follows: "Yukos, once the largest oil company, was destroyed and its property sold out and ended up in Rosneft' and Gazprom. Was this the real cause of the attack?" Khodorkovsky offered the following response:

> In prison, I met a lot of people whose business was destroyed and taken away in a similar manner. It is interesting that the level of greed demonstrated by the state raiders was absolutely astonishing. I always find it difficult to believe that the state civil servants are capable of such things motivated solely by mercantile proprietary considerations. Nevertheless, this is the reality. In all such cases state institutions have been used as instruments for enrichment of particular individuals. That is why there is not any reason to talk about terms such as renationalization and nationalization in their classical meaning as the genuine causes of the attack.[8]

It is obvious that behind any political claims and declarations about social justice, defense of national interests, and renationalization, there always lies an economic interest.

Buckley (2012) points out that idea of re-privatization is not likely to increase the level of Russian business confidence:

> Models from other former Soviet republics are hardly auspicious. Leaders of Ukraine's 2004 Orange Revolution set out to reprivatise companies more fairly. Only one group, Kryvorizhstal steel works, was resold. But speculation over how reprivatisations might happen led to oligarch battles, investor jitters, and plunging production and growth. In Georgia, many businessmen were investigated and in some cases arrested after the country's 2003 Rose Revolution, paying fines to legitimise their property. But the process was seen as highly politicised. One foreign model is mentioned approvingly by Mr Putin: the £5bn windfall tax imposed by the UK's Labour government under Tony Blair on utilities it believed were privatised too cheaply by the Conservatives. But that was limited to 30 companies, sold only a decade earlier. Russia's case is vastly more complex. Loans-for-shares involved only 12 businesses. Anders Aslund, a Swedish economist who advised the Russian and Ukrainian governments in the early 1990s, points out the auctions led directly to change of control in only four. One, Sidanco, went bankrupt (parts now belong to TNK-BP); Mr Khodorkovsky's Yukos was mostly sold to state-controlled Rosneft after his imprisonment, while Sibneft's owner, Roman Abramovich, sold it to state-controlled Gazprom in 2005. Of the four, only Norilsk Nickel has not changed hands.[9]

The structure of property is more fundamental than institutional changes. Here, this study refers specifically to property relations rather than property rights or distribution of property. Mosaics in the forms of the national economy and changes of political regimes do not strengthen the system of property relations, but instead shake it. On the surface it is expressed, for instance, in that the change of political leadership can lead to necessarily losing some property documents, which makes the process of legitimization of private property in Russia even more complex.

The main obstacle for development in modern Russia and other former Soviet republics is the high level of concentration of property rights on the means of production. All means of production are consolidated and concentrated in the hands of a few. Furthermore, the process of consolidation continues. These few enjoy luxurious lifestyles even when their businesses do not function effectively. As a result, the economy is characterized by low productivity. This became possible as a result of privatization. Why, then, did it not happen in developed western societies? Maybe it did not happen thanks to the anti-monopolistic legislation, such as antitrust laws in the US?

Laws are nothing more than a superstructure, a part of the institutional structure, a derivative. The reason is that in the West, the large enterprises were organized, created, and built in a manner to attract the capital of many individuals, stockholders, shareholders, partners, or whatever other terms may be used. This was necessary because at that time there were no individuals or families with capitals significant enough to create the large production and infrastructure facilities that were demanded by the growing level of technological sophistication. Accordingly, the property rights over the large companies were shared by many. The shareholders wanted dividends; they controlled the top management and demanded profit. Then came the stock market. The control and profitability were universalized and made nearly perfectly regulated by laws.

In distinction of the West and its evolutionary development of shared property rights, in the former Soviet Union, at the time of privatization in the early 1990s, all the large enterprises were already built during the Soviet era. They all belonged to one owner: the state. The task was not to create new value, but to distribute already created values. The distribution was declared based on the principle of an equal portion or share going to everyone. This approach was in the best spirit of socialism, but at the same time it was somewhat strange to start the market reforms with such a bold capitalistic move of privatization based on the equally bold socialist principle of equal distribution. This confusion, however, was not at the core of the transition, because all the property eventually went to the hands of a relatively small group of individuals. Any different results would be impossible, simply because it is exactly this group of individuals who initiated the disintegration of the socialist production. They did it specifically with the goal of privatizing and appropriating the wealth and means of production created by the people during the preceding decades.

VCIOM conducts annual studies of the sources of income of the population in Russia. The results of the answers given by the respondents to the question "Please, tell us sources of income of your family over the last month" during the 2000s and 2010s are presented in Tables 7.1 and 7.2. The data shows that Russians assigned most weight to revenue they receive from full-time jobs both during the 2000s and 2010s. Wages from part-time jobs and informal earnings dropped in significance during this period. Monetary support from relatives and friends also loses its significance. Russians report a decline of the share of revenues that they receive from private entrepreneurship and business in the total income structure they receive. This decline is very obvious from the 2000s to 2010s, and is of no surprise. Krylova (2018, p. 1) reports that, "the number of registered

Table 7.1 Sources of income of population in Russia (percentage of respondents), 1999–2005

Sources of income	*1999*	*2000*	*2001*	*2002*	*2003*	*2004*	*2005*
Wage from full-time job	63.5	63.5	67.1	65.9	68.6	64.5	57.0
Wage from part-time job	6.9	5.7	6.1	5.9	8.3	8.5	5.2
Informal earnings	8.6	10.3	9.4	9.5	6.6	6.7	5.8
Pension	47.4	44.7	47.3	46.4	46.9	36.7	34.8
Stipend	4.2	4.9	5.2	5.6	6.4	6.9	4.1
Unemployment dole	–	–	–	1.2	1.5	1.8	1.8
Child support, other welfare payments and compensations	13.1	11.0	16.8	17.7	17.8	11.0	9.2
Alimonies	2.2	1.9	2.2	2.9	2.5	1.1	0.6
Monetary support from relatives and friends	11.2	7.5	10.4	7.9	6.3	11.2	6.9
Revenue from sale of agricultural produce	3.7	3.2	4.2	3.1	3.2	7.0	6.9
Revenue from renting out housing, garage, dacha	1.1	0.3	1.3	0.9	0.8	2.5	0.7
Revenue from sale of real estate, property	0.2	0.0	0.1	0.1	0.3	0.4	–
Revenue from private entrepreneurship, business	4.9	5.4	4.1	3.8	3.6	6.4	3.8
Interest on deposits	1.1	0.6	0.8	0.7	0.4	0.9	0.3
Revenue from stocks and bonds	0.6	0.3	0.2	0.4	0.2	0.1	0.1

Source: Composed by the author from the data presented in VCIOM. (2005). *The Way We Thought in 2004: Russia on the Crossroads*. Moscow: EKSMO, Algoritm, pp. 166–167; Express monthly all-Russian survey. Moscow: VCIOM. Retrieved May 31, 2018, from https://wciom.ru/research/research/express/; https://wciom.ru/database/

Table 7.2 Sources of income of population in Russia (percentage of respondents), 2011–2017

Sources of income	*2011*	*2012*	*2013*	*2014*	*2015*	*2016*	*2017*
Wage from full-time job	69	–	69	73	68	–	–
Wage from part-time job	1	–	5	6	4	–	–
Informal earnings	3	–	5	4	6	–	–
Pension	20	–	33	34	36	–	–
Stipend	0	–	3	3	2	–	–
Unemployment dole	–	–	–	–	–	–	–
Child support, other welfare payments and compensations	1	–	8	7	6	–	–
Alimonies	0	–	1	1	2	–	–
Monetary support from relatives and friends	1	–	4	3	4	–	–
Revenue from sale of agricultural produce	0	–	3	1	1	–	–
Revenue from renting out housing, garage, dacha	–	–	0	0	1	–	–
Revenue from sale of real estate, property	0	–	0	0	0	–	–
Revenue from private entrepreneurship, business	2	–	3	3	3	–	–
Interest on deposits	0	–	1	1	1	–	–
Revenue from stocks and bonds	0	–	0	0	0	–	–

Source: Composed by the author from the data presented in Express monthly all-Russian survey. Moscow: VCIOM. Retrieved May 31, 2018, from https://wciom.ru/research/research/express/; https://wciom.ru/database/

entrepreneurs decreased from 8.3 million in 2008 to 2.8 million in 2015," that is, two-and-a-half times.

It is interesting that the income from stocks, bonds, and vouchers constitutes almost the least significant source of income in Russian households. This source of income was mentioned by only 0.6 percent of the respondents in 1999 and declined to 0.1 percent by 2004. This means that, during the 2004 survey, only 1 out of 1000 respondents named stocks, bonds, vouchers, and other financial obligations as a source of income for his/her family. In 2005, this figure further declined to 0.06.

It appears that Russians were not converted into stockholders or individual capitalists, which means that they did not become real owners of formerly state enterprises and do not benefit from them. This situation is characteristic of the 2000s. The situation of the 2010s is quite similar. Furthermore, revenue from stocks and bonds reported by households is equal to zero, which is even less than during the 2000s. It is hard to talk about the development of stock market in Russia based on such numbers.

For the most part, Russians do not have private property, but only personal property. Their property normally does not extend beyond an apartment, dacha, small plot of land, and a car. This is the same standard set of property items that Russians enjoyed under the Soviet rule, except for now they have many more personal vehicles. There is no oil of Western Siberia and Norilsk nickel (Nornikel) in the list of property items of a typical modern Russian household. An attempt to disperse property through voucher privatization failed.

If Russians do not have any significant income from participating in joint-stock companies, then processes of predatory raiding regarding large joint-stock companies are of little concern to them. As long as they do not lose their full-time job, which they report as their primary source of income, they may be fine with management change or change of owners. Even if an individual is a minority shareholder, but does not receive any dividends on his/her shares, then it may be obvious that he/she is not very interested in such processes as additional emissions of stock. At the same time, for corporate predatory raiders such an emission may be the key action in taking over the enterprise.

Economic and political inequalities, along with high concentration of property rights on major means of production in the hands of a few owners leads not only to a decrease of incentives to the effective and efficient functioning of enterprises and the national economy overall, as well as low productivity, but also to the weakening of private property rights.

> If the state does not protect economic agents from unlawful expropriation, these agents may take matter into their own hands. One way to protect one's property is to maintain a private system, e.g., to hire a security firm or to establish corrupt relationship with a public official. An alternative way is to reveal a preference for more public protection of property rights through the political process, e.g., by voting for an appropriate candidate. In transition and developing economies, the latter option is often unavailable due to the underdevelopment of political institutions. As a result, economic agents are forced to invest in private protection. Economies of scale in private protection provide rich agents with a significant advantage over poor agents in this environment. Furthermore, the rich agents' ability to gain from redistribution due to improper protection of property rights makes them natural opponents of improvements in public protection. (Sonin, 2003, pp. 715–716; see also Sonin, 2005, p. 2)

It seems as though the strengthening of private property rights depends on strengthening the public component of the state.

Mass de-nationalization and privatization make the legitimacy of property practically impossible, at least for several generations. The only possibility for the owner of an enterprise to legitimize his/her property rights is the effective work of his/her enterprise, and, what turns out to be very important in combating predatory raiders, the support of the workers' collective. But even this formula will only guarantee the legitimacy of the entrepreneur's right to profit and support from the employees, but not the legitimacy of his/her property rights over the enterprise. In this case, the entrepreneurial talent of the owner will be considered as a source of profit, which is quite typical for the western approach and understanding of the productivity of capital. But the enterprise itself will not be considered as a source of profit. Unfortunately, the practice of conducting business in Russia shows that the majority of owners of enterprises also involved in managerial functions are economically ineffective and do not have the respect and support of the workers' collective. Thus, it is too early to talk about the legitimacy of property rights on the means of production and legitimacy of profit obtained by the owner.

Concluding Remarks

Russia undergoes transition from a relatively simple societal organization with a centrally planned socialist economy and totalitarian political regime to a complex society. A complex society is distinct with its multiplicity of forms of economic and political organizations. The system of property rights in a given complex society is complicated as well. This complexity does not guarantee a high level of productivity for the economy. To the contrary, complex societies may be characterized by low levels of productivity. While institutions facilitate the decrease in transaction costs, societies with complex organizational structure of socioeconomic relations allocate significant human and financial resources to regulatory functions. The state assumes the function of guaranteeing the continuity and sustainability of the plurality of forms of societal organization. If the state fails to adhere to this role of the guarantor, transaction costs increase.

The threat of predatory raiding has the potential to become the single most important source of additional transaction costs in Russia. Private companies pay taxes to the state to guarantee their security in every non-economic respect. In addition, companies bear the cost of organizing and monitoring financial security as well as maintaining the physical security of property and monitoring the territory of their enterprises. Predatory raiding, which may eventually decimate the country's business population and damage its business ecosystem as a whole, is also responsible for inflated transaction costs in the cost structure of privately owned enterprises in Russia.

A high level of concentration of property rights on the means of production remains the main obstacle for economic and democratic development in modern Russia. Russia needs both further privatization of state property and a much more significant dispersion of property rights among the large and diverse population strata. However, recent processes demonstrate opposite trends. The process of consolidation and concentration of property rights on the means of production continues. While business and political elites enjoy luxurious lifestyles even when their businesses do not function effectively by world standards, the living standards of the majority of the population in Russia stagnate at relatively low levels. In addition to the negative impact of high transaction costs, the high concentration of property rights on the means of production also lowers total factor productivity in the economy.

Mass de-nationalization and privatization the way it was done in Russia make the legitimacy of property practically impossible for generations to come. The only possibility for the owner of an enterprise to legitimize his/her property rights is the effective work of the enterprise. This, along with support that may come from the workers, may be crucial in opposing hostile attempts of predatory raiders. However, in the best-case scenario, the entrepreneur or the owner will enjoy the legitimate right on profit and support from the employees, without really having the legitimacy of property rights over the enterprise.

Notes

1. Larina, Ekaterina. (2001). Bureaucracy faces the knife—and many questions. Most agree reform is needed, but little else is certain. *The Russia Journal*, 9, December 7–13, 2001. Retrieved July 7, 2009, from http://www.russialist.org/archives/5588-9.php
2. Moskva snova suditsya s set'yu "Makdonalds," dva restorana kotoroj prodolzhayut platit' za arendu 1 rubl' v god [Moscow continues court disputes with McDonalds, two restaurants of which continue to pay a rent of only 1 ruble a year]. *Newsru.com*, July 7, 2009. Retrieved July 7, 2009, from http://realty.newsru.com/article/10jul2009/mcdonalds

3. Meriya Moskvy zovet investorov arendovat' avarijnye usad'by za 1 rubl' v god [Moscow Mayor's Office calls on investors to rent dilapidated mansions for one ruble per year]. *Newsru.com*, January 24, 2012. Retrieved January 24, 2012, from http://realty.newsru.com/article/24jan2012/onepuble
4. Kessler, Glenn. (2005). Rice Cites Yukos In Moscow Talks. *Washington Post*, April 21, 2005, p. A14. Retrieved April 20, 2010, from http://www.washingtonpost.com/wp-dyn/articles/A5104-2005Apr20.html
5. On *propiska* see, for instance, Vishnevsky, Anatolij. (1998). *Serp i rubl'* [Circle and ruble]. Moscow: OGI, p. 101.
6. Vlast' davit na menya postoyanno. Tyur'moj. Interv'yu Reuters s Mikhailom Khodorkovskim (original'naya russkaya versiya) [State Authorities put pressure on me all time. By prison. Reuter's interview with Mikhail Khodorkovsky (the original Russian version)]. *Khodorkovsky.ru*, September 18, 2011. Retrieved September 18, 2011, from http://khodorkovsky.ru/mbk/articles_and_interview/2011/09/18/16606.html

   Khodorkovsky v interv'yu Reuters predrek Rossii novy krizis i porassuzhdal o mesti [Khodorkovsky predicted a new crisis for Russia and talked about revenge in an interview given to Reuters]. *Newsru.com*, September 18, 2011. Retrieved September 18, 2011, from http://www.newsru.com/russia/18sep2011/hodorkovsky.html

   Forget reform if Putin stays in power – Khodorkovsky. *Reuters*, September 18, 2011. Retrieved September 18, 2011, from http://uk.reuters.com/article/2011/09/18/uk-russia-politics-khodorkovsky-idUKTRE78H0RD20110918
7. Vlast' davit na menya postoyanno. Tyur'moj. Interv'yu Reuters s Mikhailom Khodorkovskim (original'naya russkaya versiya) [State Authorities put pressure on me all time. By prison. Reuter's interview with Mikhail Khodorkovsky (the original Russian version)]. *Khodorkovsky.ru*, September 18, 2011. Retrieved September 18, 2011, from http://khodorkovsky.ru/mbk/articles_and_interview/2011/09/18/16606.html

   Khodorkovsky v interv'yu Reuters predrek Rossii novy krizis i porassuzhdal o mesti [Khodorkovsky predicted a new crisis for Russia and talked about revenge in an interview given to Reuters]. *Newsru.com*, September 18, 2011. Retrieved September 18, 2011, from http://www.newsru.com/russia/18sep2011/hodorkovsky.html

   Forget reform if Putin stays in power – Khodorkovsky. *Reuters*, September 18, 2011. Retrieved September 18, 2011, from http://uk.reuters.com/article/2011/09/18/uk-russia-politics-khodorkovsky-idUKTRE78H0RD20110918
8. Vlast' davit na menya postoyanno. Tyur'moj. Interv'yu Reuters s Mikhailom Khodorkovskim (original'naya russkaya versiya) [State Authorities put pressure on me all time. By prison. Reuter's interview with Mikhail Khodorkovsky

(the original Russian version)]. *Khodorkovsky.ru*, September 18, 2011. Retrieved September 18, 2011, from http://khodorkovsky.ru/mbk/articles_and_interview/2011/09/18/16606.html

Khodorkovsky v interv'yu Reuters predrek Rossii novy krizis i porassuzhdal o mesti [Khodorkovsky predicted a new crisis for Russia and talked about revenge in an interview given to Reuters]. *Newsru.com*, September 18, 2011. Retrieved September 18, 2011, from http://www.newsru.com/russia/18sep2011/hodorkovsky.html

Forget reform if Putin stays in power—Khodorkovsky. *Reuters*, September 18, 2011. Retrieved September 18, 2011, from http://uk.reuters.com/article/2011/09/18/uk-russia-politics-khodorkovsky-idUKTRE78H0RD20110918

9. Buckley, Neil. (2012). A windfall tax will not lift Russian business confidence. *Financial Times*, February 24, 2012. http://www.ft.com/intl/cms/s/0/59eaaeb2-5e28-11e1-b1e9-00144feabdc0.html#axzz1nWt9yef5

References

Barnes, A. (2007). Industrial Property in Russia: The Return of the State and a Focus on Oil. *SAIS Review, 27*(2), 47–62. Retrieved July 22, 2012, from http://muse.jhu.edu/journals/sais_review/v027/27.2barnes.pdf

Blasi, J., Kroumova, M., & Kruse, D. (1997). *Kremlin Capitalism: Privatizing the Russian Economy.* Ithaca, NY: Cornell University Press.

Buckley, N. (2012). A Windfall Tax Will Not Lift Russian Business Confidence. *Financial Times*, February 24, 2012.

Danner, P. (1996). Gain-Seeking: The Economoral Nexus. In E. O'Boyle (Ed.), *Social Economics: Premises, Findings and Policies* (pp. 47–56). New York: Routledge.

Denisova, I., Eller, M., Frye, T., & Zhuravskaya, E. (2012). Everyone Hates Privatization, but Why? Survey Evidence from 28 Post-Communist Countries. *Journal of Comparative Economics, 40*(1), 44–61.

Frye, T. (2010a). *Building States and Markets after Communism: The Perils of Polarized Democracy.* New York: Cambridge University Press.

Frye, T. (2010b). Corruption and the Rule of Law. In A. Aslund, S. Guriev, & A. C. Kuchins (Eds.), *Russia after the Global Economic Crisis* (pp. 79–94). Washington, DC: Peterson Institute for International Economics.

Gould, J. (2011). *The Politics of Privatization: Wealth and Power in Postcommunist Europe.* London: Lynne Rienner Publishers.

Hedlund, S. (2008). The Property Rights Hurdle: Reconciling EU and Russian Traditions. In J. Pickles (Ed.), *Globalization and Regionalization in Socialist and Post-Socialist Economies* (pp. 233–253). New York: Palgrave Macmillan.

Krylova, Y. (2018). *Corruption and the Russian Economy: How Administrative Corruption Undermines Entrepreneurship and Economic Opportunities.* New York and London: Routledge.
O'Brien, T. (1998). George Soros Has Seen the Enemy. It Looks Like Him. *The New York Times*, December 6, 1998.
Pirani, S. (2010). *Change in Putin's Russia: Power, Money, and People.* New York: Pluto Press.
Proudhon, P.-J. (1994). *What Is Property?* Cambridge: Cambridge University Press.
Radygin, A., & Arkhipov, S. (2000). Sobstvennost', korporativnye konflikty i effektivnost' [Property, Corporate Conflicts, and Effectiveness]. *Voprosy ekonomiki, 11*, 45–59.
Rosefielde, S. (2008). Property Rights: The Cost to the EU of Russia's Accession. In J. Pickles (Ed.), *Globalization and Regionalization in Socialist and Post-Socialist Economies* (pp. 254–267). New York: Palgrave Macmillan.
Semenov, A., & Sizov, Y. (Eds.). (2002). *Korporativnye konflikty. Prichiny ih vozniknoveniya i sposoby preodoleniya.* Moscow: URSS.
Smallbone, D., & Welter, F. (2009). *Entrepreneurship and Small Business Development in Post-Socialist Economies.* London: Routledge.
Sonin, K. (2003). Why the Rich May Favor Poor Protection of Property Rights. *Journal of Comparative Economics, 31*(4), 715–731.
Sonin, K. (2005). Institutsional'naya teoriya beskonechnogo peredela [Institutional Theory of Endless Redistribution]. *Voprosy ekonomiki, 7*, 1–15. Retrieved May 9, 2009, from http://fir.nes.ru/~ksonin/VESonin.pdf
Volkov, V. (2005). Po tu storonu sudebnoj sistemy, ili Pochemu zakony rabotayut ne tak, kak dolzhny [On the Other Side of the Justice System or Why Don't Laws Work as They Should]. *Neprikosnovennyj zapas, 4*(42). Retrieved January 10, 2012, from http://magazines.russ.ru/nz/2005/42/vv6.html
Woodruff, D. (2005). Nestabil'nost' chastnoi sobstvennosti v Rossii: ekonomicheskie i politicheskie prichiny [The Instability of Private Property in Russia: Economic and Political Causes]. *Russkie Chteniia.* Vypusk 1. Moskva: "Gruppa Ekspert," pp. 206–219. Retrieved January 10, 2012, from http://personal.lse.ac.uk/woodruff/_private/materials/kogdanelzia.pdf
van Zon, H. (2008). *Russia's Development Problem: The Cult of Power.* New York: Palgrave Macmillan.

CHAPTER 8

Organizational Forms of Raiding: Client, Organizer, and Executor

The Business of Hostile Takeover

Raiding is a specific business, which can also be considered as a separate service market or a branch of the national economy. This branch is growing, and its dynamics are strong. Predatory raiding is a highly specialized type of activity, and there are firms that specialize in these kinds of services. This rule of specialization applies equally to the market systems and transitions systems. Large corporations acting aggressively on the M&A market can have an entire development department in their structure that deals specifically with the company's growth, including expansion brought about by the means of predatory raiding. In corporate predatory raiding, there are outsiders and insiders. Outsiders are organizations and institutions from outside the sector. Insiders are organizations and institutions that are part of the sector. Insiders are competitors that compete with the target firm and have an interest to acquire it. Outsiders are in search of well-established profitable enterprises or enterprises with assets that can be sold on the market within a short period of time.

Unfortunately, studies of corporate M&A, presented by Russian scholars, do not reflect organizational structures of the predatory raiding component, focusing instead predominantly on legal aspects of the predatory raiding phenomenon (see, for instance, Bazylev, 2015; Belen'kaya, 2001; Bodrova, 2014; Iontsev, 2003; Kireev, 2008; Labutin, 2008; Lopashenko, 2007; Mel'nikova, 2013; Molotnikov, 2006; Polushkin, 2008; Savchuk, 2001; Vladimirova, 1999). Maybe this shortcoming stems from the violent

A. L. Osipian, *Political and Economic Transition in Russia*,
https://doi.org/10.1007/978-3-030-03831-1_8

nature of Russian predatory raiding, which is no match to sophisticated financial tricks done on the Wall Street. Predatory raiding in Russia is directly linked to violent entrepreneurship, investigated in most detail by Volkov (2002a, 2002b, 2003, 2005), and more recently by Stephenson (2015).

In order to research the business of predatory raiding, it may be necessary to establish who is modern Russian raider or, figuratively speaking, to paint the portrait of a modern predatory raider. The media gives descriptions of violent actions of predatory raiding, but rarely so socio-economic portraits of predatory raiders themselves. Nevertheless, some basic classifications of raiders may be extracted from preliminary studies of the predatory raiding phenomenon.

According to the results of research conducted in 2008 by the Center of Political Technologies, modern raiders in Russia can be classified based on the following four types. Type one is the new class of entrepreneurs, or raiders who order raids. These are normally people with good education, who know law and psychology, and undoubtedly, know modern legislation well. These are businessmen who happened to be a little bit late to privatization, and so they now take over someone else's property. Type two consists of the white collars of the criminal community. These are people who survived in the wild 1990s. They are absolutely hidden and try to avoid publicity. Raiders of this type normally have mechanisms of influencing the judiciary and executive branches of the state authorities, and the law enforcement agencies as well. Type three consists of freelance stormtroopers and professionals. Violent takeovers are done by this type of raiders. They simply execute someone else's will. Wild or freelance stormtroopers are usually young men, 23 to 30 years old, who come to large cities from the provinces. For 1500 to 3000 Russian rubles, they will burn and kill. At the same time, professionals know very well how to clothe absolutely illegal actions in quasi-legal mantra. These are the wild ducks of the raiding market. Type four is state bureaucrats. According to the opinions expressed by the absolute majority of the respondents, the state bureaucrat is the most widespread type of raider in today's Russia. Experts are certain that the concept of state racket formed a long time ago.[1] This study can offer a somewhat similar typology, as presented in Table 8.1.

Economically active bureaucrats existing within the structural frame of the predatory state exploit their opportunities to influence businesses and offer this ability to influence the sale to competing businesses. Furthermore, they want a share in raided businesses and a share of the raiding business itself. Economically active bureaucrats merge with predatory raiders in

Table 8.1 Typology of raiders in Russia

Type	*Characteristics*
New class of entrepreneurs	Economically aggressive Well educated Willing to expand their business at the expense of their competitors
White collars of the criminal community	Capable of influencing civil servants, including courts and police, in order to secure favorable decisions and their enforcement Consider bribe as a necessary extra cost of doing business Avoid publicity
Stormtroopers	Foot soldiers or musclemen of violent storming that normally act in teams Prefer pushing and pooling tactics and avoid heavy fights Many have past criminal records
Professionals	Have economic, finance, and/or legal education Relatively well paid
State bureaucrats	Hold offices of state authority and use this authority for private gain Help raiders to gain or register ownership May be final beneficiaries of the raiding operation

Source: Composed by the author

order to share in their profits. Given the impunity of state bureaucrats for committed economic and other serious crimes, it is hard to say whether they also share the cost of preparing and conducting raiding attacks. Frye (2014) points to the ability of state bureaucrats to authorize and execute violence used in raiding businesses and emphasizes the serious level that this abuse of authority has reached in Russia.

> The issue of control over the state wielders of violence is also critical for contemporary Russia. Headlines of "corporate raids" by business people in collusion with state officials to appropriate the property of economic rivals no longer shock. Indeed, even President Putin has criticized those who engage in "extortion masquerading as state service." These are hostile takeovers in the most literal sense of the term. (Frye, 2014, p. 87)

As this study has noted earlier, predatory raiding is a specific business, which can be separated as a particular branch or type of service. In Russia, predatory raiding is a growing and rapidly developing industry. Corporate predatory raiding is performed by specialized firms. This rule works in market systems and in transition economies as well. Large corporations conducting aggressive consolidations can engage special development departments in corporate raiding, among other activities. Predatory raiders do not necessarily take over enterprises for themselves. Predatory raiders may just be intermediaries or guns for hire. The state authorities acknowledge the existence of such a market, as well as firms that offer their services on this market. In 2007, the First Vice-Mayor of Moscow Yuri Roslyak commented that "there is an entire market segment with its prices and predetermined, elaborated, and agreed schemes, which are realized by hour."[2] Raided firms are handed to the clients, taken for resale, or are sold out in pieces. There are even cases when predatory raiders offer the previous owners the opportunity to buy back their enterprises or assets at a reduced price.

As a result of the growing competition on the market for corporate control in Russia, the qualitative characteristics of the institutional environment in the property redistribution and behavior of its participants change. This change applies both in the market sector and in the nonmarket sector of enterprise asset redistribution. In the market sector, this asset redistribution takes a form of traditional M&A. In the nonmarket sector, asset redistribution manifests itself in corrupt or predatory raiding, green mail, and violent entrepreneurship. Tarkhanova (2008, p. 8) points out that, in distinction of foreign models, Russian institutions of predatory raiding are characterized by the division of functions of the client who orders the raid and the executor who performs the raid, raiding is moving to outsourcing, creation of specialized raiding chains and services, decreasing cost of the raid, increasing the number of raiding takeovers, low transparency, tougher competition among predatory raiders for small and medium business targets. What one can see here is the division of functions among the participants of the raiding movement and the development of more complex raiding mechanisms overall.

It is not unusual for scholars to view M&A as acts of exchange that take place on the stock market. The problem, however, is that Russia still has a largely undeveloped stock market. Skidanova (2010, p. 16) says that M&A, in essence, represent an act of exchange, the process of redistribution of property rights, which can be considered as a redistributive model of distributional behavior of economic agents, realized on a legitimate basis, such as friendly M&A, and on nonlegitimate bases, such as hostile corporate takeovers or raiding. As can be seen from these two excerpts, the authors actively advance the idea of predatory raiding as a corporate hostile takeover that takes place on a nonlegitimate basis that may be found in Russia. This type of a corporate hostile takeover exists in a nonmarket sector of firms' assets redistribution.

The vacuum in state regulation and enforcement has been filled by various specialized raiding companies that offered services of hostile takeovers as well as companies that offered protection services against predatory raiders. Since predatory raiding has become a highly profitable business, raiders started to multiply. As happens in nature, the growth in the population of prey led to an increase in the number of predators. The process of privatization brought to life hundreds of thousands of new private businesses in the 1990s, of which many were potential targets of predatory raiders.

> Various companies emerged that specialized in seizing property or protecting it from raiders. According to data from the Ministry of Internal Affairs, there were no less than 100 raider companies in the country in 2005. Even if some authors saw positive elements in this activity, most raider companies were predators, reminding one of the Middle Ages when lawyers were used by a strong lord to seize the property of a weaker lord, as Rabelais vividly described in his *Gargantua and Pantagruel*. Yurii Borisov, and expert on raiding, suggested that the profitability of these companies was often astronomic. (Shlapentokh, 2007, p. 144)

Respondents of the Center of Political Technologies see the existence of all the companies that specialized exclusively on predatory raiding as the most dangerous trend in raiding. They have serious legal services departments and may be called investment companies. However, three of the respondents are convinced that there is no such thing as raiding per se and that it is difficult or nearly impossible to give a definition for raiding. One of the respondents, an MP in the State Duma,[3] asserts that raiding does not exist. What does exist is a set of crimes, committed by an individual or a group with the goal of acquiring someone else's property. According to the views expressed by this small portion of the respondents, raiding is a problem characteristic of a certain stage in the process of development of the state as a system and mechanism of control over social compliance with certain norms and rules. If one is to analyze raiding, one is to see that fraud, robbery, or gangster methods are used during raids, and these are already described in the Criminal Code.[4]

The task of the state in combating predatory raiding is similar to that in combating contract killings. The major stake for the state is not punishing the executors, but organizers and their clients. The state should seek to punish those who order hostile takeovers and those who organize them. The organizational structure of predatory raiding more and more often involves the state authorities and its representatives. The use of the state functions is necessary to realize a hostile takeover and to legalize the property rights of the new owner on the raided firm or property.

The then mayor of Moscow, Yuri Luzhkov, acknowledged the presence of corruption among bureaucrats and underlined its role in the development of predatory raiding. Mayor Luzhkov admitted that raiding is facilitated by corrupt bureaucrats and law enforcement officers, who ease the task of raiders significantly. Each document should be signed by a bureaucrat. We need a wide public discussion in order to choose amendments to administrative and criminal legislation that would make the punishment for organizers of raiding harsher and prevent hostile takeovers.[5] Hence, the emphasis is placed on the need to punish the organizers of raider attacks, not just performers or executors.

Typically, at best, stormtroopers are arrested and may even be detained, while organizers and especially customers or clients of the raider attacks remain beyond the reach of justice. Those who storm the enterprise are normally punished with administrative fines for minor legal violations and disorderly conduct. Unless the law moves up the vertical organizational structure of the predatory raiders, the hope to put into action the legal component of the anti-raiding campaign will remain a hope rather than a rational expectation. Legal consideration is not the only consideration here. Economically speaking, the task of law enforcement and judicial authorities is to maximize transaction costs of raider organizations. The concentration of and an increase of transaction costs at the level of the perpetrators, that is, lower-level raider hierarchy, have its limits. Such an increase targeting the foot soldiers is unlikely to lead to any significant decline in raider attacks. Only the reach to higher levels, including the organizers and sponsors of raider attacks, and a significant increase of their transaction costs can bring positive results in the fight against corporate raiding.

In nature, food chains normally form a hierarchy. In this hierarchy, organisms each depend on the ones below them as a source of food. Predatory raiders also depend on firms and asset owners as their prey. But the raiding organizations themselves may form hierarchies. The simple structure of a raider organization may be described as follows. At the top, there are organizers of the raiding attacks. They select people for a hostile takeover of the targeted firm, ordered by the clients. Corporate lawyers, who specialize in M&A and who are aware of the legal situation of the targeted firm and the existing loopholes in the legislation, prepare the legal component of the attack. These lawyers can also have useful connections in the commercial arbitrage courts that can be used by predatory raiders. Predatory raiders also pay their patrons in the state offices. These state bureaucrats know the paperwork and proper procedures and can also be involved in the preparation of fraudulent documents. The public relations (PR) unit works on presenting the hostile takeover in the necessary light, including mass media and social networks. Their task is to make the authorities believe that the public and the labor collective support new owners. Stormtroopers are used for the physical takeover of the enterprise. This simple structure of the raiding organization is often outlined in the media reports.[6]

Holding on to the raided company is also an important task. The previous owner can attempt to take his/her enterprise back by force through staging a response storming. For this reason, predatory raiders usually employ a private security company to guard the targeted firm. Private security companies often employ former law enforcement officers who remain connected with the acting law enforcers. This is one of the ways in which predatory raiders are linked to the state apparatus and specifically to law enforcement agencies. The structure of a raiding organization is presented in Fig. 8.1.

The raiding company Investitsionnaya kompaniya "Rossiya" [Russia Investment Company], investigated by the police in 2009, had its own hierarchy, including intelligence, counter-intelligence, stormtroopers and enforcement, economists, and lawyers. In addition, they used a group of sexual minorities in order to blackmail managers of targeted firms. Representatives of this group turned to law enforcement agencies with the claim that they were raped by such and such manager of a targeted firm.

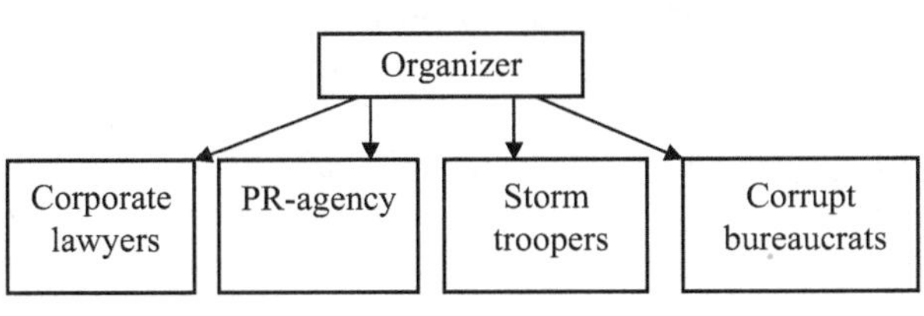

Fig. 8.1 Structure of a raiding organization

The criminal cases filed against this company contain several such cases of blackmail.[7] Hierarchical structure, specialization, division of functions, and the use of outside resources all point to a high level of organization of the raiding business.

Chronicles of Ancient Sieges or the War of High Fences

In food chains, the predator dies if it does not obtain food, so it evolves whatever is necessary in order to eat the prey: speed, stealth, camouflage to hide while approaching the prey, a good sense of smell, sight, or hearing to find the prey, immunity to the prey's poison, poison to kill the prey, and the right kind of mouth parts or digestive system. Likewise, the predator is part of the prey's environment, and the prey dies if it is eaten by the predator, so it evolves whatever is necessary to avoid being eaten: speed, camouflage to hide from the predator, a good sense of smell, sight, or hearing to detect the predator, thorns, or poison to spray when approached or bitten.[8] In human activities, these same functions and characteristics become more sophisticated and complicated. In business, property, and land raiding, both predators and prey develop a host of features and tactics to achieve their contradictory goals. These include both offensive and defensive ones.

Normally, the public perceives the state as the single major protector of private property. In most instances, the state apparatus is assigned with the monopolistic right to protect personal, state, and private property, including with the help of all necessary force. In reality, however, this perception may frequently be misleading. According to Markus (2015, pp. 22–23), "While the government can, theoretically, protect private property more efficiently than private actors themselves can, few states resemble the rational, power-wielding sovereign with long-term horizons that would allow effective self-restraint on predation." As a result of the government's inaction in regards to property rights protection, private forces come into play. These private forces may be engaged on both the attacker's and defendant's sides. Due to its insufficiencies or unwillingness, the state may refuse to lead the war against those trying to plunder someone else's property. As a result, property owners are left with the need to design and exercise their own defenses. Then comes the other war, the war of high fences.

During the Soviet era, plants were strikingly open to outsiders, but in a physical, not an economic, sense. Since then, the situation has changed drastically. The era of predatory raiding is the era of war of high fences. In the Soviet era, high fences were intended to prevent *nesuny* from carrying out the products, parts, or instruments from the plant or factory. Today, even higher and reinforced fences are intended to prevent raiders from storming the enterprise and taking over it. The stakes are much higher now, and so are the erected fences. In earlier days, the enterprise could lose some insignificant amount of the product, because *nesuny* were quite reasonable in their appetites for state property. Today, predatory raiders can appropriate the entire enterprise along with all of its workers, except, perhaps the director and the security staff dedicated to him/her.

The decorative fences of factories with nominal lifting traffic gates and sleepy gatekeepers, normally old retirees, are now being replaced with fortress-high concrete walls, traffic control barriers, iron gates, and checkpoints manned by security personnel armed like terminators. The fences were intended to keep outsiders safe from production facilities; now they are intended to keep enterprises safe from the outsiders. Typical Soviet fences are covered with thick bushes with breaches made in them by *nesuny* and used by others to cut through instead of going around. These porous fences surrounded even some of the defense industry plants. Now these are all memories of the past.

There is no need to be particularly inventive in organizing the defense of a modern enterprise. The period of ancient wars and medieval ages gave humankind a lot of practical ideas about fortification. Artificial ponds, waterways and deep ditches, or high concrete fences, topped with barbed wire, are supplemented with even more sophisticated inventions. For instance, Moscow's suburbs now extend to parks and natural preserves, where construction and development is banned. Such projects are often referred to as illegal and hostile takeovers of land and raiding of state territories. In response, the Minister of Nature once voiced a plan of removing all of the illegal houses and villas built along rivers and canals with the help of opening dams and waiting on spring floods. This idea is similar to that of Sodom and Gomorrah, when Jewish settlers near these two cities built a dam in order to swipe away the enemy's troops with water flood by opening the dam, if needed. The people's deputies or MPs, covered with legal immunity, are now used as an improvised Trojan horse, with which ancient Greeks managed to take over Troy.

In the Soviet era, the nominal fences surrounding construction sites, made of wooden planks, were normally erected very slowly, with the reason of keeping pedestrians safe from bricks and construction debris falling on their heads. Now they gave way to high fences made of concrete or even metal-plastic and erected swiftly overnight. Then, as is in H. G. Wells' novel "The War of the Worlds," there is a noise that comes out from a pit behind a fence. And suddenly a structure is raised up high, as a tripod of Martians. The developers like to dig deeper into the ground and then build for centuries to stay, so their structures would not be removed by any court decision. In such a way, numerous new office buildings and apartment high rises are built in the middle of already existing large apartment complexes. This is called precise or pointed construction development, *tochechnaya zastroika*. A typical situation of confrontation is when tenants protest so-called high precision developments, because they swallow small parks, kindergartens, playgrounds, and such. The police normally support those who paid more, meaning of course that they paid more to the city authorities for construction permission.[9] When it comes to the battle with local tenants, it is hard to tell, who are raiders and who are construction workers.[10]

Similar to the workers, soldiers, and sailors of the revolutionary Petrograd rushing to storm the Winter Palace, modern "proletarians" of the already market-integrated Petersburg rush to storm enterprises. The scale, of course, is no longer the same: then it was the Winter Palace, and now it is only a meat processing plant, textile factory, or cosmetic parlor. The former presented political demands while the latter limited themselves to narrow economic interests. In the case of revolutionary workers and soldiers, it was raiding in its highest form. It was the takeover not of property, but of authority and power. Moreover, it was a takeover of the unlimited dictatorial state power, with which one can decide independently how to alienate, appropriate, distribute, and redistribute all property in the country. In the case of modern predatory raiders, the quests are for particular pieces of property that were not appropriated or properly secured during the initial redistribution of the early 1990s.

Modern predatory raiders appear quite backward compared to the raiders of the revolutionary days, not only in terms of their goals and targets, but also in terms of their arms and organization. Revolutionary soldiers and sailors considered taking over such key objects as telephone and telegraph stations, while modern predatory raiders concentrate their attention on such positions as the main entrance and the director's office, because that is where the cash, seals, charter documents, and titles of property are. It is sometimes surprising how courageously the director holds on to his armchair not only in the indirect sense, but in the direct sense as well. The "carrying out of the body," that is, the physical removal of the director from his office, would mean defeat.[11] The major similarity between the raiders of the two eras is that in both cases they want to enter the room where the board of directors or the leadership of the country is sitting and say, "Your time is over." Modern raiders normally act under the cover of a court order, and do it so delicately as if it were a fig leaf. But the revolutionary soldiers and sailors also had a license from a congressional body for the removal of the Provisional Government [Vremennoe pravitel'stvo] in October of 1917.

Reinforced gates and high walls represent passive forms of defense, while security personnel armed with batons and pepper sprays represent active forms of defense. Fire extinguishers and fists are not the only weapons used for defense against predatory raiders. The defense of enterprises is held with the use of Molotov cocktails as well, as is shown in the video footage of a raiding storming by D'yakonov.[12] Tenants of dormitories and other housing projects that belong to particular enterprises defend their dwellings with the help of welded metal grates, repelling the assaults of the police and court bailiffs.[13] One can point out the inactive behavior of the evicted tenants, as they appear nearly defenseless. They rely more on attracting the attention of local authorities and the media to their problem rather than on actual defense techniques. They organize demonstrations and refer to the Constitution instead of physically fighting for their housing.

There is also a need to disprove the myth that violent raiding in Russia was characteristic of the 1990s and 2000s and by now is gone or left behind in the turbulent 2000s. This study refers to video footage of violent storming and forceful entries committed by raiders.[14] Property and documents of previous owners are being thrown out onto the streets.[15] Armed raiders are seen threatening workers who hold the defense.[16] Stormtroopers are blocking employees from entering firms.[17] These video recordings clearly indicate that violent raiding in Russia continues throughout the regions. The videos demonstrate hostile takeovers of large enterprises, such as plants and factories,[18] while raiding of small businesses, cafeterias, apartments, garages, land parcels, and other valuable assets continues as well.

Raiders use detachments of lightly armed foot soldiers, numbering from a few dozens to a few hundred.[19] Foot soldiers can also be equipped with helmets and bulletproof vests.[20] Mobile groups of stormtroopers form the infantry of predatory raiders. The quality of stormtroopers varies from students of athletic programs and sports colleges to street thugs to armed professionals. Prices for the services of these stormtroopers vary accordingly. Sometimes raiders have to form a live shield in order to block the entrance of the enterprise and prevent its former directors and employees from entering.[21] The arms used by predatory raiders are limited to light firearms and, rarely, automatic shotguns, supplemented with knives and clubs.[22] In terms of arms, stormtroopers are not on par with the police. As a result, they normally try to avoid open confrontation with law enforcement officers. The only exception, perhaps, is the hostile takeover of the meat processing plant in St. Petersburg, where a special military detachment was involved in the storming.[23] Shlapentokh (2007) offers a more detailed account of this story that also points to the move of predatory raiders from Moscow to the regions. The struggle for the economically attractive plot of land was the basis for the dispute over the food company in St. Petersburg:

> In the struggle for property, Moscow corporations, which generally had closer ties to the central administration and its "administrative resources," including military power, often attempted to seize assets in other regions. A good example was the change in ownership of a meat-producing company known as Samson located in St. Petersburg. The company's most coveted asset was a piece of land. A Moscow company, Salonin, wanted to use this land for building residential houses and office space. The Petersburg company did not recognize the right of the Moscow firm, referring to a previous court decision in its favor. Using its connections to the "power structures" (*the siloviki*), the Moscow firm then recruited a special military unit from Chechnya to physically oust the directors of the Petersburg company. (Shlapentokh, 2007, p. 145)

The latest trend in the equipment and actions or tactics of stormtroopers is that they are not armed at all in order to avoid being charged for violence by the police. Their physical actions are more of pushing and pulling rather than a fistfight. All of these are precautionary measures used in order to avoid legal penalties and police interference in the conflict. Stormtroopers try to outnumber those holding the defense, pushing them away from the territory rather than beating them up.

Concluding Remarks

To conclude this chapter, this study would like to highlight the following. Predatory raiding is a specific business, which can be separated as a particular branch of the economy, occupation, or type of service. Raiding is a growing and rapidly developing industry in transition economies. Firms specialize in raiding, that is, corporate raiding is a complex activity performed by specialized firms. Predatory raiders either take over enterprises to own them or to sell them. Both roles are problematic for the economy. For the former, predatory raiders are usually ineffective managers; for the latter, they serve as intermediaries. Raided firms are handed over to the clients, go for resale, or are sold out in pieces. There are even cases when raiders offer the previous owners the opportunity to buy back their enterprises.

The task of the state in combating predatory raiding is similar to that of combating contract killings. The major stake for the state is punishing not only the executors of unlawfully staged hostile takeovers, but first of all the organizers and their clients. The organizational structure of raiding more and more often involves the state authorities and its representatives. The emphasis is placed on the need to punish the organizers of raider attacks, not just performers. However, organizers—and especially customers or clients of predatory raiders—typically remain beyond the reach of legal justice. The concentration of an increase in transaction costs at the level of the perpetrators, that is, lower-level raider hierarchy, has its limits and will not lead to any significant reduction in raider attacks. Only the reach to higher levels, including the organizers and sponsors of criminally loaded hostile takeovers, and a significant increase in their transaction costs can bring positive changes in the fight against predatory corporate raiding in Russia.

Notes

1. Reiderstvo kak sotsial'no-ekonomicheskij i politicheskij fenomen sovremennoj Rossii: otchet o kachestvennom sotsiologicheskom issledovanii. Issledovanie "Tsentra politicheskih tehnologij" pod rukovodstvom Bunina. Moskva, 2008. [Raiding as a socioeconomic and political phenomenon of the modern Russia: A report on the qualitative sociological investigation. An investigation conducted by the Center of Political Technologies led by Bunin]. Moscow, May 2008. Retrieved June 12, 2009, from http://www.politcom.ru/; http://www.compromat.ru/main/mix1/raiderycpt.htm
2. FNS vvela v internete servis dlia zashchity kompanij ot reiderov [The Federal Tax Services office (FNS) introduced an internet service intended

to protect companies from raiders]. *Newsru.com*, March 26, 2007. Retrieved May 9, 2009, from http://www.newsru.com/finance/26mar2007/fns_raiders.html

3. State Duma is the Lower Chamber of the Russian Parliament.
4. Reiderstvo kak sotsial'no-ekonomicheskij i politicheskij fenomen sovremennoj Rossii: otchet o kachestvennom sotsiologicheskom issledovanii. Issledovanie "Tsentra politicheskih tehnologij" pod rukovodstvom Bunina. Moskva, 2008. [Raiding as a socioeconomic and political phenomenon of the modern Russia: A report on the qualitative sociological investigation. An investigation conducted by the Center of Political Technologies led by Bunin]. Moscow, May 2008. Retrieved June 12, 2009, from http://www.politcom.ru/; http://www.compromat.ru/main/mix1/raiderycpt.htm
5. Yuri Luzhkov: "Malyj biznes vo mnogom obespechivaet zhiznedeyatel'nost' finansovoj sistemy stolitsy" [Yuriy Luzhkov: "Small business to a large extent maintains the proper functioning of the financial system of the capital]. *Moskovskij Komsomolets*, September 2, 2007. Retrieved May 9, 2009, from http://www.mk.ru/daily/83784.html
6. Sila est' – zakona ne nado [If there is force, there is no need for law]. *MBnews.ru*, December 11, 2008. Retrieved July 22, 2009, from http://www.notheft.ru/sila-est-zakona-ne-nado
7. D'yakonov, Pavel. (2009). V Rossii vynesen pervy prigovor professional'noj kompanii reiderov [First court sentence is handed to a raiding company in Russia]. *Peterburg-Pyatyj kanal*, May 21, 2009. Retrieved July 22, 2009, from http://www.notheft.ru/v-rossii-vynesen-pervyj-prigovor-professionalnoj-kompanii-rejderov
8. Predator-Prey Relationships. NESCI. Retrieved June 12, 2017, from http://necsi.edu/projects/evolution/co-evolution/pred-prey/co-evolution_predator.html
9. See video report: Police fights with local community members near a new construction site in Moscow. August 17, 2007. Retrieved July 29, 2009, from http://www.youtube.com/watch?v=dbzwbHpyWXM&NR=1
10. See video report on the exodus of the besieged from the fortress. The construction workers leave the site after being stormed by the police special forces. Retrieved from http://www.youtube.com/watch?v=dMegGDrGE5w&feature=related
11. See video report: Raider is the robber in law: Hostile takeover of a plant in Ural. *Svobodnaya pressa*, Retrieved July 29, 2009, from http://www.svpressa.ru/issue/video.php?id=876
12. D'yakonov, Pavel. (2009). V Rossii vynesen pervy prigovor professional'noj kompanii reiderov [First court sentence is handed to a raiding company in Russia]. *Peterburg-Pyatyj kanal*, May 21, 2009. Retrieved July 22, 2009, from http://www.notheft.ru/v-rossii-vynesen-pervyj-prigovor-professionalnoj-kompanii-rejderov

13. See video report from the scene: The last defense line. Retrieved July 29, 2009, from http://www.youtube.com/watch?v=adlR_ra3V4c
14. See video footage of a group of people taking over the headquarters of Volgogradenergosbyt energy public utility company in Volgograd, Russia in August 2011. Police, investigators with a search warrant, representatives of both directors, and armed private security personnel are all present on the site. This appears to be a classical "koshmarit' biznes" spectacle merged with raiding. Reiderskij zakhvat Volgogradenergosbyta [Hostile takeover of Volgogradenergosbyt]. *YouTube*, August 17, 2011. Retrieved May 14, 2018, from https://www.youtube.com/watch?v=YuvwQuqI5FY
15. See video footage of a group of people storming the expanded clay plant in Ul'yanovsk, Russia in April 2012. The new managers try to convince workers to leave, saying it was a shortened work day. Reiderskij zakhvat keramzitovogo zavoda. g. Ul'yanovsk [Hostile takeover of expanded clay plant in Ul'yanovsk]. *YouTube*, April 4, 2012. Retrieved May 14, 2018, from https://www.youtube.com/watch?v=S1fg1JZnSfM
16. See video footage of a group of people storming a technical oil plant in Ufa, Bashkortostan Republic, Russia, in August 2015. Na zavode v Bashkirii proizoshel vooruzhennyj konflikt [Armed conflict took place on a plant on Bashkiriya]. *YouTube*, August 24, 2015. Retrieved May 14, 2018, from https://www.youtube.com/watch?v=Wc7edxfdCvE
17. See video footage of a group of stormtroopers blocking employees from entering Uralmostostroj bridge construction company, paper plant Natur Papir, and Holiday Inn Chelyabinsk Hotel, in Chelyabinskaya oblast, Russia, in August 2015. Reiderskie zakhvaty v Chelyabinskoj oblasti [Hostile takeovers in Chelyabinskaya oblast]. *YouTube*, August 29, 2015. Retrieved May 14, 2018, from https://www.youtube.com/watch?v=rs8D2kMh3cU
18. See video footage of a group of people storming Ufalejskij metallurgy machine-building plant in Verkhy Ufalei, Russia, in March 2015. Ufalejskij zavod metallurgicheskogo mashinostroeniya podvergsya atake reiderov [Ufalejskij metallurgy machine-building plant was attacked by raiders]. *YouTube*, March 4, 2015. Retrieved May 14, 2018, from https://www.youtube.com/watch?v=r-F81XIOy4w
19. See video footage of a group of people storming plant "Bazalt" in Russia. October 21, 2008. Retrieved July 29, 2009, from: http://rutube.ru/tracks/1153651.html?related=1&v=69e294f54d6067aac904bfbb67202f0a
20. See video report: Court. Raiding. *3 Kanal*. June 8, 2009. Retrieved July 29, 2009, from http://www.youtube.com/watch?v=VyvwC5VehQs
21. See video footage of hostile takeovers. Retrieved from http://www.youtube.com/watch?v=tejzH0UMzzE
22. See video footage of a group of stormtroopers detained by police in Moscow for attempted hostile takeover in October 2013. Police confis-

cated eight traumatic pistols, knives, clubs, portable radio stations, bullet-proof vests and so on. Ataka reiderov [Raiding attack]. *YouTube*, October 3, 2013. Retrieved May 14, 2018, from https://www.youtube.com/watch?v=TMS7013W4qA

23. Donskov, Nikolay. (2006). Zachem na kombinate golovorezy?: v Peterburge "spor khozyajstvuyushchikh sub'ektov" razreshaet chechenskij spetsnaz [Why are there guerillas in the meat processing plant?: In Petersburg, a dispute between two firms is being resolved by the Chechen special military forces]. *Novaya gazeta*, 72, September 21, 2006. Retrieved June 23, 2009, from http://2006.novayagazeta.ru/nomer/2006/72n/n72n-s03.shtml

References

Bazylev, D. (2015). Sostavy prestuplenij, vkhodyashchie v ponyatie reiderskikh zakhvatov [Crimes Considered as Hostile Takeovers]. *Biznes v zakone, 4*, 69–71.

Belen'kaya, O. (2001). Analiz korporativnykh sliyanij i pogloshchenij [Analysis of Corporate M&As]. *Upravlenie kompaniej, 2*(3), 49–54.

Bodrova, E. (2014). Reiderstvo kak factor destabilizatsii rossijskoj ekonomiki [Raiding as a Destabilizing Factor of the Russian Economy]. *Vlast, 4*, 41–45.

Frye, T. (2014). Legality and Violence in Russia: An Introduction. *Post-Soviet Affairs, 30*(2–3), 87–88.

Iontsev, M. (2003). *Korporativnye zahvaty: sliyanija, pogloshchenija, grinmejl [Corporate Raiding: Mergers, Acquisitions, Green-mail]*. Moscow: Os'-89.

Kireev, A. (2008). *Reiderstvo v rossijskoj ekonomike: sushchnost', tendentsii i vozmozhnosti protivodejstviya [Raiding in the Russian Economy: Essence, Trends, and Possibilities for Resistance]*. Doctoral dissertation, Institute of Economics and Mathematics RAN (TsEMI), Moscow.

Labutin, A. (2008). Reiderstvo [Raiding]. *Vestnik TISBI*, 1. Retrieved July 25, 2009, from http://www.law.edu.ru/doc/document.asp?docID=1284343

Lopashenko, N. (2007). Reiderstvo [Raiding]. *Zakonnost, 4*, 7–12.

Markus, S. (2015). *Property, Predation, and Protection: Piranha Capitalism in Russia and Ukraine*. New York: Cambridge University Press.

Mel'nikova, T. (2013). K voprosu o soderzhanii ponyatiya "nedruzhestvennoe pogloshchenie" v rossijskom grazhdanskom prave [On the Issue of the Category of Hostile Takeover in Russian Civil Law]. *Yurist, 14*, 33–36.

Molotnikov, A. (2006). *Sliyanija i pogloshchenija. Rossijskij opyt*. Moscow: Vershina.

Polushkin, O. (2008). Reiderstvo: Puti resheniya aktual'nyh problem [Raiding: The Ways to Solve Modern Problems]. *Zakon i pravo, 2*, 62–65.

Savchuk, S. (2001). Analiz osnovnykh motivov sliyanij i pogloshchenij [Major Reasons for M&A]. *Menedzhment v Rossii i za rubezhom, 5*.

Shlapentokh, V. (2007). *Contemporary Russia as a Feudal Society: A New Perspective on the Post-Soviet Era*. New York: Palgrave Macmillan.

Skidanova, L. (2010). *Reiderstvo kak sotsial'no-ekonomicheskij fenomen [Raiding as a Socio-Economic Phenomenon]*. PhD dissertation, Moscow State University, Moscow.

Stephenson, S. (2015). *Gangs of Russia: From the Streets to the Corridors of Power*. Ithaca, NY: Cornell University Press.

Tarkhanova, Z. (2008). *Funktsionirovanie instituta reiderstva v RF [Functioning of the Institute of Raiding in the RF]*. Dissertation, Severo-Osetinsky State University, Vladikavkaz.

Vladimirova, I. (1999). Sliyanija i pogloshchenija kompanij [Companies M&A]. *Menedzhment v Rossii i za rubezhom, 1*.

Volkov, V. (2002a). *Violent Entrepreneurs: The Use of Force in the Making of Russian Capitalism*. Ithaca, NY: Cornell University Press.

Volkov, V. (2002b). Silovoe predprinimatel'stvo: ekonomiko-sotsiologicheski analiz [Violent Entrepreneurship: Economic and Sociological Analysis]. *Ekonomicheskaya sotsiologiya, 3*(1–5).

Volkov, V. (2003). Silovoe predprinimatel'stvo: ekonomiko-sotsiologicheski analiz [Violent Entrepreneurship: Economic and Sociological Analysis]. *Ekonomicheskaya sotsiologiya, 4*(1–3).

Volkov, V. (2005). *Silovoe predprinimatel'stvo – ekonomiko-sotsiologicheski analiz [Violent Entrepreneurship: Economic and Sociological Analysis]*. Moscow: Izdatelski dom GU VSHE.

CHAPTER 9

Foot Soldiers and Firepower: Prices on Raiding Services

ChOPs and MVD: The Right to Defend

The right to protect private property is no longer monopolized by the state. Private security firms can legally operate on the market of security services. However, arming a private security firm may be a problem, since owning and the use of arms is strictly regulated and in many instances prohibited. Thus, private security firms are no match for the police. The drastic imbalance in the firepower is compensated for by the number of stormtroopers involved. Predatory raiders act with the expectation that the police will not shoot, because the use of firearms by the police in Russia is very strictly limited by law. In cases of direct confrontation with the police, stormtroopers try to push police officers and keep them away from key positions, such as the director's office and the main entrance gates. In the US, there would normally be no such pushing and shoving, because it would be considered an assault on a police officer. However, in the former Soviet states, there is more liberty in this regard, because of the exceptionally strict regulations on the use of firearms by the police, inherited from the Soviet era. If predatory raiders fail to agree on the hostile takeover with the police and court bailiffs, keeping them away from the storming, then the police would attack the premises of the raided company in order to remove the stormtroopers and reinstate the lawful or previous director to his rightful place.[1]

A. L. Osipian, *Political and Economic Transition in Russia*,
https://doi.org/10.1007/978-3-030-03831-1_9

Stormtroopers often come from strong-arm entrepreneurs or, simply put, criminal gangs. According to Kireev (2007, p. 40),

> Strong-arm groups ... are made up mainly of veterans of the war in Afghanistan, former athletes, and former (and, not infrequently, also current) members of various state quasi-military special units. Raider structures rarely keep strong-arm entrepreneurs on staff; even in cases when they play (as a rule, subordinate) roles in providing "muscle" in carrying out raiding schemes (above all, maintaining physical control of seized assets).

The law enforcement officers can also take part in hostile takeovers on the side of predatory raiders. According to information aired in the report of the "*3 Kanal*," the Ministry of the Interior reports 44,000 cases in 2008 where police officers in Russia were held responsible for different types of violations. About half of these police officers were directly or indirectly helping predatory raiders.[2] The investigational units of the police can also be used for predatory raiding, including unauthorized searches and the taking away of financial documentation, computers, cell phones, and USB drives.[3] Sometimes the police are used for simple bullying, harassment, or intimidation of businessmen, if hired by their competitors. This is what the then Russian President Dmitry Medvedev called ***koshmarit' biznes***. Medvedev's expression became famous as a result of media outlets repeating it numerous times, and it is still used when describing the pressure of different state agencies on businesses.

Volkov (2005) points out that "Some units of the Ministry of the Interior, and especially those that have the authority to launch criminal investigations in economic crimes, transformed formally state services into the business of creating competitive advantage and providing services to businesses regarding the redistribution of property." Such types of behavior, based on viewing the state office as a kind of economic asset, appears to be quite rational. Half of all the law enforcement officers receive supplemental incomes and are involved in business, and around 18 to 20 percent of them do this business while on duty. Supplemental income of the law enforcement officers in 2004 was equal to anywhere from $1.5 billion to $3 billion, that is, half of all the state expenditures on internal security (Kolennikova, Kosals, & Ryvkina, 2004). Low salaries and long working hours are used routinely to excuse this situation with supplemental income.

A Russian businessman, Yuri Fink, appealed to Dmitry Medvedev with his raiding story, realized with the help of law enforcement agencies, and said that a hostile takeover is,

> [a] simple procedure: it is sufficient to have good connections with law enforcement agencies, that is with people who are sufficiently corrupt. Much more than a million dollars was spent in order to imprison me in "Butyrka" and really conduct an investigation. Not a single hostile takeover occurs without some help from law enforcement agencies.[4]

This businessman was charged with fraud, but later released due to the newly introduced amendments in the Criminal Code, intended to reduce the number of detentions of businessmen who are accused of economic crimes.

The then President Medvedev suggested reducing the punishment for economic crimes.[5] The Russian government chose a paternalistic approach and a protective stance in regard to small businesses in order to show the regime's concern with improving business environment, competition, and entrepreneurial opportunities. Medvedev met with representatives of small- and medium-sized businesses in February of 2010 and told them about the lowering of administrative barriers, and specifically about the mitigation of criminal responsibility for economic crimes not connected to violence:

> I hope that what I suggest will allow at least partial blocking of the opportunities for corrupt officers of law enforcement agencies to use detention to help raiders. We know that there is a sufficient number of such cases. First, those that detain businessman at the mere hint of his competitor and then release him from detention for "cash," that is what is going on. This lawlessness has to stop. I will introduce the law project to the State Duma within the next few days.

President Medvedev suggested setting a bail of 100,000 rubles (at that time approximately $3500) for minor crimes and 500,000 rubles ($17,500) for significant crimes or felonies.[6] The bail can be submitted with real estate, stocks and bonds. Such measures will serve the goal of decriminalizing society and will help in combating corruption and improving the investment climate in the country. Despite some improvements in this area, the issue of jail time versus bail money for businesspeople remains an issue in 2018.[7]

Media reports that only 10 to 16 percent of police-initiated criminal cases on economic crimes had resulted in court rulings. Of those cases initiated by the police, only 40 to 60 percent of cases, depending on the article, get resolved. Of those resolved, 60 to 80 percent never reach the court. Of those cases that reach the court, 20 to 30 percent fall apart in court. Such is the statistics for the period of 2000 to 2009. When it comes to one of the most popular articles, fraud, the figures for 2007 are as follows: 211,277 open criminal cases, of which 50,788 were transferred to the court and 34,241 court rulings were handed down. The report concludes that 177,036 entrepreneurs were under investigation, and some were detained, without a good cause. The news report itself is titled "Nine out of ten criminal cases on economic crimes in Russia are fictitious."[8] The statistics on the types of economic crimes in Russia in 2010 is presented in Table 9.1.

The increasing technical capabilities of both the predatory raiders and the owners defending their enterprises require a certain legal field of action. The right to self-defense is now important not only for individuals

Table 9.1 Types of economic crimes in Russia, 2010

Article of the Criminal Code	*Crimes*	*Share percentage*
Fraud 159	69,445	56.8
Embezzlement or gross waste 160	38,008	31.1
Tax evasion 199	3847	3.1
Smuggling 188	3224	2.6
Attempted tax evasion 198	1759	1.4
Abuse of authority 201	1458	1.2
Commercial bribery 204	1424	1.2
Unlawful entrepreneurship 171	1241	1.0
Unlawful use of trademark 180	442	0.4
Violation of bankruptcy procedures 195	398	0.3
Intentional avoidance of loan repayment 177	393	0.3
Intentional bankruptcy 196	288	0.2
Money laundering or legalization of property obtained unlawfully 174	108	0.1
Avoiding customs dues 194	91	0.1
Illegal banking 172	84	0.1
Extortion 163	69	0.1
Coercion in signing contract or not signing 179	13	0.0
Total	122,292	100.0

Source: Composed from the data presented in Volkov, V., Dmitrieva, A., Paneyakh, E., & Pozdnyakov, M. (2011). Aktivnost' pravookhranitel'nykh organov RF po vyyavleniyu prestuplenij v sfere ekonomicheskoj deyatel'nosti, 2000–2011 gg. [Productivity of law enforcement agencies in investigating economic crimes, 2000–2011]. Moscow: The Institute for the Rule of Law, European University in St Petersburg. Retrieved January 10, 2012, from http://www.enforce.spb.ru/images/analit_zapiski/pm_econ_crime_1111.pdf

but for enterprises as well. On August 1, 2007, Putin signed into law "On the amendments to Federal Law on the supply of products for federal needs" and article 12 of the Federal Law on arms. The law was passed by the State Duma on July 4, 2007, and was approved by the Senate on July 11, 2007. The amendment that allows large state corporations Transneft' and Gazprom to form their own armed forces was introduced into the federal law.[9] In fact, the law now allows creating corporate armies.[10] These newly formed private armies will have to defend the production and transport infrastructure of so-called natural monopolies. At the same time, the legal status of private armies and their use outside Russia remains unclear. The presence of large detachments of Russian mercenaries in Syria and their participation in the military conflict will essentially lead to more legal provisions on the issue of private armies in Russia.

According to the amendments signed into law in 2007, strategic enterprises, strategic joint-stock companies and their branches, involved in exploitation of main oil pipelines and own these pipelines, including the firm that owns the Unified system of gas supply can acquire firearms and equipment after receiving a proper license from the state. They have the right to buy arms, as well as other special equipment, necessary to guarantee the safety and security of goods supplied under the state contract, objects of extracting, processing, transporting, and storage of such products, and other property and equipment needed for fulfilling the state contracts.[11] Armed private law enforcement and security agencies are common in the US, but in Russia this type of security services has only been developing over the last three decades.

At present, the security services of Gazprom and its branches protect 91 percent of all objects, while 5.5 percent are guarded by private security firms and the remaining 3.5 percent by mixed forces, including the police. In addition to the Federal State Unitary Enterprise "Okhrana" [Federal'noe gosudarstvennoe unitarnoe predpriyatie, FGUP], there are 16 other federal agencies that have special security units. "Okhrana" is the direct descendant of the police branch that performed the security functions for different facilities. There are also over 20,000 private security firms, generally known by their abbreviation of ChOPs [Chastnoe okhrannoe predpriyatie, ChOP] and more than 4000 security service departments in large companies.

Many private security firms are suspected of helping predatory raiders during hostile takeovers, which is of no surprise.[12] Predatory raiders need private security firms not only for violent storming, but also to hold the occupied enterprise. Private security firms are hired to stage and to repel the attacks on the enterprises. The job of a security guard is perhaps one of the most common types of employment in Russia. The need to guard private property creates the demand for the profession of security guard, and therefore the army of private security services continues to grow. By some unconfirmed estimates, Moscow alone employs around 400,000 security guards. It is time to add to the calendar of state holidays in Russia the day of the private security guard, in addition to the day of the teacher, the day of the health worker, the day of cosmonautics, and the day of knowledge. There is already the day of system administrator in Russia and even the day of the court bailiff celebrated on November 1.[13] And why does the country need the day of knowledge, if working as a private security guard does not require much knowledge? After all, this employment is not cosmonautics or rocket science. The old Soviet propaganda machine may be used as well. It would be easy to replace the slogans on the posters and placards of the World War II era, denoting the Soviet warrior-liberator as the private security guardsman, or a ChOP employee, and marking German Nazi aggressors as predatory raiders.

Redistribution of human resources, from the function of production to the function of maintaining the physical security of property and the legal security of property rights is a regressive process for the society. The Soviet system was focused on material production, and people were considered as necessary elements to the production process. At the same time, due to the totalitarian nature of the ruling political regime, institutes that would protect property rights and human rights were undeveloped. The disintegration and decomposition of the existing Soviet system of societal production leads to change in priorities, a variety of mismatches, and misallocations of resources and time.

The dissonance between stated goals and real practices in Russia is widespread. For instance, college students working part time as private security guards in department stores is a normal practice. At the same time, they study medicine or engineering only as much as their free time allows, or even solve their academic problems with the help of bribes. Cash or gifts for faculty members can guarantee high marks on examinations. The irony of this is that students work more and study less and then spend part of their salary on these gifts and bribes. The result of such shifted priorities from education to work is a low-quality service rendered in professional organizations due to low qualifications of undereducated specialists. This is because while attending colleges, they considered their education as a mere formality as compared to making real money on the side. The same is true for many professions and sectors of the economy. Simply put, when a society concentrates its resources on guarding already created assets, it becomes unclear who will produce new assets for the society. Higher transaction costs and misallocation of the resources, supported by widespread corruption, makes a society less productive.

Prices on Raiding and Related Services

An important indicator of the phenomenon of predatory raiding is the pricelist on services needed for staging a hostile takeover. The National Anti-Corruption Committee (NAK) presents the figures for the minimum rates for predatory raiders in order to secure a much-needed support of state bureaucrats, the so-called administrative resource. The NAK was trying to identify the prices of corruption services by surveying businessmen and lawyers employed in the sector of anti-raiding technologies. The survey reached 100 such representatives. The unofficial purchase of copies of the BTI [Byuro tekhnicheskoj inventarizatsii, the Bureau of Technical Inventory Registration] needed for the appraisal of assets costs predatory raiders at least $5000. Introducing changes to the charter documents, regarding the change of founders or directors of the targeted company, costs from $10,000 and above. Initiating a criminal investigation against managers and major shareholders costs at least $30,000, while the recall of already initiated criminal investigations against predatory raiders costs at least $50,000. $50,000 is also the minimum price for controlled tenders. This service includes the bidding process in a tender with the buyout of all the copies of the official newspaper edition that announces the tender and places the call for bidders, as well as the guaranteed win for a certain bidder and lobbying for a reduced price. The cost of this service increases depending on the value of the state contract placed for bidding. Obtaining a favorable court decision will cost at least $35,000, while the delay of a court hearing and setting a new, later date starts at $10,000.[14]

Fedorov (2010, p. 78) presents an approximate financial budget of a hostile takeover of an enterprise by predatory raiders. To strike a deal with tax inspectors costs $3000. Changing entries in the state register costs starting $10,000 in Moscow or $1000 in a province. A court decision regarding seizing or attaching property, seizing the register, banning the meeting of shareholders, annulling the results of the shareholder meeting, and so on costs $10,000–$20,000 in regions or $30,000–$200,000 in

Moscow. Execution of the court order by the court bailiff services costs starting $15,000 in Moscow or $5000 in a province. Notarial certification of signatures on documents costs $3000–$10,000. Obtaining a copy of the sale agreement from the Registration Chamber in Moscow costs up to $30,000, and $5000 in province. "Neutralizing" law enforcement agencies (police and prosecutors) costs $30,000–$60,000. Violent storming costs $300–$500 per stormtrooper involved, plus an additional $100–$200 per stormtrooper for guarding the enterprise after the storming. Appointing a loyal director costs $150,000–$250,000.

Firestone (2008, p. 1209) refers to some internet publications and offers the following pricelist:

> In 2005, one alleged raider, who has never been charged or convicted for raiding, published an article on his website explaining how to take over a business and listing the prices he charged for various services, including: assessing a target's capacity to resist an attack ($3,000 to $10,000); altering a target company's corporate register (starting at $10,000 in Moscow and $1,000 in the regions); and initiating a criminal case against a target (starting at $50,000 in Moscow and $20,000 in the regions outside Moscow). One researcher recently conducted an anonymous survey of raiders and identified the following standard prices in Moscow (prices outside Moscow are less) for the following services:
>
> - altering a target company's corporate documents: 10,000 euros and up;
> - notarizing documents: from 3,000 to 10,000 euros;
> - obtaining a court ruling: from 30,000 to 200,000 euros;
> - "neutralizing" of police and prosecutors: from 30,000 to 60,000 euros;
> - effecting a forcible seizure of a business: 300 to 500 euros for each armed attacker.

Referring to media reports and data presented by the Moscow Center of Political Technologies (see Bunin, 2008), Shelley and Deane (2016, p. 11) present a list of average prices for specific corrupt actions.[15] According to the report by the National Anti-Corruption Committee and Phoenix Group, based on interviews with more than 100 businessmen and lawyers in Russia, it costs from $5000 to $10,000 to falsify a company's documents; $10,000 to secure a delay in court proceedings; and $50,000 to close a criminal investigation opened against the business owner. In low-profile cases, decisions of judges can be bought through direct bribing or by offering a share in illegal proceeds from the raiding operation. Size of bribes varies across different regions. For example, a false court ruling obtained in the capital costs from $50,000 to $200,000, while the price at the regional level ranges from $10,000 to $20,000.

According to the investigation conducted in 2008 by the Center of Political Technologies, there is a price list on all the services used by predatory raiders during attacks. This price list became possible due to the total corruption in Russia. For instance, an ungrounded or unlawful court decision in Moscow costs from $50,000 to $200,000; in the regions, it can cost from $10,000 to $20,000. Obtaining a copy of a requested document about the sale from the Registration Chamber in Moscow will cost predatory raiders $30,000, and $5000 in the periphery. Neutralization of law enforcement agencies, including police and prosecutor's office will cost from $30,000 to $60,000. Launching a criminal case against an entrepreneur who owns a targeted firm will cost from $50,000 and above.[16] The stated prices are based on perceptions conveyed or voiced by the interviewed experts. As such, they may be labeled as speculations rather than facts. Nevertheless, as a Russian proverb goes, "There is no smoke without fire," and the very fact that such price lists are circulated in the media and discussed by scholars points to the seriousness of the problem.

The existence of price lists points not only to the corruptness of the state apparatus, but also to the division of functions in the business of corporate predatory raiding. The division of functions, in its turn, points to the high level of development and systemic character of predatory raiding in Russia. The large scale of predatory raiding and the involvement of state bureaucrats and entire groups of bureaucrats in the business of predatory raiding also points to its systemic character. The process of institutionalization of predatory raiding occurs because it is closely linked to the state. State bureaucracies have their strict hierarchies, including both formal and informal arrangements. Raiding companies may have such formal hierarchies too. Specialization and division of functions among participants of the predatory raiders' movement point to this trend.

Tkachenko and Lobodenko (2007, p. 213) also present some prices on services used by raiders for hostile takeovers, but the sources of such information are not specified by the authors. This study will not list these prices here simply because they are not very different from those already presented above, and because their original sources are similarly unknown or unreliable. The problem of obtaining reliable data, including prices on corrupt services, persists throughout the research on corruption and makes predatory raiding a challenging topic to address. Nevertheless, this study will present a summary table for predatory raiding-related services, purchased in exchange for bribes or other illegal payments.

These price lists and services, illegal by default, published in different media sources or on websites of alleged predatory raiders who speak up do not necessarily constitute scientific information, but rather food for thought. Such sources of information are rather liable than reliable. Nevertheless, such information moves from publication to publication, gets printed and reprinted, cited and recited, and finally acquires some features of credible information, being presented as reliable. The lack of any reliable scientific information and data on such illegal deeds is of no surprise. This study will limit the discussion of prices to what has been already presented above. This study will not try to capture and present all available price lists, for there are plenty in mass media publications and on the internet.

Prices on predatory raiding–related services in Russia, presented in Table 9.2, indicate that raiding is not a cheap business. Cost of a hostile takeover can easily mount to half-a-million dollars. These may be regarded as transaction costs in the business of predatory raiding. At the same time, not paying these prices will likely result in failed attempts at hostile takeovers. Investing in a predatory raiding attack may be afforded by large firms or professional raiding companies. Small, locally operating violent criminal gangs are unlikely to have the financial means for organizing successful raiding attacks. They may be part of the predatory raiding organization, but cannot act successfully on their own.

There are prices not only for predatory raiding-facilitating services, including those of corrupt courts, law enforcement agencies, and state bureaucrats, but on the predatory raiding activities as well. By these "prices" this study means the punishment that awaits predatory raiders if they are convicted of raiding-related crimes. Thus, taking part in criminally flavored predatory raiding may be a risky enterprise. Legislators want to make predatory raiding equal to robbery.[17] Likewise, Bogdanov (2008) reports that predatory raiding in Russia will be equated to robbery.[18] MPs and entrepreneurs are drafting a law, according to which predatory raiding will be punished with up to 20 years in prison. Similar ideas are being presented and discussed by legislators and entrepreneurs in the regions. Significant prison terms are anticipated not only for predatory raiders, but also for those who help predatory raiders in their hostile takeovers, including judges and other state officials. A ten-year sentence may soon become a reality for judges who help predatory raiders.[19]

Table 9.2 Prices on predatory raiding–related services in Russia

Major categories	*Services*	*Price range*
Charter documents	To falsify targeted company's documents	
	Unofficial purchase of copies of the BTI for the appraisal of company's assets	$5000 and above
	Introducing changes to the charter documents, regarding the change of founders or directors of the targeted company	$10,000 and above
	Obtaining a copy of the sale agreement from the Registration Chamber	$5000 (up to $30,000 in Moscow)
Notary public	Notarial certification of signatures on fraudulent documents	$3000–$10,000
Courts	Obtaining unlawful favorable court decision	$35,000 and above
	Delaying a court hearing and setting a new, later date	$10,000 and above
	Court decision regarding seizing or attaching property, seizing the register, banning the meeting of shareholders, annulling the results of shareholders meeting	$10,000–$20,000 ($30,000–$200,000 in Moscow)
	Appointing a loyal director through a court decision	$150,000–$250,000
Court bailiff services	Execution of the court order by the court bailiff services costs starting $15,000 in Moscow or $5000 in a province	$5000 and above ($15,000 and above in Moscow)
Prosecutors	Buying inaction of prosecutors	$30,000–$60,000
Police	Initiating a criminal investigation against managers and major shareholders	$30,000 and above
	Recall of already initiated criminal investigations against raiders	$50,000 and above
	"Neutralizing" police and other law enforcement agencies	$30,000–$60,000
Tax Administration	Making a deal with tax inspectors	$3000
Stormtroopers	Violent storming	$300–$500 per stormtrooper
	Guarding the enterprise after the storming	$100–$200 per stormtrooper
Private legal services	Assessing a target company's capacity to resist hostile takeover	$3000–$10,000

Source: Completed by the author

As of the summer of 2009, the founding statute was no longer on the list of formal documents for establishing limited liability companies (LLCs). It was excluded from the charter documents.[20] This was done in order to complicate the task of predatory raiders. It is hard to understand what is going on in the interactions between the business environment and the legislative process. It is either an attempt by present owners to secure themselves from predatory raiders and losing their property, or an attempt to preserve the status quo, when the function of predatory raiders as cleaners of the market will be blocked by the newly introduced anti-raiding laws. Predatory raiders may well end up paying damages for attacking other businesses. Allegedly, many lawsuits are being filed not in order to resolve a corporate dispute, but in order to receive some guarantees from the court and cause problems for their competitors.[21] Obviously, predatory raiders use the existing legal system in order to advance their agenda, but so do those who want to keep their property safe.

Concluding Remarks

With the emergence of private property, the need to protect it becomes obvious. The emergence of private property on a massive scale in an extremely short period of time, as was the case with Russian mass privatization of the 1990s, necessitates the protection of this property on an equally massive scale. At the same time, the state was no longer capable of or willing to protect property. With this, the right to defend private property is no longer the monopoly of the state. Private security firms partially replace the state in its function of protecting private property. These firms can now legally operate on the Russian market of security services. Before predatory raiding appeared on the agenda of the Russian business community, private security services were already numerous. At present, working for private security services is one of major occupations in the country, totaling over two million employees.

In addition to private security agencies, state law enforcement officers also take part in protecting private property in their spare time. The legality of such practices is dubious, but the facts reported in the media point to frequent occurrences of such practices. In addition to protecting private property, private security agencies also take part in hostile takeovers, performing the function of violent stormtroopers. What is more surprising is that some law enforcement officers can also take part in hostile takeovers on the side of predatory raiders. This situation does not prevent the

Russian government to demonstrate a paternalistic approach and take a protective stance in regard to small businesses. Government agencies do so in order to assure foreign investors the security of their investments. However, given the scope of predatory raiding in Russia, the ruling political regime's concern with improving the business environment, encouraging competition, and creating entrepreneurial opportunities appears to be more of a public declaration.

Corruption in the law enforcement agencies, judiciary, and other related state bureaucracies not only hinders the anti-raiding effort, but helps predatory raiders to target successful and financially sound businesses. Although it is hard to quantify corrupt dealings of state officials due to their natural secrecy, both the media and scholars report some price lists. Such price lists reflect services needed to stage a successful hostile takeover in a corrupt environment of the Russian business ecosystem. Predatory raiding is a costly activity, which can hardly be done by amateurs and without serious initial investment. The division of functions in the business of predatory raiding points to the high level of development and the systemic character of this economic phenomenon.

Notes

1. See the video report about the police storming a ferrous ash disposal area in the city of Zlatoust in Russia on September 26, 2008, as a result of the court dispute. The ferrous disposal area contains colored metals and other useful and expensive materials that are the byproducts of the production of the Zlatoust metallurgic complex. Retrieved from: http://rutube.ru/tracks/1048253.html
2. Court. Raiding. *3 Kanal*, June 8, 2009. Retrieved July 29, 2009, from http://www.youtube.com/watch?v=VyvwC5VehQs
3. See for instance: Police is storming a private bank in Moscow using axes and sledge hummers. Masked policemen are breaking in through the bulletproof glass and arresting private security. They also attempt to get through armored doors. It is unclear why the police are performing locksmith functions. Date unknown. Retrieved from: http://www.ochevidets.ru/rolik/7551/
4. Dmitry Medvedev poobeshchal, chto biznesmenov budut sazhat' znachitel'no rezhe [Dmitry Medvedev promised businessmen a much lower rate of their imprisonment]. *Zagolovki*, February 27, 2010. Retrieved February 27, 2010, from http://www.zagolovki.ru/daytheme/medvedev/27Feb2010

5. Medvedev predlagaet smyagchit' nakazaniya za ekonomicheskie prestupleniya [Medvedev is suggesting to reduce punishment for economic crimes]. *Newsru.com*, February 26, 2010. Retrieved February 26, 2010, from http://www.newsru.com/arch/finance/26feb2010/medvedev.html
6. Dmitry Medvedev poobeshchal, chto biznesmenov budut sazhat' znachitel'no rezhe [Dmitry Medvedev promised businessmen a much lower rate of their imprisonment]. *Zagolovki*, February 27, 2010. Retrieved February 27, 2010, from http://www.zagolovki.ru/daytheme/medvedev/27Feb2010
7. Glava RSPP Shokhin prizval vypustit' brat'ev Magomedovykh iz SIZO, chtoby ne pugat' drugikh predprinimatelej [Head of RSPP, Shokhin, calls for the release of Magomedovs from jail in order to avoid a scare among other businessmen]. *Newsru.com*, April 5, 2018. Retrieved April 5, 2018, from https://www.newsru.com/russia/05apr2018/shohin.html
8. Devyat' iz desyati ugolovnyh del po ekonomicheskim prestupleniyam v Rossii – fiktivnye [Nine out of ten criminal cases on economic crimes in Russia are fictitious]. *Newsru.com*, February 17, 2010. Retrieved February 17, 2010, from http://www.newsru.com/finance/17feb2010/krim.html
9. Putin podpisal zakon, pozvoliayushchij "Transnefti" i "Gazpromu" sozdat' korporativnye armii [Putin signed the law that allows "Transneft" and "Gazprom" to create corporate armies]. *Newsru.com*, August 1, 2007. Retrieved May 9, 2009, from http://palm.newsru.com/russia/01aug2007/gazpromarmy.html
10. Gazprom i Transneft' poluchat pravo imet' sobstvennye vooruzhennye sily [Gazprom i Transneft' will be granted the right to have their own military forces]. *Babr.ru*, March 27, 2007. Retrieved June 10, 2009, from http://news.babr.ru/?IDE=36823
11. Vpervye v Rossii sozdayutsya korporativnye armii [First time in Russia corporate armies are created]. *Evangelie.ru*, July 16, 2007. Retrieved June 10, 2009, from http://www.evangelie.ru/forum/t35744.html
12. Novgorodskoe ohrannoe agentstvo "FFF" podozrevaetsya v reiderstve [Novgorod private security agency "FFF" is suspected of raiding]. *Novgorodinform*, October 10, 2008. Retrieved July 22, 2009, from http://www.novgorodinform.ru/crime/16615.html
13. Rossijskoe pravitel'stvo ofitsial'no uchrezhdaet Den' programmista – 256-j den' v godu [Russian government officially establishes the day of the computer programmer]. *Newsru.com*, July 24, 2009. Retrieved July 25, 2009, from http://www.newsru.com/russia/24jul2009/256.html
14. Reiderstvo i korruptsiya: uslugi i tseny [Raiding and corruption: services and prices]. *Notheft.ru*, September 5, 2008. Retrieved July 22, 2009, from http://www.notheft.ru/rejderstvo-i-korrupcija-uslugi-i-ceny

15. Osadchuk, S. (2008). Bribe to Illegally Seize a Firm Put at $30,000. *The Moscow Times*, September 8.

Reiderstvo kak sotsial'no-ekonomicheskij i politicheskij fenomen sovremennoj Rossii: otchet o kachestvennom sotsiologicheskom issledovanii. Issledovanie "Tsentra politicheskih tehnologij" pod rukovodstvom Bunina. Moskva, 2008. [Raiding as a socioeconomic and political phenomenon of the modern Russia: A report on the qualitative sociological investigation. An investigation conducted by the Center of Political Technologies, led by Bunin]. Moscow, May 2008, p. 64. Retrieved June 12, 2009, from http://www.politcom.ru/; http://www.compromat.ru/main/mix1/raiderycpt.htm

16. Reiderstvo vstanet v odin ryad s korruptsiej [Raiding will stand in one line with corruption]. *Nezavisimaya gazeta*, May 23, 2008. Retrieved July 26, 2009, from http://www.notheft.ru/rejderstvo-vstanet-v-odin-rjad-s-korupciej

17. Deputaty namerevayutsya uzhestochit' nakazaniya za "reiderstvo" [MPs want to introduce harsher punishments for "raiding"]. *Notheft.ru*, March 13, 2009. Retrieved July 22, 2009, from http://www.notheft.ru/deputaty-namerevajutsja-uzhestochit-nakazanija-za-%C2%ABrejderstvo%C2%BB

18. Bogdanov, V. (2008). Reiderstvo uravnyayut s razboem: deputaty i predprinimateli gotovyat zakonoproekt, po kotoromu zakhvat predpriyatij obojdetsya v 20 let tyur'my [Raiding will be equated to robbery: MPs and entrepreneurs are working on the project of the law, according to which raiding will be punished with up to 20 years in prison]. *Rossijskaya gazeta*, №4612, March 14, 2008. Retrieved July 26, 2009, from http://www.rg.ru/2008/03/14/reider.html

19. Desyat' let za reshetkoj budet skoro svetit' sud'e za pomoshch' reideram [Ten-year sentence will soon become a reality for judges who help raiders]. *Simbirskij kur'er*, March 19, 2008. Retrieved July 26, 2009, from http://www.notheft.ru/desjat-let-reshetkoj-budet-skoro-svetit-sude-pomoshh-rejderam

V Sankt-Peterburge sobirayutsya likvidirovat' antireiderskuyu komissiyu [There is an intention to liquidate the anti-raiding commission in Sankt-Petersburg]. *Notheft.ru*, March 6, 2009. Retrieved July 22, 2009, from http://www.notheft.ru/v-sankt-peterburge-sobirajutsja-likvidirovat-antirejderskuju-komissiju

20. Uchreditel'nyj dogovor budet isklyuchen iz chisla uchreditel'nykh dokumentov obshchestv s ogranichennoj otvetstvennost'yu letom etogo goda [The founding statute will no longer be on the list of formal documents for LLCs, starting summer of this year]. *Notheft.ru*, March 30, 2009. Retrieved July 22, 2009, from http://www.notheft.ru/uchreditelnyj-dogovor-budet-iskljuchen-iz-chisla-uchreditelnyh-dokumentov-obshhestv-s-ogranichennoj-

21. S reiderov vzyshchut ubytki za ataki na chuzhoj biznes [Raiders may well end up paying damages for attacking other businesses]. *Newsru.com*, September 5, 2011. Retrieved September 5, 2011, from http://www.newsru.com/finance/05sep2011/sigma.html

References

Bunin, I. (2008). *Reiderstvo kak sotsial'no-ekonomicheskij i politicheskij fenomen sovremennoj Rossii: otchet o kachestvennom sotsiologicheskom issledovanii. Issledovanie "Tsentra politicheskih tehnologij" pod rukovodstvom Bunina.* Moskva, 2008. [Raiding as a Socioeconomic and Political Phenomenon of the Modern Russia: A Report on the Qualitative Sociological Investigation. An Investigation Conducted by the Center of Political Technologies]. Moscow, May 2008. Retrieved June 12, 2009, from http://www.politcom.ru/; http://www.compromat.ru/main/mix1/raiderycpt.htm

Fedorov, A. (2010). *Reiderstvo i korporativny shantazh (organizatsionno-pravovye mery protivodejstviya) [Raiding and Corporate Blackmail].* Moscow: Volters Kluwer.

Firestone, T. (2008). Criminal Corporate Raiding in Russia. *The International Lawyer, 42*(4), 1207–1230.

Kireev, A. (2007). Raiding and the Market for Corporate Control: The Evolution of Strong-Arm Entrepreneurship. *Problems of Economic Transition, 50*(8), 29–45.

Kolennikova, O., Kosals, L., & Ryvkina, R. (2004). Kommertsializatsiya sluzhebnoj deyatel'nosti rabotnikov militsii [Commercialization of the Service by the Law Enforcement Officers]. *Sotsiologicheskie issledovaniya, 3*, 73–83.

Shelley, L., & Deane, J. (2016). *The Rise of Reiderstvo: Implications for Russia and the West.* Washington, DC: Terrorism, Transnational Crime and Corruption Center. Retrieved January 12, 2017, from http://www.reiderstvo.org/sites/default/files/The_Rise_of_Reiderstvo.pdf

Tkachenko, N., & Lobodenko, M. (2007). Mekhanizm provedennya rejders'kyh atak ta shemy zahoplennya biznesu yak chinnyk ekonomichnoji nebezpeky diyal'nosti sub'yektiv gospodaryuvannya [Mechanism of Conducting Raiding Attacks and Schemes of Taking Over Business as a Factor of Economic Insecurity for Economic Agents and Firms]. *Nauchnye trudy DonNTU. Ekonomicheskie nauki, 31*(3), 211–215.

Volkov, V. (2005). Po tu storonu sudebnoj sistemy, ili Pochemu zakony rabotayut ne tak, kak dolzhny [On the Other Side of the Justice System or Why Don't Laws Work as They Should]. *Neprikosnovennyj zapas, 4*(42). Retrieved June 10, 2009, from http://magazines.russ.ru/nz/2005/42/vv6.html

Volkov, V., Dmitrieva, A., Paneyakh, E., & Pozdnyakov, M. (2011). *Aktivnost' pravookhranitel'nykh organov RF po vyyavleniyu prestuplenij v sfere ekonomicheskoj *deyatel'nosti, 2000–2011 gg. [Productivity of Law Enforcement Agencies in Investigating Economic Crimes, 2000–2011]*. Moscow: The Institute for the Rule of Law, European University in St Petersburg. Retrieved January 10, 2012, from http://www.enforce.spb.ru/images/analit_zapiski/pm_econ_crime_1111.pdf

CHAPTER 10

Conclusion

Scholars are only now catching up with the actual phenomenon of corporate predatory raiding in Russia, while the phenomenon itself peaked some time before 2010. Maybe this peak was linked to the aftermath of the 2008 financial crisis, but only to a certain extent. Moreover, as predatory raiding continues, and conditions for raiding to continue do not change, other peaks are possible. It is the same old Russian Empire, same Putin, same oligarchs, and same criminals. This study shows that predatory raiding in Russia is not on the declining trajectory. The interest in the problem of predatory raiding in Russia is only expected to grow among scholars. Furthermore, this study predicts that clashes over enterprises and land will only intensify and the number of international or transnational scandals related to raiding will grow.

The issue of raiding is always tied to property rights. Corporate raiders deal with property within a certain frame of property rights established in a given country. Raiding facilitates property redistribution, but Russian predatory raiding does this in quite an unusual way by using informal ways and illegal means. This type of redistribution can hardly be identified as having a positive impact on the national economy, and on the investment climate in particular. Russian predatory raiders achieve their goals primarily by breaking laws or using legal loopholes. They also use shares, buy-outs, bankruptcies, and other financial instruments and methods, as do their western counterparts. The destabilizing effect of predatory raiding on the economy is manifested in the skewed redistribution of property,

A. L. Osipian, *Political and Economic Transition in Russia*,
https://doi.org/10.1007/978-3-030-03831-1_10

already biased and ineffective due to the poorly designed and executed mass privatization of the 1990s.

The roots of raiding in Russia are economic rather than legal, indeed. Thus, introducing some characteristics of "classical" or Wall Street–type raiding in the introduction in order to highlight this difference later in the text was helpful in discovering the phenomenon of predatory raiding that plagued modern Russia. At the same time, it is also true that some parts of the book may at first glance appear somewhat unrelated to this argument. The explanation to this seemingly surprising mismatch is simple. Russia is to a significant extent a feudal society, and thus noneconomic forces play a significant role in country's development, including the phenomenon of predatory raiding.

Under the Soviet rule, totalitarian Communist regime held the monopoly on the role of the predator. The totalitarian political regime preyed on its own population. The state predation was exercised through the total control over the lives of the Soviet people, including in both economic and noneconomic spheres. In addition to the state as the major and indeed the only overwhelming predator, there were also parasites. These parasites fed off the Soviet economy, lived off the people's body, by embezzling in the course of production and distribution. The predominance of embezzlement under the Soviet socialism is explained by the monopoly of the state over productive assets.

Grand-scale and petty embezzlement were not the only forms of parasitism. Other widespread forms of parasitism included gift-giving as a camouflaged bribery, as well as nepotism and cronyism. These forms of parasitism were present in job placements and promotions, as well as when receiving education in public universities and healthcare in closed hospitals. Under the conditions of near-total deficit, access to consumer goods and services and even obtaining membership in the Communist Party were all affected by parasitism.

Modern Russian state retains the role of the major predator, inherited from the Stalinist regime. Rarely, if at all, a corporate predatory raider can overpower a strong and successful business that operates on legal grounds. Despite the use of violence in a storming of the targeted enterprise, violence is not the major resource used by predatory raiders. As the state holds the monopoly on overwhelming power, coercion, and legal justice, the predatory state serves as the major resource for predatory raiders. Corporate predatory raiders buy the right to use this overwhelming external force from corrupt bureaucrats and politicians. Predatory raiders and corrupt bureaucrats form an unlawful symbiosis in order to expropriate profitable businesses and other valuable assets from their lawful owners.

M&A, so familiar to the market agents in the western corporate world, are done in a much different way in Russia. Moreover, they may differ not only in the ways they are done, but in their very nature. Less effective owners may acquire assets of more effective entrepreneurs by the means of coercion and by using other noneconomic tools and instruments. Large corporations conducting aggressive consolidations can engage special development departments in predatory corporate raiding. Raided firms are handed over by predatory raiders to the clients who ordered and paid for the hostile takeover or, alternatively, these firms can go for resale. The hijacked firms can also be dismantled or restructured and sold out in pieces.

Even the state may be used as a tool of predatory raiding. Corruption in the law enforcement agencies, judiciary, and other state bureaucracies not only hinders the anti-raiding effort, but also offers predatory raiders a helping hand in the form of certain state-rendered services. And there is a price list on such services, as reported in some media outlets. The existence of price lists points not only to the corruptness of the state organs, but also to the division of functions in the business of raiding. The process of the institutionalization of predatory raiding occurs because it is closely linked to the predatory state.

Business competition that takes place in modern Russia is based on the use of noneconomic factors, including direct violence. The high level of corruption allows raiders to buy prosecutorial investigations, court decisions, and police enforcement in order to organize hostile takeovers of private businesses and public property. The state interference in economic life is considered a norm and as long as this state of affairs continues, predatory raiders will be able to involve the state as an external force needed for a hostile takeover. Predatory raiding in Russia is unnatural because, unlike in social Darwinism, raiders welcome the external force, the interference of the predatory state.

Redistribution of human resources, from the function of production to the function of security of property and property rights, is a regressive process for the society. The high level of concentration of property rights on the means of production prevents economic and social development in Russia. Most means of production are consolidated and concentrated in the hands of just a few oligarchs. Furthermore, the process of consolidation of capital and means of production continues. As a result, the economy is characterized by low levels of total factor productivity. In distinction of the West and its evolutionary development of shared property rights, in Russia, at the start of privatization in the early 1990s, all large enterprises were already created. The task was not to create a new value, but to distribute already created values. The distribution was declared as the equal portion or share going to everyone. This approach was in the best spirit of socialism, but at the same time it was somewhat illogical to start the market reforms with such a bold capitalistic move of privatization based on the equally bold socialist principle of equal distribution.

What is the future of predatory raiding in Russia? Large and effective, and well-functioning enterprises will become invulnerable to predatory raiding attacks, especially those conducted on the grounds of corruption and violence. A major part of the Russian economy consists of large industrial enterprises, many with a full production cycle. Large enterprises will be capable of repelling attacks of predatory raiders. They are able to improve their own security and influence the local and central authorities, including law enforcement agencies and branch ministries.

Representatives of local authorities, politicians, judges, prosecutors, and law enforcement agencies will realize that it is no longer beneficial to them, their agencies, and the localities in general to leave the important enterprises unprotected or help predatory raiders destabilize the situation around these enterprises. If key enterprises will be destabilized, then, the economies of entire cities and regions may also be destabilized. The rational approach will force the local authorities to refrain from seeking immediate benefits of corruption in favor of more stable and sustainable values, such as preserving the public office and support of continuous economic development in the region, including through the protection of important large enterprises and investments.

As far as the medium-sized and small enterprises are concerned, they can fence themselves from raiders and racketeers through self-organization and collective defense. The historically formed forms of simple cooperation in small businesses may serve as a basis for cooperation in mobilizing against predatory raiders and forming a collective defense business association. Joining associations at the local level rather than based on the market segments or branches of the economy will not violate the principles of free competition. Entrepreneurs unite in order to oppose raiding attacks. It is easier for large companies to withstand raiding attacks. As a result, predatory raiding serves as a stimulus for further mergers and enlargement of firms. This trend encourages monopolization and further concentration of the private property on the means of production in the hands of just a few oligarchs. Such a trend is deemed to be negative for the level of productivity and thus for the national economy overall.

Further development of predatory raiding will be based not only on the advancement of the raiding movement from the center to the periphery or from large cities to distant areas, that is, geographic expansion, developing in space, and extending the list of targets, including land. It will also include the larger roster of participants and active redistributors of property. Here, one will not only see aggressive forces such as organized criminal groups, investment banks, large financial-industrial groups, corrupt law enforcement agencies, and shell firms, but also those distant from real world entities such as cultural foundations, art centers, and the church. For some of these organizations, raiding is an expression of pretentions on the return of their former property, or restitution, while for others it is a defense strategy, based on the principle that "the best defense is a good offense."

The negative impact of the phenomenon of raiding on the institute of property is obvious. But the danger of the phenomenon of raiding is not only in the unlawful distribution and redistribution of property and discrediting of the state institutions and the rule of law. Raiding is also dangerous because it is being converted into a culture and perceived by the masses as a norm of behavior. The culture of raiding is based on the right of taking away someone else's property without one's consent, including violent hostile takeovers. Raiding endangers not only the right of ownership over movable property and real estate, but also the inviolability of the home, as guaranteed by the Constitution.

In modern Russia, the culture of raiding goes far beyond the seizure of buildings that belong to enterprises and institutions with the use of fake documents. Raiding is counterproductive because it breeds instability and positions itself against consistency and development of long-lasting values. In essence, raiding threatens the process of forming property relations regarding the means of production. On the one hand, there is the process of forming a capitalist economic structure. On the other hand, there is a simultaneous process of undermining its foundation, namely, the system of corporate private property rights. It is likely that in the long run, private property relations will be strengthened through the process of creative destruction, a part of which is predatory raiding.

Either very low or virtually absent legitimacy of swiftly acquired property creates grounds for eternal instability and social tensions. This instability causes economic uncertainties and negatively impacts not only domestic businessmen, but foreign investors as well. The mass privatization of the 1990s turned out to be the goose that lays golden eggs for Russian oligarchs. The masses are dissatisfied with such outcomes, however. The waves of privatization continue to come, and thus the issue of the legitimacy of property remains high on the agenda of the property owners, the general public, and the state. As long as the problem of predatory raiding persists, so does the issue of securing property rights.

Oligarchs are being called to demonstrate the sense of social responsibility and conducting business in a socially responsible manner. This campaign is led in the spirit of Putin's promise to "pull everything out of stomach and give away to poor," addressed to socially irresponsible businesspeople. What it means is that the low level of legitimacy of accumulated wealth should be compensated for with the voluntary-forceful donations that would benefit the state and the society in general. The predatory state exercises pressure over businesspeople with the goal of sharing the social responsibility.

The ruling political regime hints at the possible revision of the privatization results or even a partial renationalization in order to make businesspeople more cooperative and loyal to the regime. It seems apparent that the theme of eggs, from throwing eggs at politicians and using them as an example of the developing legal aspects of property rights to acquiring Faberge eggs for publicly displayed collections and the eternal chicken and egg problem, will continue to challenge the minds of economists and politicians for quite some time. The task of legitimization of property and productive assets acquired in the process of the mass privatization of the 1990s would require the most immaculate reputation of any given current property owner. How to gain this reputation and whether it is at all possible to gain such a reputation in contemporary Russia remains an open question.

Author Index[1]

[1]Note: Page numbers followed by 'n' refer to notes.

A. L. Osipian, *Political and Economic Transition in Russia*,
https://doi.org/10.1007/978-3-030-03831-1

Subject Index[1]

[1] Note: Page numbers followed by 'n' refer to notes.

A. L. Osipian, *Political and Economic Transition in Russia*,
https://doi.org/10.1007/978-3-030-03831-1

FSC
www.fsc.org
MIX
Papier | Fördert gute Waldnutzung
FSC® C083411

Kolibri 360 GmbH
Ferdinand-Jühlke-Straße 7
99095 Erfurt, Deutschland
produktsicherheit@kolibri360.de